THE WEDDING IN CANA

The Power & Purpose of the First Sign of Jesus Christ

The Wedding in Cana

The Power & Purpose of the First Sign of Jesus Christ

Fr George Koshy

ST VLADIMIR'S SEMINARY PRESS
YONKERS, NY 10707
2017

Library of Congress Cataloging-in-Publication Data

Names: Kōśi, Jōrjj, author.

Title: The wedding in Cana : the power and purpose of the first sign of Jesus Christ / George Koshy.

Description: Yonkers, NY : St Vladimirs Seminary Press, 2017. | Includes bibliographical references.

Identifiers: LCCN 2016059164 (print) | LCCN 2017008685 (ebook) | ISBN 9780881415469 | ISBN 9780881415476

Subjects: LCSH: Turning water into wine at the wedding at Cana (Miracle) | Bible. John, II, 1–11—Criticism, interpretation, etc. | Jesus Christ—Miracles.

Classification: LCC BS2615.6.M5 K67 2017 (print) | LCC BS2615.6.M5 (ebook) | DDC 226.5/06—dc23

LC record available at https://lccn.loc.gov/2016059164

COPYRIGHT © 2017
ST VLADIMIR'S SEMINARY PRESS
575 Scarsdale Rd, Yonkers, NY 10707
1–800–204–2665
www.svspress.com

ISBN 978–0-88141–546–9 (paper)
ISBN 978–0-88141–547–6 (electronic)

For
Bavukutty Abu Shemmashen and Feba,
Gibu,
and Alexis

The Orthodox Study Bible

On the third day there was a wedding in Cana of Galilee, and the mother of Jesus was there. Now both Jesus and His disciples were invited to the wedding. And when they ran out of wine, the mother of Jesus said to him, "They have no wine." Jesus said to her, "Woman, what does your concern have to do with Me? My hour has not yet come." His mother said to the servants, "Whatever He says to you, do it." Now there were set six water pots of stone, according to the manner of purification of the Jews, containing twenty or thirty gallons apiece. Jesus said to them, "Fill the water pots with water." And they filled them up to the brim. And He said to them, "Draw some out now, and take it to the master of the feast." And they took it. When the master of the feast had tasted the water that was made wine, and did not know where it came from (but the servants who had drawn the water knew), the master of the feast called the bridegroom. And he said to him, "Every man at the beginning sets out the good wine, and when the guests have well drunk, then the inferior. You have kept the good wine until now!" This beginning of signs Jesus did in Cana of Galilee, and manifested His glory; and His disciples believed in Him.

The New Oxford Annotated Bible

On the third day there was a marriage at Cana in Galilee, and the mother of Jesus was there; Jesus also was invited to the marriage, with his disciples. When the wine gave out, the mother of Jesus said to him, "They have no wine." And Jesus said to her, "O woman, what have you to do with me? My hour has not yet come." His mother said to her servants, "Do whatever he tells you." Now six stone jars were standing there, for the Jewish rites of purification, each holding twenty or thirty gallons. Jesus said to them, "Fill the jars with water." And they filled them up to the brim. He said to them, "Now draw some out, and take it to the steward of the feast." So they took it. When the steward of the feast tasted the water now became wine, and did not know where it came from (though the servants who had drawn water knew), the steward of the feast called the bridegroom and said to him, "Every man serves the good wine first; and when men have drunk freely, then the poor wine; but you have kept the good wine until now." This is the first of his signs, Jesus did at Cana in Galilee, and manifested his glory; and his disciples believed in him.

From the Peshitta

And on the third day there was a feast in Kotna, a city of Galila; and the mother of Jeshu was there: and Jeshu and his disciples were called to the feast. And the wine failed, and his mother saith to him, to Jeshu, They have no wine. Jeshu saith to her, What (is it) to me and to thee, woman? Not yet hath come mine hour. His mother saith to the servitors, Whatever he telleth you, do. Now there were six water-pots of stone set there, unto the purification of the Jihudoyee, which contained each two quarantals or three. Jeshu saith to them, Fill these water-pots with waters; and they filled them to the top. He saith to them, Draw now, and carry to the chief of the guests. And they carried. And when that chief of the guests had tasted those waters which were made wine, and knew not whence it, (but the servitors knew, who had filled them with waters,) the chief of the guests called the bridegroom, and said to him, every man at first the good wine produceth, and when they are satisfied, then that which is inferior; but thou hast kept the good wine until now. This is the first sign that Jeshu wrought in Kotna of Galila, and manifested his glory; and his disciples believed in him.

John Wesley Etheridge, *The Syrian Churches: Their Early History, Liturgies and Literature* (London: Elibron Classics, 2005; repr. of London: Longman, Green, Brown, and Longmans, 1846), 479–80

The New American Bible (Catholic Book Publishing Company)

On the third day there was a wedding in Cana in Galilee, and the mother of Jesus was there. Jesus and his disciples were also invited to the wedding. When the wine ran short, the mother of Jesus said to him, "They have no wine." (And) Jesus said to her, "Woman, how does you concern affect me? My hour has not yet come." His mother said to the servants, "Do whatever he tells you." Now there were six stone water jars there for Jewish ceremonial washings, each holding twenty to thirty gallons. Jesus told them, "Fill the jars with water." So they filled them to the brim. Then he told them, "Draw some out now and take it the headwaiter." So they took it. And when the headwaiter tasted the water that become wine, without knowing where it came from (although the servers who had drawn the water knew), the headwaiter called the bridegroom and said to him, "Everyone serves good wine first, and then when people have drunk freely, an inferior one; but you have kept the good wine until now." Jesus did this as the beginning of his signs in Cana in Galilee and so revealed his glory, and his disciples began to believe in him.

Jewish New Testament

Two days later, there was a wedding at Kanah in the Galil; and the mother of Yeshua was there. Yeshua too was invited to the wedding, along with his talmidim. The wine ran out, and Yeshua's mother said to him, "They have no more wine." Yeshua replied, "Mother, why should that concern me—or you? My time hasn't come yet." His mother said to the servants, "Do whatever he tells you." Now six stone water-jars were standing there for the Jewish ceremonial washings, each with a capacity of twenty or thirty gallons. Yeshua told them, "Fill the jars with water," and they filled them to the brim. He said, "Now draw some out, and take it to the man in charge of the banquet;" and they took it. The man in charge tasted the water; it had now turned into wine! He did not know where it had come from, but the servants who had drawn the water knew. So he called the bridegroom and said to him, "Everyone else serves the good wine first and the poorer wine after people have drunk freely. But you have kept the good wine until now!" This, the first of Yeshua's miraculous signs, he did at Kanah in the Galil; he manifested his glory, and his talmidim came to trust in him. Afterwards, he, his mother and brothers and his talmidim went down to K'far-Nachum and stayed there a few days.

Translation by David H. Stern (Jerusalem, Israel: 78 Manahat, 1981)

Contents

Foreword

It is a pleasure to introduce this work by the Very Rev. Dr George Koshy, a priest of the Northeast American Diocese of the Malankara Orthodox Syrian Church and also an alumnus of St Vladimir's Seminary. Fr George's recent book, *Marriage, The Mystery of Love: An Eastern Christian Perspective* (Thiruvalla: CSS Books, 2016), offers a vision of the transformation of human love in the sacrament of marriage, grounded in the sacrificial act of the cross, as reflective of and an entry into the heavenly beauty of the kingdom of God. Based on scriptural, liturgical, theological, spiritual and ethical insights, Fr George addressed various contemporary questions regarding marriage to offer a companion on those setting out on this path.

In the present volume, Fr George focuses his attention on the Gospel of John, and specifically the marriage feast in Cana. This episode, at the beginning of the Gospel, offers a unique and important lens that brings into focus many themes that occur throughout the Gospel, climaxing in the Passion: "the first of his signs" manifesting his "glory," "the third day," "the hour," the "woman," the changing of water into wine, the best wine, and, of course, the marriage itself. Fr George offers us twelve meditations on different aspects of this episode, bringing to bear insight drawn from the Scriptures, the Fathers, Liturgy and its hymnography, modern theologians and scriptural scholars. We are taken from the historical setting, locating Cana in first-century Palestine, through the Gospel reading, with explorations of its resonances with other passages of Scripture, its connection to the gospel proclamation itself, and to its place in the tradition thereafter, thereby opening up the riches that this little episode contains—offering the "best wine"—to all those who seek the mystery of the kingdom.

This volume has been a labor of love for Fr George over many years. It is wonderful to see it, finally, in print. May it enrich its readers as it has enriched Fr George himself.

—Very Rev. Dr John Behr

Preface

While I was a student at the Orthodox Theological Seminary in Kottayam, India, a retreat led by the late Catholicos Baelius Mar Thoma Mathews II (then Metropolitan Mar Coorilos) instilled in me a sense of the depth and width of the the first and "foremost" *sign* performed by our Lord at Cana. Half a century later, the robust reflections he shared with us reverberate within me still. The seeds that the sign sowed in me took root and began to sprout, and over time I began to scribble thoughts that arose, as well as ideas and inferences I heard or read on the passage. Reading further, the interpretations of the sign and the theological insights of the holy fathers as well as of theologians and scholars of Holy Scripture illumined my mind and broadened the horizons of my understanding. This book, containing more than a dozen meditations, is the fruit of sustained contemplation on the wonder that took place in Cana.

There are many who helped me to bring this to fruition and I gratefully record my thanks to all of them. In particular, I would like to mention the names of Mr Joseph Alexander, a member of the St George Orthodox Church of Westchester, and Ms Olga Savin, both whom edited my initial draft, as well as the Rev. Dr Timothy (Tenny) Thomas, Rev. Dn Philip Mathew, and my sons Rev. Dn Givargis Koshy and Gibu George. I am indeed thankful to my wife for giving me the time and providing me enough inspiration to focus on this project and to my parents for inculcating in me an interest and excitement in spiritual matters.

The Very Rev. Dr John Behr, the dean of St Vladimir's Seminary, a leading voice of Orthodoxy in the world, encouraged me to publish my work after reading the manuscript. His support really bolstered my enthusiasm to move forward and have it printed. I am thankful to the St Vladimir's Seminary Press team and especially to the Rev. Dr Benedict Churchill for their efforts in producing this book.

I prayerfully remember the late Catholicos Baselius Mar Thoma Mathews I, whose presence and prayers accompany me always. I am thankful to the late Metropolitan Dr Paulos Mar Gregorios, my teacher who sent me abroad for higher studies, as well as the two institutions of my theological studies, the Orthodox Theological Seminary in Kottayam and St Vladimir's Seminary in New York. It is a pleasure to mention my parish, the St George Orthodox Church of Westchester (Port Chester, New York), "my joy and crown" (Phil 4.1), for their love and support despite my shortcomings.

It has been my humble hope and prayer throughout my life to undergo a transformation from the ordinary to the extraordinary, from earthly to spiritual, just as happened to the water at the wedding scene at Cana. The same is my wish and prayer for the readers of this book.

—Fr George Koshy
The Feast of the Resurrection, 2017

I
The Sign of the Wedding in Cana and Its Significance

The Importance of the Initial Sign at Cana

The wedding sign occurred centuries ago at a Jewish wedding feast in Cana, a village about six miles from Nazareth in the land of Galilee. The event at the wedding feast at Cana concerns the changing of water into wine; however, its meaning transcends time, space, and race and can relate to everyone in one way or another. As described in the second chapter of the Fourth Gospel, this sign is, in a way, the substance of the whole Gospel, summarized in one scene and in one sign. Though the sign narrative is very concise in style, it profoundly but succinctly captures the whole saga of salvation and sanctification.

The wedding which Jesus Christ, his mother, and his disciples attended took place "at Cana in Galilee" (Jn 2.1). Cana is a rural and remote village and, strangely enough, it is mentioned only in the Fourth Gospel, and that is also limited to three occasions (2.1; 4.46; 21.2). The first reference in relation to the wedding is in 2:1, and the second reference is in the narrative about the healing of the nobleman's son, where it begins with, "So Jesus came again to Cana of Galilee where he had made the water wine" (4.46). In the third and last reference about Cana (21.2), we read, "Nathanael of Cana in Galilee." Does this likely mean that this was where Nathanael was born and raised? Probably, yes. Though, he may have simply been residing in that village during those times.

"Jesus would go forth to Galilee," according to John 1.43. Yet, when Cana is mentioned in 2.1 and 21.3, it is always referred to as "Cana in Galilee." This is a clear indication that people in those days needed a more definite sense of its location, and that mentioning "Cana" alone was not enough. William Barclay is of opinion that "Cana" was mentioned together with "Galilee" in order to distinguish "Cana in Galilee" from Cana in Coelho-Syria.[1] Thus, it can also mean that there were other places with the same name in other Jewish and non-Jewish areas.

The name Cana does not appear in Hebrew Scripture of the Old Testament. Cana was likely derived from Canaan, the land of the Gentiles. Quoting from the Prophet Isaiah (8.23), Matthew mentions Galilee as "Galilee of the Gentiles" (4.15). In the Peshitta[2] Bible, the name of the village is not Cana, but Kothenay (Qathena), which may correspond to "Canaan," but it may also be another name for Cana. According to Sebastian Brock, a different form of the name is given in the Peshitta Bible as likely reflecting an early oral tradition: "thus the marriage feast to which Jesus was invited is not at Cana, but at Qatna (which has not been successfully identified)."[3]

Many modern scholars identify Cana as "Khirbet Qanah, a deserted site about 5.5 miles northwest of Kefar Kenna."[4] The very word "Cana" means "place of reeds," and there is a place still identified as Cana which "is appropriate, for it overlooks a marshy plain where reeds are still plentiful."[5] Some scholars also suggest Kefar Kenna,

[1] William Barclay, *The Gospel of John*, vol. 1, *The Daily Study Bible* (Edinburgh: The Saint Andrew Press, 1964), 80.

[2] Ancient Bible in Syriac language used by the Syrian Churches.

[3] Sebastian P. Brock, *The Bible in the Syriac Tradition* (Piscataway, NJ: Gorgias Press, 2006), 110.

[4] Daniel J. Harrington, *John's Thought and Theology* (Wilmington, DE: Michael Glazier, Inc., 1990), 28.

[5] George Arthur Buttrick et al., eds., *Interpreter's Dictionary of the Bible, vol. 1*, A–D (Nashville, TN: Abingdon Press, 1962), 493.

which was more than two miles from Nazareth. Eusebius of Caesarea (*c.* 260–340) and Jerome (+420) preferred Khirbet Qanah or Khirbert Qana. Jerome stated that he saw Cana from Nazareth, because of its proximity.[6] There is also some evidence that suggests the village of Cana was "located near the legendary birthplace of Dionysius,[7] the Greek god of fertility, whose feasts were celebrated with huge outpourings of wine."[8] Scholars dispute the exact location where the wedding took place, and varying traditions exist, as well. Nevertheless, Cana was thought of as a small, ordinary village of little distinction in Galilee, which was situated a few miles northwest of Nazareth. A traveler from Judea to Galilee had to pass through Cana to reach Nazareth or Capernaum. There is a place, at present, identified as Cana, and a church is there, claiming to be the location where Jesus performed the sign, and this is a favorite for modern day pilgrims and tourists to the Holy Land. Vaselin and Lydia W. Kesich observe, "Outside of Nazareth, about three miles to the northeast, is the city of Kefr Kenna. Many tourists visit this site because it is popularly identified with Cana in Galilee, where Jesus attended a marriage celebration with his disciples and his mother and changed water into wine (John 2). Many scholars, however, dispute this identification, favoring another place, Khirbert Qana, about nine miles north of Nazareth."[9]

Believed to have written the Gospel, John the Apostle, the youngest among the twelve and also "the beloved disciple of Christ" (Jn 13.23; 21.7, 20), had the prudent and penetrating eyes of an eagle to see beyond the obvious and the natural.[10] For Augustine of Hippo (*c.* 354–430), the evangelist is "like an eagle" who "abides among Christ's

---

[6]Barclay, *The Gospel of John*, 80.

[7]Dionysius was the god of wine and drunken revelry in Greek mythology.

[8]Wes Howard-Brook, *Becoming Children of God: John's Gospel and Radical Discipleship* (Maryknoll, NY: Orbis Books, 1994), 77–78.

[9]Veselin and Lydia W. Kesich, *Treasures of the Holy Land* (Crestwood, NY: St Vladimir's Seminary Press, 1985), 19.

[10]This Gospel has always been interestingly compared to an eagle (one among the four living creatures of the Apocalypse), the bird with sharpened eyesight and keen watchfulness.

sayings of the sublimer order and in no way descends to earth but on rare occasions."[11] Although at a glance the Gospel appears to be simple and straightforward, one has to delve deep to ascertain the depth and the width of the meaning of its words, phrases, context, and contents. John Chrysostom of Constantinople (*c.* 340–407) observes, "If men were exactly and with ready mind to receive and keep them, they could no longer be mere men nor remain upon the earth, but would take their stand above all the things of this life, and having adapted themselves to the condition of angels, would dwell on earth just as if it were heaven."[12] The leader of the Reformation, Martin Luther (1483–1546), observed, "Never in my life have I read a book written in simpler words than this, and yet the words are inexpressible."[13] William Barclay writes, "John did not see the events of Jesus' life simply as events in time; he saw them as windows looking into eternity."[14] The Gospel narratives are allegorical and, at the same time, intuitive and mystical in content. Because of the depth and profundity of the Gospel it has been called "the Spiritual Gospel."[15]

Unlike the Synoptic Gospels, which present miraculous events and incidents performed by Jesus Christ as miracles, the Gospel of John presents stories of a miraculous nature as signs. Hence the Fourth Gospel is also known as the Book of Signs or the Gospel of Signs.[16] Though narrated in all four Gospels, even the miracle of multiplying five loaves and two fish to feed the hungry multitude is presented as a sign rather than a miracle in the Gospel of John. The signs in this Gospel were also miraculous events, at the same time they were mysterious manifestations of divine revelation that were often revealed

[11]Augustine, *Harmony of the Gospels*, 4.11 (NPNF[1] 6:231).

[12]Chrysostom, *Homilies on the Gospel of John* 1.1 (NPNF[1] 14:1).

[13]A. M Hunter, *The Gospel according to John: The Cambridge Bible Commentary* (London: Cambridge University Press, 1965), 14.

[14]Barclay, *The Gospel of John*, "Introduction," xxv.

[15]*The Orthodox Study Bible: New Testament and Psalms*, ed. Peter E. Gillquist (Nashville, TN: Thomas Nelson, 1997), 201.

[16]Neal M. Flanagan, *The Gospel According to John and the Johannine Epistles* (Collegeville, MN: Liturgical Press, 1983), 13.

only to a specific group of believers who witnessed them and were amazed by what they watched. They encouraged the faithful followers of the "new way" to sustain their faith in Christ and for their spiritual edification. Every sign in the Gospel conceals a plethora of phenomenal mysteries pertaining to the process of divinization initiated and fulfilled by the Son of God.

The Gospel of John presents the sign at the wedding in Cana as the first act performed by Jesus Christ during his public ministry, and in many ways, it is one of the most beloved. Chronologically, this is the first sign mentioned in the Gospel. At the same time, the sentence construction could also suggest that it was the "first" or "the most important" sign performed by Jesus Christ. Raymond F. Collins observes that the sign at Cana is the "first in the sense that it is the paradigm of all signs."[17] John Chrysostom noted that there are those who say they do not have enough proof that it was the first miracle Jesus performed, because it occurred "in 'Cana of Galilee,' as allowing it to have been the first done there, but not altogether and absolutely the first, for He probably might have done others elsewhere."[18] However, John Chrysostom clearly negated such a suggestion and established the Cana sign as the "beginning of the miracles."[19] Michel De Goedt observed that the marriage at Cana is "a primordial sign which, in some manner, contains within its symbolism the meaning of all other signs" and then writes, "It is not only the first sign, but as the text says, 'the beginning of signs, *arche ton simeion.*'"[20]

The Gospel passage narrating the sign (2.1–12) appears different from narratives that include other signs. "John 2:1–12 stands as an independent literary unit with a clear introduction and a definite conclusion. John 2:1 points to the exact beginning of a new section: the

[17]Raymond F. Collins, *These Things Have Been Written* (Louvain: Peeters Press, 1990), 195.

[18]St John Chrysostom, *Homilies on the Gospel of St. John* 21.2 (NPNF[1] 14:73).

[19]Ibid.

[20]Max Thurian, *Mary, Mother of the Lord, Figure of the Church*, trans. Neville B. Cryer (London: The Faith Press, 1963), 131. Thurian cites from M. De Goedt, *Bases bibliques de la maternité spirituelle de Marie* (Paris, 1960).

reference of the 'third day' indicates the change of time and the reference of 'Cana in Galilee' points to the change of place."[21] The main characters in the initial sign were Jesus, the mother of Jesus, the servants, the disciples, the master of the feast, and the bridegroom. The sign consists of several conversations: between the mother of Jesus and Jesus, between the mother of Jesus and the servants, between Jesus and the servants, and between the master of the feast and the bridegroom. The Cana sign introduces the major themes in the Gospel: "the third day" resurrection (2.1); "the hour" of suffering and the crucifixion" (2.5); the re-creation and the purification process of creation; transformation and superabundance in the Messianic time, etc. In many ways the sign summarizes the mission of Jesus Christ and points to all other signs performed by him in the process of divine manifestation during his public ministry. Though there are seven signs recorded in John's Gospel, the Synoptic Gospels do not mention the sign performed at the wedding in Cana, and thus it remains unique.

An unusual feature of the wedding at Cana is that Jesus initially appeared to be astonishingly reluctant to perform any miracle at the wedding. The only other instance where Jesus was reluctant to act is in the Synoptic Gospels when the Canaanite woman asked him to heal her demon-possessed daughter. She humbly and prayerfully pleaded before Christ, comparing herself to a dog waiting to be fed by breadcrumbs that fall from the master's table (Mt 15.21–28; Mk 7.24–30). The mother of Jesus is present at the wedding in Cana, and this is the first time she appears in the Fourth Gospel. It was Mary who prompted her Son to perform the miracle or at least informed him about the deficiency and the dire need there. This also confirms that Mary was present at the inauguration of the public ministry of Jesus.

Jesus attended the wedding with few of his "disciples,"[22] though few in number at the time, possibly "six disciples-two pair of brothers

[21]John Vaipil, "A Marian Re-Reading of the Fourth Gospel," *Aikya Samiksha* 7.1 (May 2010): 37.

[22]John avoids the term "apostle," "which was a term used post-resurrectional period," according to Raymond E. Brown, *The Gospel According to John I-XI*, in the Anchor Bible Series (Garden City, NY: Doubleday, 1966), 98.

who were fishermen from Bethsaida and a pair of friends, Philip and Nathanael."[23] It is also the first time in the Gospel that the term "disciples" (2.2) is used for the apostles. In John 6.13, the disciples or the apostles are identified as "the twelve."

Mary's husband Joseph does not appear in the wedding scene, likely because of his death before the event. The Fourth Gospel mentions his name only once, and in a special context: "They said, 'Is not this Jesus, the son of Joseph, whose father and mother we know?'" (Jn 6.42). However, these words could also mean that Joseph was alive at that time.

In the Synoptic Gospels, the initial act performed by Jesus after the inauguration of his public ministry is not the same as the one in John's Gospel. Matthew begins the ministry of Jesus with the Sermon on the Mount. Mark mentions the exorcism in the synagogue at Capernaum as the starting point. According to Luke, Jesus initiated his public ministry by delivering the sermon in the synagogue on the Sabbath, after reading from the scroll of the Prophet Isaiah. For John, however, the inaugural event was the sign of changing water into wine at the wedding feast in Cana. From his presenting the sign as the initiation of Jesus Christ's public ministry, one can sense the importance that John attributes to the sign.

For many, the wedding in Cana is a very familiar and favorite passage in the New Testament. Strangely enough and as already noted, the first three Gospels do not narrate this sign. John's Gospel recounts other important events, especially signs and miracles, such as the raising of Lazarus from the dead, which are not mentioned in the Synoptic Gospels. One probable reason that some of the signs like the wedding in Cana are recorded only by John is that at the time, only a few among the twelve were called to be apostles (Jn 1.35–51). John was among the first whom Jesus called, and he was probably fortunate enough to witness the event. Moreover, as Jesus entrusted his mother to John during his passion on the cross she stayed with John after the

---

[23]R. C. Foster, *Studies in the Life of Christ* (Grand Rapids, MI: Baker Book House, 1971), 352.

resurrection. Thus it is also reasonable to speculate that Mary might have told John the Cana story during those times, including her conversation with her Son at the wedding feast.

John's purpose of writing his Gospel, according to some of the early writers, was to add what was missing in the other Gospels. The second-century Muratorian Canon says about this Gospel: "The Fourth Gospel is that of John, one of the disciples. When his fellow-disciples and bishops entreated him, he said, 'Fast now with me for the space of three days, and let us recount to each other whatever may be revealed to us'. On the same night it was revealed to Andrew, one of the apostles, that John should narrate all things in his own name as they called them to mind. And so, although different points are taught to us in the several books of the Gospels, there is no difference as regards the faith of believers, since in all of them everything is related under one imperial Spirit. . . . John professes himself to be not only the eye-witness, but also the hearer; and besides that, the historian of all the wondrous facts concerning the Lord in their order."[24] That also is a probable reason why the sign is narrated only in the Fourth Gospel.

The sign is described with just under a dozen sentences, but it is elaborate with precisely chosen words that have great symbolic and mystical meaning. Terminology, matter and manner, place and participants, time and context, and manifestation of the revealed glory all relate to the mystery and the majesty that blossom with profound realities and revelations. Thus, as Raymond Brown mentions, a few biblical scholars have suggested that the wedding feast in the Gospel was more a parable than an actual event.[25] Yet, the fact that this passage speaks about a specific time, identifies the location by name, and mentions the presence of persons like Jesus, his mother, and the apostles undoubtedly negates the likelihood of any such hypothesis.

---

[24]Joel C. Elowsky, *John 1–10*, Ancient Christian Commentary on Scripture, New Testament vol. IVa (Downers Grove, IL: Inter Varsity Press, 2006), Introduction, xx (hereafter ACCS NT IVa).

[25]Brown, *The Gospel According to John I-XII*, 101.

Moreover, John again refers to the wedding in Cana in chapter four "where he had made the water wine" (4.46), which also confirms that the sign was a real event.

Recent archeological discoveries have also helped to confirm the sign at Cana as a historical event. One discovery that received worldwide media attention was uncovering the location of the biblical village of Cana where the wedding took place, as well as shards of large stone jars, quite possibly used for the wedding miracle.

The Sign at Cana and Its Place in the Lectionary of the Church

The sign at Cana occupies a prominent place in the lectionary of almost all Churches, both in the West and in the East. In many ancient Churches, including the Indian Orthodox Church (West Syrian-Antiochian tradition), the Gospel passage of the wedding at Cana, a "third-day" event (Jn 2.1), is read at the Divine Liturgy on the first Sunday of Great Lent. At the conclusion of Great Lent, the Church celebrates the feast of all feasts, the resurrection, also a third-day event. Great Lent is a time to prepare for the greatest third-day event, the resurrection of Christ. It is also the season of repentance—a time specifically set apart in the annual liturgical cycle of the Church for *metanoia*, a personal transformation through prayer, fasting, repentance, and renunciation. As water was changed into wine, so throughout the days of Great Lent the faithful are to experience a total and complete transformation through fasting, forgiveness, prayer, and charitable works. Because it reminds the members of the Church of this third-day event through the sign at Cana, this is certainly an apt Gospel passage to read as the Church begins its Lenten journey toward the solemn celebration of the resurrection.

Incidentally, this tradition's Scripture readings at Divine Liturgies on the Sundays of Great Lent are about the miracles of Jesus Christ. The reading for the First Sunday of Lent is about the changing of water into wine, while all the other readings recount the healing miracles of Christ. Jesus begins his public ministry with a sign of water, a sign of nature. The other signs in the Gospel deal with the healing of men and women. Sickness, inherited by human beings because of disobedience and the fall, deforms and weakens the mind, body, and spirit. The purpose of the coming of Christ was to heal humanity from its spiritual and physical bondage as well as sickness, to make it "whole" once again. Healing is transformation. Jesus Christ's ministry of transformation starts with water, the initial creation, and ends with the transformation of human beings, the crown of creation. Healing is the central theme of the gospel, and it was the deeper message of our Lord, and of his apostles' preaching (Mt 10.1, 8; Mk 3.15; Lk 4.18).

In the Old Testament, marriage and wine are both symbols of the kingdom of God. Lent has always been a time to experience in this world a foretaste of the kingdom of God and to enjoy the life in paradise that Adam and Eve lost through disobedience. The scripture passage of the wedding in Cana, read at the very beginning of Great Lent, teaches and reminds the faithful about the kingdom of heaven.

After his baptism, Jesus went into the desert to fast and he was tempted there. His being tempted makes this, too, a timely reading for Great Lent, which is concerned with regeneration and transformation. The reading of the "wedding in Cana" is important in the Syrian tradition, not only to mark the beginning of Great Lent, but also the last Sunday of the Epiphany season, which celebrates the baptism of Christ. As water was the first creation, Jesus' entry into the River Jordan was the initiation of the process of re-creation. At the time of the baptism of Jesus, the Holy Trinity was revealed: the Holy Spirit descended on Jesus Christ like a dove, and the heavenly Father witnessed and proclaimed, "This is my beloved Son in whom I am well pleased" (Mt 3.17).

In the Byzantine tradition, the Gospel passage of the wedding at Cana is read on Monday after Thomas Sunday (also known as New Sunday in the Syrian tradition), probably because of the relationship of this event to the resurrection or third-day event. In the Eastern Orthodox tradition, the annual cycle of daily lectionary readings begins on Pascha (Easter) Sunday. Scripture portions about the resurrection are read on Holy Saturday evening and at morning prayers for Pascha, but the Gospel for the Paschal Liturgy is John 1.1–18, which begins the cycle with a continuous reading from the same Gospel.

The Scripture reading of the sign during the Paschal season, especially in the early Church, was valuable and very meaningful in another aspect. It was a time for instructing the newly baptized, who are introduced to the signs and the mysteries of the Church through baptism. The wedding-in-Cana narrative is a suitable passage for them as it is a sign with great significance and meaning.

> They had already received the fundamental teachings of the Faith. Now they were in the proper state to have their initiation explained. They had been baptized and chrismated; they had received communion. What did it all mean? That is the question that the post-baptismal instruction addressed, and its basis was John's Gospel. Why John? Because it was recognized that the Christ's miracles are really "signs" (*sēmeion* is the Greek word that John uses) that point to the sacramental basis of the Christian life. There are signs in which water is not only a necessary element for cleansing or for satisfying thirst, but is also symbolic of the water of baptism.[26]

The sign at Cana helps those who had already been baptized and those who were about to be baptized in their spiritual instruction and edification as it was a mysterious event that dealt with rudiments of the faith and different aspects of the "new way" (Acts 19.23; 24.22). New believers were able to see and to believe in the divinity of the Lord through the sign in which the divine glory of the Lord was manifested at the wedding in Cana.

During the fourth century, the Church of Rome celebrated Epiphany, the adoration of the Magi, and the sign of the marriage at Cana on the sixth of January.[27] In the Western liturgical tradition these

[26]Archbishop Dmitri (Royster), *The Miracles of Christ* (Crestwood, NY: St Vladimir's Seminary Press, 1999), 71–72.

[27]A Monk of the Eastern Church [Lev Gillet], *The Year of Grace of the Lord* (Crestwood, NY: St Vladimir's Seminary Press, 1992), 104.

three events were revelations or epiphanies of Jesus as the Messiah.[28]
"Our liturgical tradition has seen three moments as a kind of 'rolling
epiphany' or disclosure of Jesus as our Messiah."[29] Here the author
speaks about the Roman Catholic tradition. The divine was manifested at the baptism of our Lord and at the wedding in Cana. "The
element of 'water' is the link between the event that took place at Cana
and that which took place on the banks of the Jordan."[30] Given the
explicit and important link between Epiphany and the sign at Cana,
and because of these parallels, the passage about the wedding in Cana
was also read on Epiphany.

In some Western Churches (Protestant), the wedding sign passage
is used liturgically on the days after Epiphany and read on one of the
Sundays after Epiphany, at the beginning of the annual cycle, because
the event at Cana was an epiphany, a revelation, a transformation. It
was the first act of the public ministry of Christ through which his
glory was revealed as a transforming divine power that is brought
to the attention of the faithful at the very beginning of the annual
lectionary cycle.

In many Church traditions, the wedding at Cana narrative is the
Gospel reading for the service of the sacrament of marriage. It is the
only instance recorded in Scripture of the presence of Christ at a marriage celebration, making it a truly appropriate and meaningful reading for the sacrament of matrimony. Not only was Jesus Christ present
at the wedding, but he also performed the miraculous transformation
of water into wine. It was his presence at the wedding that saved the
family from shame and blessed the members with surplus and with
ton kalon oinon, "the good wine" (Jn 2.10). Just as the water kept
in the jars was changed into wine, so the bride and the bridegroom
were transformed at Cana into husband and wife. Thus a miraculous
transformation also happens to a bride and a bridegroom, who come

[28]Gregory Dix, *The Shape of the Liturgy* (London: Adam & Charles Black, Decree
Press, 1964), 357.

[29]Joseph S. Krempa, *Captured Fire: Cycle C* (New York: St Pauls, 2005), 75.

[30]A Monk, *The Year of Grace*, 104.

from two different families and were raised in different circumstances, but who become one as husband and wife, for "the two shall become one flesh" (Mt 19.5).

Yet in some ancient Church traditions, the Gospel reading for the sacrament of marriage is from Matthew (19.1–12), where Jesus spoke to the Pharisees who came to test him on marriage and divorce. Though the passage speaks about marriage and against divorce, the solemn occasion of the celebration of the mystery of marriage is not the most auspicious occasion for speaking about divorce, especially since divorce and separation that destroy the sacred union of marriage are prevalent in our culture and communities today. In the Armenian Apostolic (Orthodox) Church, both Gospel readings (Mt 19.1–6; Jn 2.1–12) are used during the sacrament of marriage.[31]

The wedding-at-Cana passage was also important in another sense, especially in the early years of the Church. John Meyendorff observes, "The story of the marriage in Cana in Galilee has been often invoked in the past against puritanical, pseudo-monastic sectarian trends, which considered marriage as impure and recommended celibacy as the only acceptable Christian ideal. This use of the passage is certainly fully legitimate: if Jesus, himself, and his Mother accepted the invitation to a wedding feast, marriage is certainly blameless."[32] Set against the background of many heretical teachings about marriage prevalent in those times, the wedding-in-Cana narrative emphasized both the place and the importance of marriage, as well as of marital life itself.

Hence, there is no surprise in the repeated usage of the Cana wedding narrative in the Gospel lectionaries of various Church traditions in different seasons (Epiphany, Great Lent, days and Sunday following Easter, etc.) and occasions, especially during the sacrament of matrimony.

[31]Zenob Nalbandian, *The Sacrament of Marriage in the Armenian Apostolic Church* (New York, NY: St Vartan's Press, 1987), 47, 50.

[32]John Meyendorff, *Marriage: An Orthodox Perspective* (Crestwood, NY: St Vladimir's Seminary Press, 1993), 40.

The Christological Importance of the Sign

The primary purpose of the sign at Cana seems to be Christological, and the wedding in Cana is basically centered on Christ. "As is frequently the case in John, the point of the story is Christological: Jesus' freedom from human control but his choice to act on behalf of humans."[33] Theologians assign importance to the sign because of its relationship to the redemptive work of Jesus. The sign and the context of the sign reveal that the eschatological time had begun in and through Christ.

The name "Jesus" is used six times in the narrative of sign by which the glory of Jesus was revealed to his followers. John says in the narrative, "Jesus did this as the beginning of his signs in Cana in Galilee and so revealed his glory, and his disciples began to believe him" (2.11). Some of the disciples had already acknowledged Jesus as Son of God, King of Israel, and Messiah foretold by the prophets. Yet, Jesus' response to them was, "You will see greater things than these" (1.50). The disciples at the wedding witnessed what Jesus had promised—the "glory as of the only Son from the Father" (1.14). The glory of the Messiah was revealed at that initial act of changing water into wine.

The Cana sign is also full of images and symbolism from the Hebrew Scriptures of the Old Testament. Only in the context of Jewish customs and practices can one fully grasp the depth of the meaning of words, symbols, and actions in the sign. The sign will take one to the time of Moses, who transformed the water in the rivers of Egypt into blood. "Moses who also at the beginning of his ministry manifested through himself God's power and glory so that the people might believe in him and respond to the act of salvation to which he was to lead them. This is why the Gospel according to John refers to this implicitly by saying 'that he manifested his glory; and his disciples believed in Him' (Jn 2.11)."[34]

The sign possibly has some connections with Elijah's miraculous supply of food and oil (2 Kg 4.42–44) and Elijah's oil (1 Kg 17.1–16).

[33]Bonnie Thurston, *Women in the New Testament: Questions & Commentary* (New York, NY: The Crossroad Publishing Company, 1998), 82.

[34]Matthew the Poor, "The Wedding in Cana," *Sourozh* 37 (August 1989): 14.

The amazing action at the wedding inaugurates Jesus' public ministry with superabundance as a sign of the messianic age excitedly awaited by the Jewish community. "The Christology of the story of water-become-wine would seem to be more functional than ontological. The Johannine account shows Jesus as the giver of the messianic gifts much more clearly than it points to him as the Incarnate Word."[35]

It is interesting to note that Roger Aus finds many similarities between the wedding in Cana and the banquet scene in the Old Testament book of Esther (1.1–8). In contrast to what happened at Cana, the banquet arranged by King Xerxes (Ahasuerus) was royal and majestic. It was attended by servants, a headwaiter, and many guests, and there was plenty of wine. Racial purity was an issue in that celebration, which relates to the water, kept for purification in the jars at the wedding scene in Cana. The king's banquet was a show of his superior power and glory, whereas the wedding in Cana illustrated the revelation of the glory of the Son of God. To quote Roger Aus, "The author of John 2.1–11 basically retained the characteristics he found in the Esther 1 traditions available to him. He too has a bridegroom, servants, a headwaiter and guests (Mary, Jesus and the disciples)."[36]

Contrary to the false teachings of the time, the sign affirmed the reality of the incarnation—the Son of God, "was incarnate that we might be made God."[37] Many false teachings about Jesus Christ prevailed, especially on the incarnation, when John penned the Gospel, and they were a significant threat to the true faith. A major heresy among them was Gnosticism, a generic term for the several branches of heterodox teachings. Its main teaching included that matter was evil and not real, and, therefore, everything material and of this world was to be rejected and condemned. Subsequently, followers of the various sects within Gnosticism questioned the reality of the incarnation of Jesus Christ. For them, worldly desires and pleasures were to

[35]Collins, *These Things Have Been Written*, 162.
[36]Roger Aus, *Water into Wine and the Beheading of John the Baptist* (Atlanta, GA: Scholars Press, 1988), 15.
[37]St Athanasius, *On the Incarnation* 54, trans. and ed. John Behr, Popular Patristics Series 44B (Yonkers, NY: St Vladimir's Seminary Press, 2011), 107.

be shunned. They glorified asceticism and were against marriage and using things, such as wine.

Yet, throughout the Fourth Gospel, we see references to the reality of Jesus' humanity. In Cana, Jesus attended a wedding and miraculously transformed water into wine. At the temple in Jerusalem, he was angry with those who had turned the temple into a marketplace (Jn 2.15). A thirsty Jesus asked for water to drink at his meeting with the Samaritan woman near Jacob's well (Jn 4.7). After the resurrection, Jesus also appeared to his disciples on the shore of the Sea of Tiberias and invited them to eat the breakfast he had prepared for them (Jn 21.12). John opens his Gospel by affirming the incarnation with great conviction in these words, "The Word became flesh and made his dwelling among us, and we saw his glory, the glory of the Father's only Son, full of grace and truth" (1.14). To sum up, "John's purpose in emphasizing so strongly the material, incarnational, and sacramental dimensions of God's redemptive work was to counteract a heresy known as *Gnosticism*."[38]

The theme of Jesus' humanity continued in the marriage scene at Cana, which he attended with his disciples. His mother was also there. One of the main items provided at the feast was wine, and Jesus miraculously changed water into wine to replenish the exhausted supply. The incarnation and the events at the wedding proved that the material world and things of this world were sacred and to be taken seriously. "All things came to be through him and without him nothing came to be" (Jn 1.3). By attending a marriage ceremony with his mother and his disciples, Jesus Christ revealed the reality of his humanity; and by changing water into wine, he revealed the reality of his divinity. At Cana, the fully divine and fully human person of Christ was clearly revealed, though much later, this reality, the divinity and humanity of the incarnate God, was to become a subject of great divisions within the Church.

---

[38]George Cronk, *The Message of the Bible* (Crestwood, NY: St Vladimir's Seminary Press, 1982), 163.

John wrote the Gospel in Greek at a time when the influence of Hellenic philosophy had infiltrated almost all areas of the social and religious fabric of Jewish life. In Greek mythology, as already mentioned, the pagan deity Dionysus was considered to be the god of wine. Stories were prevalent at that time about Dionysius miraculously changing water into wine. To those Greeks who knew about the power of the god Dionysius, John revealed with certainty that the true power of transforming water into wine rested not with Dionysius, but with Jesus Christ, God incarnate, who was the one with authority over all creation.[39] By narrating what happened at Cana, John was teaching the faithful that changing water into wine was not the folklore or the myth that they were well acquainted with, but an event that was witnessed by many, including the apostles.

To introduce the Only-begotten Son to the Hellenic world, the author presented Jesus in the beginning of the Gospel as the *Logos*, the pre-existent and incarnate Word of God. The all-powerful Word of God was familiar to the Jews, especially during later centuries of the pre-Christian era. On the other hand, the concept of the Logos was well-developed and well-known in Hellenic thought and philosophy. For the Greeks, the Logos was both Word and Reason, as well as the divine creating, guiding, and driving force behind the universe. It is also plausible that the wedding in Cana is narrated only in the Fourth Gospel because of its familiarity among the Greeks in various stories related to Dionysius, the god of wine. The Gospel was written so people would "believe that Jesus is the Messiah, the Son of God" (Jn 20.31), and even though Jesus had performed many other signs (Jn 20.31), only those signs that helped them believe in Jesus were included in the Gospel. It should also be noted that during those times in many cultures, especially in the Middle East, wine was seen in relation to the deities. "In the Greco-Roman world wine represents the presence and benevolence of the deity."[40]

[39]Barclay, *The Gospel of John*, 89.
[40]Wai-Yee Ng, *Water Symbolism in John: An Eschatological Interpretation,* Studies in Biblical Literature 15 (New York, NY: Peter Lang, 2001), 68.

The Gospel of John thus drew on sources, allusions, and images from the Old Testament, from prevailing Jewish thought, and also from Greek beliefs and practices. John Marsh summarizes all the sources and allusions behind the sign at Cana as follows:

> But now, at the beginning of the Gospel, John tells of the first sign. In doing so he has characteristically drawn together allusions from many sources, from the Old Testament, from Rabbinic thought and literature, possibly from Hellenistic concepts and beliefs, and certainly from the area of Christian experience, particularly sacramental experience. In light of this, it would be foolish to insist upon asking which of several interpretations is the right one; John almost certainly intended his allusions to be manifold, picking up religious experience from several fields in order to point to the reality that lay at the heart of the Christian's faith in God through Christ.[41]

John's intent when writing the Gospel was to point out that everything was fulfilled in Jesus Christ, and to this end he utilized all available cultural, intellectual, and religious ideas. Even the initial sign performed by Christ at the very beginning of his public ministry was a visible proof that "the Word became flesh and made his dwelling among us, and we saw his glory, the glory as of the Father's only Son, full of grace and truth" (Jn 1.14). "Jesus first manifested his glory in a Jewish setting, but in a way that anticipated a revelation to the wider Greco-Roman world."[42]

The Cana Sign in the Writings of the Church Fathers and Early Christian Writers

The Fathers of the Church saw a significant and symbolic event in the sign at Cana. They used the sign to explore and to explain the very

[41]John Marsh, *Saint John: The Pelican New Testament Commentaries* (London: Penguin Books, 1971), 142.

[42]Craig R. Koester, *Symbolism in the Fourth Gospel: Meaning, Mystery, Community* (Minneapolis, MN: Fortress Press, 1995), 80.

purpose of the incarnation of Jesus, as well as to reveal his redemptive vision and mission. Through the sign, they were able to comprehend cohesively that exhilarating experience which followers of Christ are expected to have in this world and in the world to come. By meditating on the different stages and nuances of the sign at Cana, we can also see the same theological, liturgical, and sacramental significance of that simple but elegant event experienced by the early Fathers of the Church.

Irenaeus of Lyons (*c.* 135–202) observes a specific difference between the wine that was served and consumed and the wine that Jesus made out of water at the wedding. He writes, "It was a good thing which was made by God's creation in the vineyard, and was first drunk as wine. None of those who drank of it spoke badly of it, and the Lord also took some of it. But better wine was that which was made by the Word directly and simply out of water for the use of those who were invited to the wedding."[43] Irenaeus alludes to the two kinds of wine that served as symbols of the old and the new covenants. If the quantity of wine served first was neither sufficient, nor of the best quality, the quantity of wine supplied at the end was both sufficient and of a much better quality. Irenaeus also observes in Jesus' response to Mary that the Son of God did everything in a timely manner, waiting for that hour known to his Father.[44] Clement of Alexandria (*c.* 150–215) related the sign to the Holy Communion. He warned also against those who abused wine finding comfort that Jesus miraculously made superb wine—and a large quantity of it!—at the wedding.[45]

Origen of Alexandria (*c.* 185–254) saw the presence of Christ at the wedding in relation to the union of Adam and Eve in the garden of Eden. He writes, "Jesus being Maker of man and woman does not refuse to be called to a marriage; it was he who after forming

---

[43]Irenaeus of Lyons, *Against Heresies* 11.5, in *Early Christian Fathers*, ed. Cyril C. Richardson (New York, NY: Simon & Schuster, 1996), 380.

[44]Irenaeus, *Against Heresies* 3.16.7, *John 1–10* (ACCS NT IVa), 92.

[45]Clement of Alexandria, *Paedagogus* 2.2, "On Drinking," in The Ante-Nicene Fathers, vol. 2, ed. Alexander Roberts and James Donaldson (Grand Rapids, MI: Eerdmans, 1979), 245.

Eve brought her to Adam. Therefore in the Gospel he says about the union, 'what God has joined together let no man put asunder.' Let the heretics therefore be put to shame who reject marriage, since Jesus was called to a marriage and his mother was there."[46] Eusebius of Caesarea (*c.* 260–340) noted that the first miracle took place in Cana of Galilee as prophesied by Isaiah (9.11).[47] For him, the wedding miracle was a sign of the mystical wine that transforms "bodily joy to a joy of mind and spirit."[48]

Theodore of Heraclea (*c.* 355) saw in the sign the eschatological wedding on the third day.

> According to the *theoria* (of this passage), the Word of God descended from heaven in order that the bridegroom, having made the punishment of the human nature his own, might persuade (his bride) to become pregnant with the spiritual seed of wisdom. He convened the wedding on the third day, that is, in the last times of the age. For he struck the transgression that was in Adam and again bandaged us on the third day, that is the last times when, becoming human for us he took on the whole fleshly nature that he resurrected in himself from the dead. Therefore, because of this (John) mentions the third as the day when he consecrated the wedding.[49]

It is interesting to note that Ephraim the Syrian (*c.* 306–373) views the Cana sign in the context of the Virgin Birth. He writes, "Why then did our Lord change the nature (of water) in the first of his signs? Was it not to show that the divinity, which had changed nature in the depths of the jars, was that the same (divinity) that had changed nature in the womb of the virgin?"[50] He continues:

---

[46]Origen, *Fragment 28 on the Gospel of John, John 1–10* (ACCS NT IVa), 89.
[47]Eusebius of Caesarea, *Proof of the Gospel* 9.8.8, ibid.
[48]Ibid.
[49]Theodore of Heraclea., *Fragments of John* 12, ibid.
[50]Ephraim the Syrian, *Hymns on Virginity* 33.1–2, ibid., 95.

He made wine from water, therefore, in order to give proof concerning how his conception and his birth took place. He summoned 'six water jars' as witness to the unique virgin who had given birth to him. The water jars conceived in a novel way, not in keeping with their custom, and gave birth to wine. But they did not continue to give birth. Similarly the Virgin conceived and gave birth to Emmanuel, and she did not give birth again. The giving birth by the jars was from smallness to greatness and from paucity to abundance; from water indeed to good wine. In her case, however, it was from greatness to weakness and from glory to ignominy.[51]

The Virgin Mary occupies an important position in Ephraim's hymns and writings. He links many scriptural passages to her to substantiate the place of the Mother of God in the economy of incarnation. The wedding in Cana narrative is a prominent one among them. In *Hymns on Virginity*, Ephraim writes,

> Let Cana thank you for gladdening her banquet!
> The bridegroom's crown exalted you for exalting it,
> And the bride's crown belonged to your victory.
> In her mirror allegories are expounded and traced,
> For you portrayed your church in the bride,
> And in her guests, yours are traced,
> And in her magnificence she portrays your advent.
> Let the feast thank him, for in multiplying his wine
> Six miracles were beheld there:
> The six wine jugs set aside for water
> Into which they invited the King to pour his wine.[52]

---

[51]Ephraim the Syrian, *Commentary on Tatian's Diatessaron* 5.6–7, ibid., 95. (From C. McCarthy, trans. and ed., *Saint Ephrem's Commentary on Tatian's Diatessaron: An English Translation of Chester Beatty Syriac MS 709. Journal of Semitic Studies* Supplement 2 [Oxford: Oxford University Press for the University of Manchester, 1993], in Joel C. Elowsky, *John 1–10*, ACCS NT IVa).

[52]Ephraim the Syrian, *Hymns on Virginity* 33.1–2, ibid., 95–96.

According to Ephraim, praise of God is basically a gift from God. It is evident from His Hymn on the wedding feast at Cana that is compared to the Eucharist. To quote,

> I have invited you, Lord, to a wedding feast of song,
> but the wine—the utterance of praise—at our feast has
>   failed.
> You are the guest who filled the jars with good wine,
> fill my mouth with your praise.
>
> The wine that was in the jars was akin and related to
> this eloquent wine that gives birth to praise,
> seeing that the wine gave birth to praise
> from those who drank it and beheld the wonder.
>
> You who are so just, if at a wedding feast not your own
> you filled six jars with good wine,
> do you, at this wedding feast, fill not the jars
> but the ten thousand ears with its sweetness.
>
> Jesus, you were invited to the wedding feast of others,
> here is your own pure and fair wedding feast,
> gladden your rejuvenated people,
> for your guests too, Lord need
> your songs; let your harp utter.
>
> The soul is your bride, the body your bridal chamber,
> your guests are the senses and the thoughts.
> And if a single body is a wedding feast for you,
> how great is your banquet for the whole church![53]

For Cyril of Jerusalem (*c.* 315–386) changing water into wine prefigured Holy Communion. "Jesus once changed water into wine by a word of command at Cana of Galilee. Should we not believe him

---

[53]Ephraim the Syrian, *Hymns on Faith*, XIV, quoted in Sebastian P. Brock, *Studies in Syriac Spirituality* (Bangalore: Dharmaram Publishers, National Printing Press, 2008), 26.

when he changes wine into blood? It was when he had been invited to an ordinary bodily marriage that he performed the wonderful miracle at Cana. Should we not be much more ready to acknowledge that to 'the sons of the bridal chamber' he has granted the enjoyment of his body and blood?"[54]

John Chrysostom gave good and lengthy exposition on the sign in his sermons. He viewed the presence of Christ at the wedding as servant—Christ as servant attended the wedding of his servant.[55] He also brought out through the sign the importance of the transformation of human beings. "For there are, yes, there are men who in nothing differ from water, so cold, and weak, and unsettled. But let us bring those of such disposition to the Lord, that He may change their will to the quality of wine, so that they be no longer washy, but have body, and be the cause of gladness in themselves and others."[56] Chrysostom says that what Jesus did at Cana was to honor his mother, and that there was no contradiction in Jesus' response to "the woman who had borne Him."[57]

For Chrysostom, every sacrament of marriage is the image of the marriage in Cana, where Jesus Christ is present in a special way.[58] The "golden-mouthed" Father of the Church, in his sermon on marriage, advised the faithful, reminding them about the wedding in Cana, to invite Christ at their wedding. "Let those who take wives now do as they did at Cana in Galilee. Let them have Christ in their midst."[59] According to him, the power of Jesus' miracle was revealed gradually and only to those who were able to grasp fully what had happened. For in the end, not only the servants, but the steward and the

---

[54]Cyril of Jerusalem, *Mystagogical Lectures* 4.2, ibid., 98.

[55]Chrysostom, *Homilies on the Gospel of John* 21.1, ibid., 88.

[56]Chrysostom, *Homily on the Gospel of John* 22.3 (NPNF[1] 14:78).

[57]Chrysostom, *Homilies on the Gospel of John* 22.1, *John 1–10* (ACCS NT IVa), 94–95.

[58]St John Chrysostom, "Homily XII: On Colossians 4:18," in *On Marriage and Family Life,* trans. Catherine P. Roth and David Anderson, Popular Patristics Series 7 (Crestwood, NY: St Vladimir's Seminary Press, 1997), 79.

[59]Chrysostom, *Sermon on Marriage*, ibid., 81.

bridegroom attested to the fact that the wine served last was the best. About the manifestation of glory, he writes:

> "How?" asks one, "and in what way? For only the servants, the ruler of the feast, and the bridegroom, not the greater number of those present, gave heed to what was done." How then did he "manifest forth His glory"? He manifested it at least for His own part, and if all present heard not of the miracle at the time, they would hear of it afterwards, for unto the present time it is celebrated, and has not been unnoticed. That all did not know it on the same day is clear from what follows, for after having said that He "manifested forth His glory," the Evangelist adds, "And His disciples believed on Him."[60]

Cyril of Alexandria (c. 375–444) writes about the reasons why Jesus was at the wedding. Jesus was imparting his blessings to the couple as well as preparing "grace in advance for those soon to be born" and sanctifying "their entrance into existence."[61] Through the wedding in Cana, Cyril of Alexandria brings out in his writings also the important place of the Mother of Jesus in salvation history. According to Cyril, the wedding took place in the "Galilee of the Gentiles,"[62] the reason being that the synagogues of the Jews rejected the heavenly bridegroom, but the church of the Gentiles accepted and received him. Cyril presents the mother's request to Jesus at the wedding and his response and action as complimentary. He also presents another reason for Jesus' presence at the wedding: to sanctify the mystery of marriage. "God had said to the woman . . . 'in pain you shall bring forth children.'"[63] "How else could we escape a condemned marriage unless this curse was annulled? This curse too the Savior removes because of his love for mankind. For he who is the delight and joy

---

[60]Chrysostom, *Homily 23.1* (NPNF[1] 14:80).
[61]Cyril of Alexandria, *Commentary on the Gospel of John* 2.1 (ACCS NT IVa, 90).
[62]Op. cit. 2.1 (ACCS NT IVa, 88).
[63]Op. cit. 2.2 (ACCS NT IVa, 90).

of all honored marriage with his presence so that he might expel the ancient sadness of childbearing."[64]

Augustine of Hippo (*c.* 354–430) saw Jesus Christ in the sign as the source of Scripture. He writes, "But when he turned the water itself into wine, he showed us that the ancient Scripture comes from him too; for by his order the jars were filled. This Scripture, too, is indeed from the Lord. But it has no taste if Christ is not understood in it."[65] For Augustine, the coming of Christ was to participate in a wedding; the wedding of the lamb (Rev 19.9). "The one came to attend the wedding in Cana, came to this world for a wedding. Therefore he has a bride here whom he has redeemed by his blood and to whom he has given the Holy Spirit as a pledge. He wrested her from enslavement to the devil, he died for her sins."[66] According to Augustine, Jesus made the new wine, the Gospel, from the water of the Law and the Prophets, and the Son of God was the one who gave it its taste. In Augustine's opinion, Jesus performed the miracle not out of necessity, but to manifest his glory, which would be fully revealed at the hour of his crucifixion, and for which he as Creator knew the most appropriate time.

For Maximus of Turin (380?–408/423/465?), Jesus attended the wedding in order to sanctify marriage by his presence. In his sermon on the wedding in Cana, Maximus writes:

> He went to a wedding of the old order when he was about to take a new bride for himself through the conversion of the gentiles, a bride who would forever remain a virgin. He went to a wedding even though he himself was not born of human wedlock. He went to the wedding not, certainly, to enjoy a banquet but rather to make himself known by miracles. He went to the wedding not to drink wine but to give it.[67]

[64]Op. cit. 2.2 (ACCS NT IVa, 90).
[65]Augustine, *Tractates on the Gospel of John* 9.5.3 (ACCS NT IVa, 96).
[66]Op. cit. 8.4.1, pp. 89–90.
[67]Maximus of Turin, *Sermon 23* (ACCS NT IVa, 90).

That "suddenly in a marvelous way the water began to acquire potency, take on color, emit fragrance and gain flavor"[68] in Jesus' presence is proof that he is the Creator. The sign also proved to the disciples that Jesus, the Son of the Virgin Mary in whom they already believed, was indeed the Son of the Most High.

Caesarius of Arles (c. 470–548) saw in the sign the mystery of the Trinity as well as the heavenly joy of the mystery of marriage. He observes:

> The third day is the mystery of the Trinity, while the miracles of the nuptials are the mysteries of heavenly joys. It was both a nuptial day and a feast for this reason, because the church after the redemption was joined to the spouse who was coming to that spouse. I say, whom all the ages from the beginning of the world had promised. It is he who came down to earth to invite his beloved to marriage with his highness, giving her for a present the token of his blood and intending to give later the dowry of his kingdom.[69]

The Sign in Relation to the Transfiguration: Transformation to Divinization

Jesus Christ is presented in the Fourth Gospel as the one who transforms everything. In his presence everything is elevated to a sublime and celestial level. At the wedding in Cana, water kept for purification was transformed into wine of a superb quality and was a prelude to the transforming mission of Jesus Christ's ministry. Fr Matthew the Poor, the Coptic monk, observes, "In the miracle of the wedding the notion of 'transformation' is brought into focus at the deepest and clearest level of interpretation."[70] Barclay particularly finds in the sign individual transformation. He writes, "This story in John is saying to us: 'if you want the new exhilaration, became a follower of Jesus

[68]Op. cit., p. 96.
[69]Caesarius of Arles, *Sermon 167.1*, ibid., 89.
[70]Matthew the Poor, "The Wedding in Cana," 15.

Christ, and then there will come a change in your life which will be like water turning into wine."[71] In his presence and through his action, human beings and the cosmos are also transformed, revealing in him the kingdom of God.

The sign at the wedding in Cana is linked to the transfiguration of our Lord on Mount Tabor. Both were *theophanies*, manifestations of the divinity of Christ. Fr Lev Gillet, writing as "A Monk of the Eastern Church," says, "For many Orthodox, the Transfiguration of Our Lord announces and symbolizes the metamorphosis of this world into a new world. It is a somewhat eschatological view, foreshadowed in the transformation of water into wine at Cana."[72] In both events, the disciples accompanying Christ witnessed the manifestation of the glory of the Lord. It is interesting to note that although detailed in all three Synoptic Gospels (Mt 17.1–9; Mk 9.2–10; Lk 9.28–36; also 2 Pet 1.17), the transfiguration of Jesus on Mount Tabor is missing in John's Gospel, and that strangely enough, the Cana event is narrated only in the Fourth Gospel. Yet, John was present in Cana, as well as on Mount Tabor. Why did he avoid narrating the transfiguration event in the Gospel? The answer is unclear, though he could have thought that the wedding in Cana would adequately explain Jesus' transforming power and thereby fully reveal the glory of the Lord.

Jesus Christ came into a sinful world disintegrated through the fall (Jn 1.9–11). The purpose of the incarnation was to inaugurate "a new heaven and a new earth" (Rev 21:1). He is "the way, the truth, and the life" (Jn 14.6). St Paul says, "Therefore, if anyone is in Christ, is a new creation; old things have passed away; behold, all things have become new" (2 Cor 5.17). The event of changing water into wine at Cana truly points to the mission, as well as the direction of the new creation. Evdokimov observes, "It is the miracle at the wedding of Cana, the classical image of the metabolism of the human being; it is the *metanoia*, the second birth, the very real death and the still more

---

[71]Barclay, *The Gospel of John*, 91.

[72]A Monk of the Eastern Church [Lev Gillet], *Orthodox Spirituality* (Crestwood, NY: St Vladimir's Seminary Press, 1987), 96.

real resurrection."[73] In fact, the four different events detailed in chapters two to four of John's Gospel—the wedding in Cana, the cleansing of the temple, the conversations between Nicodemus and Jesus, and the Samaritan Woman and Jesus—all illustrate the renewal and the novelty that Jesus establishes through his incarnation. The transformation that he brings to nature and matter is revealed through the sign of changing water into wine. The transformation of the temple and worship is introduced in the cleansing of the Jerusalem temple (2.13–20). In chapter three, where Jesus discusses the new birth from above with Nicodemus, we are presented with the transformation of the individual through baptism. The next chapter deals with the Samaritan woman, a person of questionable character and conduct; there we read not only about the transformation that took place in her life, but also about the discussion about her transformation by the entire Samaritan community.

The original purpose of the water in the jars at the wedding in Cana was for ablutions, but it was changed to sublime wine, a "new wine," in Christ's presence. This wine was new for several reasons. Not only was it made from water and not through traditional wine-making methods, but the transformation was unlike anything that anyone there had ever seen. It was miraculously created, breaking all traditional boundaries of making wine. Moreover, it excelled not only in quality, but in quantity, surprising and delighting the headwaiter and prompting his subtle observation that "Everyone serves good wine first, and then when people have drunk freely, an inferior one; but you have kept the good wine until now" (Jn 2.10).

The fact that the first wine served at the banquet ran out was also true of the water kept for purification. The pots where it was stored at the wedding were empty as well (Jn 2.6–7). In other words, what existed in Judaism through the Mosaic Law was exhausted and had lost its exuberance and vitality. Miraculously providing the new wine at the wedding banquet was clearly a significant symbolic act of rev-

---

[73]Paul Evdokimov, *The Sacrament of Love* (Crestwood, NY: St Vladimir's Seminary Press, 2011), 77.

elation concerning that abundant life which the Son of God was to impart to the estranged children of God. It is the fullness and the abundance of life that Jesus Christ came to share with all of creation, especially with mankind, the crown of creation.

The passage of the transformation of ordinary water to extraordinary new wine is followed by the cleansing of the Jerusalem temple where Jesus Christ spoke about the new temple. Jesus chastised and chased away the merchants and the moneychangers who converged in "his Father's house" (Jn 2.16) and had converted the holy place into a market place. He publicly declared on the steps of the temple, "Destroy this temple, and in three days I will raise it up" (Jn 2.19). It was certainly a shocking statement for listeners, for that was the most sacred place and the only temple for them. Symbolically, Jesus was replacing the old temple in Jerusalem and establishing in its place a new temple not made by human hands. The Jews believed that the temple was the place where the Almighty dwells. Jesus Christ who died and resurrected on the third day, was to become that new temple, the One who is God and the One in whom the Father dwells (Jn 14.10, 11, 38). Through Jesus and in Jesus, the temple becomes the place where God dwells in man.

Jesus Christ is God and Man, and in him perfect divinity and perfect humanity meet. The temple, representing heaven on earth and the dwelling place of God, is the place where God and man meet. Jesus is that new temple where God and man meet and in whom man is reconciled to God. While talking about the destruction of the Jerusalem temple, the symbol of Jewish faith and the center of Jewish life, Jesus Christ already alluded to himself as the temple. "But He was speaking of the temple of his body" (Jn 2.21). The same theme is presented in Revelation, "I saw no temple in the city, for its temple is the Lord God almighty and the Lamb" (21.22). The Church, the body of Christ, is the dwelling place of God. At the Last Supper, Jesus transformed wine into his own blood, and bread into his body. His body was the temple that was broken on the cross, and to this day, it is given to the "members of His body" (1 Cor 12.27) unto eternal life.

While the second chapter of the Gospel of John deals with water and wine, as well as with the cleansing of the temple, the third chapter is devoted to water and rebirth, a spiritual birth in the Holy Spirit. The central theme of chapter three is the transformation of matter (that is, water, and the temple) and mankind through a new spiritual birth. Those who want to enter the kingdom of God need to born again, and this was the main point of the dialogue between Jesus and Nicodemus, a Jewish leader ("a member of the Jewish council," 3.1) and scholar who came to meet Jesus secretly by night. Jesus said to him, "Amen, amen I say to you, no one can see the kingdom of God without being born from above. . . . Amen, amen I say to you, no one can enter the kingdom of God without being born of water and Spirit" (3.3–5). Those who enter into the Church, the new temple or the body of Christ, and participate in the new wine or are in communion with Christ, they must go first through a new birth. That new birth is the initiation ceremony into the abundant and eternal life in Christ, life in the Church.

A new worship is introduced in the fourth chapter of John's Gospel. While conversing with the Samaritan woman, Jesus says, "Everyone who drinks this water will be thirsty again, but whoever drinks the water I shall give will never thirst; the water I shall give will become in him a spring of water welling up to eternal life" (4.13–14). A new form of worship is established for those who have experienced a new birth. Jesus told the Samaritan woman, ". . . a time is coming when you will worship the Father neither on this mountain nor in Jerusalem . . . Yet, a time is coming and has now come when the true worshippers will worship the Father in the Spirit and in truth, for they are the kind of worshippers the Father seeks. God is Spirit, and those who worship him must worship in Spirit and in truth" (4.23–24).

At the time of the crucifixion of Christ, the veil in the Jerusalem temple was torn in half. The obstacles that prevented human beings from entering into the presence of the heavenly Father were thus removed by the torn veil. The children of God gained access to heaven through the Son, who opened for them a new path of worship, to "worship the Father in Spirit and in truth" (4.24). This was not limited to the Israelites, but was prepared for every child of God.

Thus the sign at Cana is a symbol of the transformation that Jesus Christ came to introduce and to establish. One of the prayers for Great Lent in the Syrian tradition says, "At the marriage feast the waters saw You and were changed into wine as a sign of the new life You raise in us by the second birth."[74] Everything is new in Christ, and He is the one who makes everything new. St Paul clearly and concisely says, "So whoever is in Christ is a new creation: the old things have passed away; behold, new things have come" (2 Cor 5.17). In the words of Matthew the Poor:

> It is noteworthy that this miracle inherently brings out the transformation *from water*—the capital stock of John the Baptist—as a power of purification and change through repentance and behavior, *to Christ Himself* as a much greater power, able to transform the very essence of human nature and its subsequent behavior. For Christ here, by subjecting water and transforming it into what is not water through the power of his word, explicitly and forcefully points out that the power to change, repent, rejoice, and find comfort, which all mankind craves, originally exists in Christ and in his word.[75]

If the sign at Cana—of water transformed into wine—was a prelude to the transformation of the new creation, then the signs, the words, and the deeds that followed reveal the same theme.

The Sign in Relation to Pascha

A reader with basic understanding of Holy Scripture can recognize that the wedding in Cana is a prelude to the crucifixion and resurrection of our Lord. The words, the context of the sign, and the time

[74]Francis Acharya, *Prayer with the Harp of the Spirit*, vol. 3, *The Crown of the Year*, part II (Vagamon: Kurishumala Ashram, 1985), 307. Translated from the original Syriac of the Penqitho.

[75]Matthew the Poor, "The Wedding in Cana," 10.

it occurred are very important to the author of the Gospel. They all convey much more than their surface meaning and are interestingly filled with biblical, theological, and mystical insights, especially in relation to the death and the resurrection of Christ. The sign's close relation to this Paschal event may be seen in the very first sentence of the narration of the sign, as it happened on "the third day" (2.1). One may speculate that the time reference possibly meant three days after Jesus' baptism or was tied to another event, such as Christ calling the disciples. However, by presenting it as a "third-day" event, the wedding in Cana was linked to the greatest of all feasts, the glorious resurrection. Since it was the initial act of Christ's public ministry narrated in the Gospel of John, Jesus was indirectly indicating to his disciples what was going to happen in the coming days of his ministry, especially his death and resurrection. The context of the sign happening at a wedding also foreshadows the wedding of the Lamb (Rev 19.7–9).

Jesus addressed his mother as "woman" at the wedding in Cana. Today, for a son to call his mother "woman" seems strange and, of course, disrespectful. So it is difficult to understand why Jesus Christ, the perfect Son, addressed his beloved mother as "woman." However, the meaning of this way of addressing someone varies according to language, culture, and the context in which it is used. Still, it can make sense only in the context of the redemptive work of Jesus Christ, especially in the events that took place at the end of his earthly ministry. "This peculiar interchange enables readers to see that Jesus' actions cannot be understood on the level of typical relations between mother and son but must be interpreted respectively in light of his death and resurrection."[76] The only other time Jesus addressed Mary as "woman" was at the foot of the cross during the crucifixion, when he entrusted her his beloved disciple John.

The first woman, Eve, and her husband, Adam, succumbed to the temptation of the serpent, thus causing creation and the crown of creation to fall away from paradise and the Creator. The Virgin Mary is the New Eve, whose seed, as promised, would crush the head of the

[76]Koester, *Symbolism in the Fourth Gospel*, 78.

serpent (Gen 3.14–15). It was her seed, Jesus Christ, who would fulfill what was promised after the fall. "The woman and her seed" are also present at the marriage feast. If Eve prompted Adam to disobey God, it was the woman Mary who prompted her Son to act in order to save the fallen world from the clutches of sin and Satan.

The relationship between the Son and the mother was elevated for all time to a higher level at the wedding in Cana. When Jesus entrusted his mother to John the Apostle, Mary was no longer only his mother, but mother of all the faithful. Just before the crucifixion, Jesus had the Last Supper with his disciples, where he gave them bread and said, "This is my body" and wine, saying, "This is my blood" (Lk 22.20; Mk 14.24; Mt 26.28). As water was transformed into wine in Cana, so would bread and wine be transformed through the Holy Spirit into the life-giving body and blood of Jesus Christ. And those who receive this body and blood would also be transformed in spirit.

Another theme that is reflected in the wedding at Cana is the "hour" or "time," which for Jesus, meant his glorification through his suffering, death, resurrection, and ascension. When the mother of Jesus informed her Son about the lack of wine at the wedding, his response was "My time has not come" (Jn 2.4; 7.6). Jesus Christ could only do his mother's bidding by revealing his divine authority. Complying with his mother's request thus marked not only the beginning of his journey toward the "hour" of the cross and death, but it also advanced the time of his "hour."

The Wedding Feast in Cana in Relation to the Feast of Pentecost

Some biblical scholars see a parallel between the sign at Cana and the coming of the Holy Spirit on the day of Pentecost.[77] They see the "third-day" in relation to Pentecost (Acts 2). The third-day to Pentecost is also connected to the giving of the Torah and the Covenant on Mount Sinai, when Moses went up to the mountain the third day (Ex 19.16), while the Israelites spent time in prayer and preparation.

[77]Joseph A. Grassi, "The Wedding at Cana," *The Composition of John's Gospel*, ed. Orton E. David (Leiden: Brill, 1999), 123–128.

The sign took place in a village of Galilee. In Acts 2.7, those who received the Spirit are presented as Galileans, "Then they were all amazed and marveled, saying to one another, 'Look, are not all these who speak Galileans?'" The Cana event passage mentions, "The mother of Jesus was there" (Jn 2.1). The only other place we read these words is in Acts 1.14, "These all continued with one accord in prayer and supplication, with the women and Mary the mother of Jesus and with His brothers."

The words of the Virgin Mary to her Son that there was no wine, could imply that she was informing Jesus not only of the absence of physical wine, but also of the lack of "spiritual wine." This can be interpreted also in light of the descent of the Holy Spirit at Pentecost. The crowd remarked about the disciples gathered on Pentecost, "They are filled with the Spirit" (Acts 2.4), while some even scoffed at them saying, "They have had too much wine" (Acts 2.13). When Jesus responded to his mother at the wedding, "My hour has not yet come," he was talking about the hour of his glorification. In the seventh chapter of the same Gospel we read more about the glorification from Jesus, "He said this in reference to the Spirit that those who came to believe in him were to receive. The Holy Spirit had not descended because Jesus had not yet been glorified" (7.39). The time of glorification was the time of the coming of the Holy Spirit. The servants obeyed at the wedding when they were told to fill the pots with water. According to Luke, the Holy Spirit descended upon people who obeyed the commands of Jesus, "Behold I am sending the promise of my Father upon you, but stay in the city until you are clothed with power from on high" (24.49). Acts 1.4 confirms that followers of Jesus did obey.

The jars at the wedding were filled to the brim with the best wine. Those who were waiting for the Holy Spirit on the day of Pentecost had the same experience when "they were all filled with the Holy Spirit" (Acts 2.4), and they were as if "filled with new wine" (Acts 2.13). Just as Jesus filled the jars with new wine, so the Holy Spirit fills those who receive him. Paul Evdokimov observes how the Word and the Spirit act together at the wedding in Cana for the nuptial Pentecost. "At Cana, in the house of the first Christian couple, the Word and the Spirit preside at the feast, and for this reason one drinks the new wine, the miraculous wine that brings with it a joy not of this world. This is the 'sober intoxication' which Gregory of Nyssa speaks of, and which the Apostles were accused of on the day of Pentecost. The nuptial Pentecost makes 'all things new.'"[78] Thus, the sign at Cana where the divine glory was manifested was an act of the Holy Trinity.

At the time of the baptism of Jesus Christ there was a divine manifestation, followed by his calling the disciples. Archimandrite Theodor Micka says that on that occasion, "a new consummation needed to be prepared: the joining of His Spirit to the spirit of man. Born out of this union would come a new spirit, the manifestation of the glory of God (2.11) and a new birth described in the next chapter (3.5) . . . 'Truly, truly I say to you (Nicodemus) except a man be born of water and of the Spirit, he cannot enter into the Kingdom of God.'"[79]

Thus at the wedding in Cana, the first act of Jesus in his public ministry not only reveals the purpose of the incarnation, but also leads to the joyous experience of the "new wine," or the Holy Spirit. The sign also leads to the sacramental mysteries of the Church, which is an act of the Holy Spirit: the visible means of "invisible grace" through which the faithful have access to the divine presence and can become part of the kingdom of God during the time of their earthly existence.

Conclusion

The sign of the wedding contains the same narrative pattern that we see in the other signs detailed in the Gospel. A situation arose at the wedding for which a normal quick fix or instant resolution was not possible. Jesus was informed of the crisis, and his initial response was

[78]Evdokimov, *The Sacrament of Love*, 128.
[79]Johanna Manley, ed., *The Bible And The Holy Fathers For Orthodox* (Menlo Park, CA: Monastery Books, 1990), 36.

not very positive in its appearance, at least in how it sounded. Yet, he did act miraculously to resolve the situation, and the ultimate result was a divine transformation. The signs one after the other in the Gospels helped Jesus' disciples to strengthen their faith in him. Howard Brook observes, "A setting in space or time is given, someone other than Jesus speaks. Jesus responds with an unexpected word and/ or deed, and reactions are sorted out. Frequently, the formula will involve the transformation of an 'earthly' reality (e.g., wine, water, birth) into a 'heavenly' one (e.g., God's bounty, commitment to the faith community). Often, it will suggest the replacement of a Jewish/ Judean religious practice with Jesus himself or an apparent practice of the Johannine community. Inevitably, it will lead some to faith and drive some away."[80]

In addition to the theological and spiritual mysteries that were expressed through the sign, it also revealed the inauguration of eschatological time. The sign also bore witness to abundant joy in the presence of Jesus Christ, as it brought the presence of the almighty Christ and the powerful mediation of the Virgin Mary while also paving the way for Jesus' miraculous act on water. The sign revealed the ineffable glory of the Son of God, which indirectly led his disciples to believe in the Messiah whom they had eagerly awaited. In fact, the first sign was also an occasion for the glory of the Son of God to be manifested. It was a sign where events of the initial creation were remembered, the history of redemption was retold, and the deification process of the children of God was revealed. The disobedience of Adam and Eve caused the fall of humanity and scarred the image of God in man. They were expelled from the garden of Eden, and there was total confusion in the cosmos: a breakdown that brought about alienation among human beings, but above all, between God and humanity. The sign symbolizes the restoration of broken relationships by Jesus Christ. The transformation of water into wine points to the restoration of nature and humanity to its original state of glory.

[80]Howard-Brook, *Becoming Children of God*, 77.

2

The Inauguration of the Public Ministry of Jesus Christ

According to the Gospel of John, as noted already, the wedding in Cana was the first sign our Lord performed. This chapter will analyze the purpose of the sign at Cana and will look at how we can understand it. Based on the context of the event, the apparent and primary goal was to save a family from embarrassment. The sign also revealed a creative act of the Creator. C. S. Lewis writes, "Every year, as part of the Natural Order, God makes wine. He does so by creating a vegetable organism that can turn water, soil and sunlight into a juice, which will, under proper conditions, become wine . . . Once, and in one year only, God, now incarnate, short-circuits the process; makes wine in a moment: uses earthenware jars instead of vegetable fibers to hold the water."[1]

Many have attempted to rationalize the sign and not to see the miracle that took place. One among them speculated that when Jesus told the servants to add water to the half-empty pots, and merely by his presence, the guests were so happy that "they took the diluted wine for a fresh supply of the finest vintage."[2] Since this sign is narrated only in St John, some commentators suggest that the event actually never happened, but was added later, "regarding the whole as a purely theological creation."[3] Raymond Brown strongly negates this

[1]Cited in Hunter, *The Gospel According to John*, 30. C. S. Lewis, *Miracles: A Preliminary Study* (New York, NY: Harper San Francisco, 2001), 221.

[2]Ibid., 30.

[3]Brown, *The Gospel according to John I-XII*, 101.

opinion, while scholars like Bultmann hold the view that there was strong pagan influence behind the story, especially with Dionysius, the Greek god of wine. The feast of Dionysius was celebrated on January 6, and the Scripture reading for the Epiphany Liturgy, according to some traditions, is the Cana narrative.[4]

The sign of changing water into wine is one of the nature miracles in the Gospel of St John. Six other nature miracles are in all four Gospels: calming of the storm (Mt 8.23–27; Mk 4.35–41; Lk 8.22–25); the multiplication of the loaves and fish (Mt 4.13–21; Mk 6.30–41; Lk 9.10–17; Jn 6.1–14); walking on water (Mt 14.22–33; Mk 6.45–52; Jn 6.15–21); cursing the fig tree (Mt 21.18–22; Mk 11.19–26); the miraculous catch of fish (Jn 21.1–14); and finding the coin in the mouth of the fish to pay the temple tax (Mt 17.24–27). With the exception of the fig tree miracle, all these miracles were performed to help people in need. If multiplying the loaves was to feed the hungry multitude, protecting the frightened disciples was the sole purpose of calming the storm at sea. However, the sign at Cana of changing water into wine is essentially and existentially different from the other nature miracles cited above. How the Apostle John presents and narrates the sign at Cana reveals far more than the act of assisting a family in distress over lacking wine: it clearly conveys that John wanted to reveal the purpose of the incarnation to the Church he established and the community to whom he wrote his Gospel. More likely, it was the apostle's goal to inculcate in them the true faith and to instruct them in the heavenly mysteries that were revealed through the life-giving words and deeds of Jesus Christ.

A Feast in the Beginning and a Feast at the End

In the Gospel of John, Jesus' public ministry is inaugurated by the sign at the wedding feast of Cana. Jesus was fully aware of his eventual death on the cross, and he was ready to fulfill the mission for which he had been sent. He was certain of his mission, knowing first and

[4]Ibid., 101.

foremost that he would accomplish the absolute act of fulfilling the will of his heavenly Father. When the disciples reminded Jesus to eat after his lengthy discourse with the Samaritan woman, he responded by saying, "My food is to do the will of the one who sent me and to finish His work" (Jn 4.34). Before his crucifixion, Jesus knelt down and prayed in the garden of Gethsemane, "Father, if it is your will, take this cup away from me, nevertheless not my will, but Yours, be done" (Lk 22.42). His last words before dying on the cross were, "It is finished" (Jn 19.30), which meant that he had fulfilled his mission. Thus, the goal and the purpose of everything Jesus did and said was to please his heavenly Father, by doing the Father's will. He was ready to start his ministry in Cana, and his presence at the wedding with his disciples was not only to participate in a joyous event, but to signify the beginning of his ministry, which culminated in and was completed on the cross.

Jesus Christ also concluded his public ministry with a meal, the Last Supper. He was one of many guests at the wedding banquet in Cana, but at the Last Supper, he was not only the host, but also the food and the drink. This meal took place during the Feast of Passover, and at the same time his passion and crucifixion were approaching quickly. He was about to face unimaginable suffering and unbearable sorrow. His followers were about to forsake him, and one of his disciples would even deny him. Those who publicly proclaimed their willingness to die with him would also soon disown and deny him. Yet, in spite of all these difficult situations, Jesus became the host and served a supper to his disciples, saying, "With fervent desire I have desired to eat this Passover with you before I suffer" (Lk 22.15). Then "He took bread, gave thanks and broke it, and gave it to them, saying, 'This is my body which is given for you; do this in remembrance of me.' Likewise, he also took the cup after supper saying, 'This cup is the new covenant in my blood, which is shed for you'" (Lk 22.19–20).

Dining is a continual theme in the New Testament, and Jesus often accepted invitations to dine. It is very significant and certainly meaningful that the first event in which Jesus Christ participated after the inauguration of his public ministry was a banquet that also involved eating and drinking. Food is essential for sustenance and thus a fundamental necessity for all living beings. Through his presence at and participation in the wedding, Jesus was teaching the transformative power of food and drink. Coincidentally, the fall of Adam and Eve involved food, but it was a forbidden fruit tasted and shared by way of Satan's temptation. Consuming the forbidden fruit not only resulted in expulsion from paradise, but also destroyed relationships among people, as well as between heaven and earth. Adam and Eve were in paradise with everything, the whole universe, at their disposal. They were given the freedom to fast, as well as to feast, but their freedom was conditional: they were not allowed to eat of the Tree of the Knowledge of Good and Evil. Ultimately, their failure was to break the fast by feasting from the forbidden fruit in paradise. Jesus Christ's experience was antithetical to that of Adam and Eve. The last thing Jesus, the second Adam, did before performing the sign of changing water into wine was to fast for a long time in the wilderness, where food was not available.

Man inevitably needs food to survive, but the food he eats to survive leads to death, physical or biological death. Through man's initial fall at the garden of Eden, the food that was supposed to supplement his eternal life and to be a means of communion with his Creator introduced death, destruction, and separation from God. The incarnate God became food at the Last Supper. Thus, he became the eternal food to overcome death as well as the food that provides everlasting and abundant life. He repeatedly declared, "I am the bread of life . . . I am the living bread that came down from heaven; whoever eats this bread will live forever; and the bread that I will give is my flesh . . . for the life of the world" (Jn 6.35, 51). The purpose of his incarnation was to redeem human beings from the fall and its consequences and to restore them to the joy of lost paradise, and to invite everyone to a "dinner," the Last Supper. Christ thus became the server at the table and the food that was served. Through his sacrificial death and resurrection, Jesus Christ reestablished shattered relationships and restored eternal life to fallen human beings.

Though food is essential for our earthly existence, it is also uniquely important for our eternal existence and abundant life. The food that we consume regularly for daily sustenance will not grant eternal life because that is part of the fallen and corrupted world. The only food that is not of this world is the food that Jesus Christ provides. It is his own body and blood, which is not corrupted by sin. This mysterious and heavenly food is "the medicine of immortality,"[5] as Ignatius of Antioch (*c.* 35/50–98/108) explained. Through his presence and participation in the wedding, Jesus was teaching the transformative power of food and drink. "And since God has created the world as food for us and has given us food as means of communion with Him, the new food of the new life which we receive from God in His Kingdom *is Christ Himself*."[6]

In the inauguration of his public ministry, Jesus Christ took part in a celebration where the food served was of the kind essential for sustenance and celebration. He did the same at the end of his public ministry by presiding over the Last Supper. He continued to do the same during the resurrection appearances to the travelers who were going from Jerusalem to Emmaus on Pascha (Lk 24.30–31), as to the disciples who were fishing at the Sea of Galilee a few days after Jesus' resurrection (Jn 21.13). Food is essential for physical life and survival. Jesus, "the bread of life," is essential for eternal and abundant life.

The Temptation to Turn Stones into Bread: The Transformation of Water into Wine

It is good to compare and to contrast what happened in the desert, where Jesus Christ was tempted by Satan to turn stones into bread, with the transformation of water into wine at the wedding celebration. The

[5]St Ignatius of Antioch, "Letters of Ignatius: Ephesians 20.2," ed. Cyril C. Richardson, *Early Christian Fathers* (New York, NY: Touchstone, 1996), 93.

[6]Alexander Schmemann, *For the Life of the World* (Crestwood, NY: St Vladimir's Seminary Press, 1995), 42–43.

two situations are entirely different as to location and circumstances, yet both were connected with food. One is a barren place with no food and drink, while a wedding usually is a place where there is plenty of food and drink. In the desert, Jesus was asked to change stones into bread that he personally needed, and thereby to reveal his power and glory. At Cana, Jesus changed water into wine to save a family from shame and to manifest the glory of God. Just before inaugurating his public ministry, Jesus went into the desert to be in communion with his Father about what lay before him. He spent forty days fasting and praying, and we may assume there was nothing to eat in the barren and dry desert. Seeing Jesus' hunger and thirst, Satan, who was hoping for an opportune moment, came and tempted him to change stones into bread. For Jesus Christ, who transforms water into wine and raises the dead, changing stones into bread would have been very easy, but he did not succumb.

The long period of hunger and thirst made the situation Jesus confronted in the desert antithetical to what Adam and Eve encountered in the garden of Eden. Everything was at the disposal of Adam and Eve, and they were warned not to eat of only the "forbidden fruit" (Gen 2.17). In the desert, Jesus was hungry and had no food, but he refused to succumb to temptation. Satan also came to Adam and Eve in the garden and tempted them to eat the forbidden fruit. In the midst of plenty, they chose the one fruit forbidden by God. So one can see in this the evident contrast between the desert experience of Jesus and that of Adam and Eve in the garden of Eden. Before the fall, food for Adam and Eve was a means of thanksgiving through eucharistic communion with God. And their disobedience to God and obedience to Satan turned it into a means of communion with Satan.

Was it an accident or was it by divine design that the first sign performed by the Messiah was associated with food, which man requires for sustenance? It is significant that the re-creation and renewal process of man started with God's first creation—water. If eating "forbidden fruit" was the reason for the man's downfall, then it is through the "new wine" and the "living bread" that the transformation and reclamation of paradise were initiated. Jesus changed water into wine, and he is the true wine that gives new life to the world through food, making it an appropriate antidote to the fruit of the forbidden tree. "I am the vine, you are the branches" (Jn 15.5). Wine is made from the fruit of the vine, and it is the essence of the fruit. The wine Jesus Christ gives is his own blood. Blood symbolizes life, and through his blood, Jesus Christ gives eternal life that overcomes death and destruction.

In Cana, Jesus Christ changed water into wine to alleviate the shame of a family whose need of food and drink became a social and spiritual problem. He did not work the sign for any personal fame or gain. Bishop Fulton Sheen beautifully presents the contrasts in what happened in the desert and in Cana:

> Thus He did at a marriage feast what He would not do in a desert; He worked in the full gaze of men what He had refused to do before Satan. Satan asked Him to turn stones into bread in order that He might become an economic Messiah. The mother asked Him to change water into wine that He might become a Savior. Satan tempted him from death; Mary "tempted" Him to death and resurrection. Satan tried to lead Him *from* the Cross; Mary sent Him *toward* it.[7]

In the desert, Jesus Christ rejected the challenge from Satan to turn stones into bread for his personal use; in Cana, he performed the sign at the behest of his mother, turning it into an occasion for manifesting the glory of God.

In the desert, Satan's tempting Jesus was a temptation to display power, which Jesus unequivocally rejected. Yet, when faced with the hunger of the multitude, who had listened for three days to his life-giving words on the Mount as well as in the valley, Jesus multiplied a few fish and loaves of bread to feed the entire multitude. Not only did he feed and satisfy them, but enough was left over to fill twelve baskets. How true is Nikolai Berdyaev's observation: "Bread for myself is a physical question; bread for my neighbor is a spiritual

[7] Fulton J. Sheen, *Life of Christ* (New York, NY: Image Books, 1977), 79.

question."[8] Adam and Eve's priority was their personal avarice, to the degree of ignoring a divine command. Jesus never performed any miracles for his own personal needs. He could have easily escaped suffering and crucifixion through a miracle! He was even challenged to come down from the cross as proof of his claim that he is the Son of God. Yet, for multitude that had gathered to hear his words, he did miraculously supply food. By providing food, especially for those who had been hungry for days, Jesus was filling not only a physical need, but also a spiritual one.

Wedding at Cana in Galilee: Funeral in Jerusalem of Judea

It is worth mentioning that the first sign in the Gospel of John was at a wedding, an event in life that is joyous and celebratory, while the last sign in the same Gospel was at a funeral, a very sad event in life, where Jesus brought Lazarus back to life (11.1–44). Both events take us back to the story of creation in the book of Genesis, where we see the happy wedding of the first couple Adam and Eve and the sad story of their spiritual death.

The presence of Jesus Christ at the marriage feast in Cana and his entering the Jerusalem temple are the two major episodes described in chapter two of the Fourth Gospel. Conspicuously, the sign performed at Cana is followed in the Gospel of John by Jesus' prophecy about the destruction of the temple in Jerusalem. Both have many similarities.

> Both the wedding story and the temple cleansing story are revelation events (manifesting the glory of the Son); both are third day stories (resurrection symbolism); both focus upon a sign; both carry a polemic against religion centering upon ceremonies (water of purification in one, temple rites in the other); in neither does being present suffice to generate faith in Jesus; both conclude with references to disciples believing. But the differences between the two and the wealth of meaning in each justify two messages, not

[8] Jim Forest, *The Ladder of the Beatitudes* (Maryknoll, NY: Orbis Books, 1999), 62.

one. In Galilee is the wedding; in Judea is the funeral ("Destroy this temple").[9]

The first story is about marriage, a familiar, celebratory event for family and community; but the second story is about Jesus at the temple, the center of Jewish worship and religious life. Worship at the temple of Jerusalem was one of the most important marks of Jewish identity and ethos; yet it was at this solemn setting that Jesus delivered his grim message about the total destruction of this sacred temple. The temple event and the story of Lazarus' death were both connected to Jerusalem in Judea, the center of religion and culture, and addressed existing conditions in the community to which Jesus belonged. The disciples saw the glory of Jesus Christ manifested in the Cana sign, and they believed in him (2.11). Yet afterwards, only after his resurrection did they also believe that his prophecy about the Jerusalem temple would come to pass. "But he was speaking of the temple of his body. Therefore, when he had risen from the dead, his disciples remembered that he had said this to them and they believed the Scripture and the word which Jesus had said" (2.21–22).

The Feast of Passover was one of the three most important feasts during which every Jew was expected to be in Jerusalem to attend festive celebrations in the temple. It was a time for the Israelites to recollect and to reflect humbly on their past experiences, as well as to express gratitude to God for the amazing way he had guided and guarded them during their bondage and the hardships they endured on their journey to the promised land. Jesus Christ declared while in the temple at Passover, "Destroy this temple and in three days I will raise it up" (Jn 2.19). He was, of course, referring to his own body and was revealing his own resurrection.

The annihilation of the existing temple, as the one and only place for the Israelites to worship and to perform the ultimate sacrifice, paved the way for a "new temple," not built by man. Moreover, a new form

---

[9]B. Fred Craddock, *John: Knox Preaching Guides* (Atlanta, GA: John Knox Press, 1983), 23–24.

of worship would be established, most importantly by the ultimate and final sacrifice of Jesus Christ. That "new temple" is Jesus Christ, and the new worship is "in spirit and in truth" (Jn 4.23–24). The new "sacrificial lamb" is the Lamb of God, Jesus Christ, as was witnessed by John the Baptist, the forerunner of the Messiah (Jn 1.29).

Jesus performed the first sign not at Jerusalem in Judea, but in the obscure village of Cana in Galilee, "A so-called no-place."[10] In general, one may assume that the typical village folk of Cana were simple and poor, as this was common in ancient times. The poor financial status of the bride and the bridegroom in that remote area might have been a reason for the insufficient supply of wine at the wedding feast. The city of Jerusalem where the temple was located was the center of Jewish social and religious life, and it housed the holy of holies. The Jews believed that it was the place for the presence of God, and every Jew was proud of Jerusalem. "Jerusalem symbolizes the home of Eden, or Paradise from where humanity fell."[11] The Psalmist sang, "If I forget you, Jerusalem, may my right hand wither. May my tongue stick to my palate if I do not remember you, if I do not exalt Jerusalem beyond all my delight" (Ps 137.5–6). Strangely enough, the prophetic books of the Old Testament predict that the Messiah, the Savior, was expected to come not from Jerusalem or Judea, but from outside of Judea, which reflects the words of the Theotokos (Bearer/Mother of God) in the *Magnificat*, "He has brought down rulers from their thrones but has lifted up the humble" (Lk 1.52).

The inauguration of the public ministry of Jesus Christ was the inauguration of the kingdom of God, and it occurred not in Jerusalem or anywhere else in Judea, but at Cana in Galilee. By inaugurating his public ministry in Galilee, Jesus expanded the kingdom of God to the outside world, beyond the borders of Jewish territory and religion. Galilee was known predominantly as a Gentile area, and Cana was

[10]Herman C. Waetjen, *The Gospel of the Beloved Disciple* (New York, NY: T & T Clark International, 2005), 114.

[11]James Puthuparambil, *Mariological Thought of Mar Jacob of Serugh (451–521)* (Baker Hill, Kottayam, Kerala, India: St. Ephraim Ecumenical Research Institute [SEERI], 2005), 220. Also available from Gorgias Press.

not a place that was spiritually or socially connected with the Jewish people. Many of them believed that Galilee was an area where Yahweh was not present at all. Wes Howard-Brook observes, "Whatever Cana may be, it is a long way from Jerusalem, where one might otherwise expect the sorts of events described in this passage to take place. Jesus begins his activity not in the headquarters of the Law, not in the center of the religious world of Israel, but on the obscure margins, hidden, quiet, yet invited."[12]

In his commentary on the Gospel of John, Cyril of Alexandria observes, "The wedding was not held in Jerusalem but outside of Judea, as it were, in the country of the Gentiles—'Galilee of the Gentiles,' as the prophet said. It is, I suppose, altogether obvious that the synagogue of the Jews rejected the Bridegroom from heaven and that the church of the Gentiles (gladly) received him."[13] Eusebius of Caesarea says that Isaiah foretold the first miracle that took place in Cana in Galilee: "Drink this first. Act quickly, land of Zebulon and Naphtali, Galilee of the Gentiles (Is 8.23)."[14] The initial sign performed in Cana profoundly symbolizes that the kingdom of God is extended beyond Judea and it is to be spread to the whole world.

It is interesting that according to John's Gospel (4.46–54), the next sign that Jesus performed was also in Cana. Jesus traveled from Judea through Samaria to reach Cana in Galilee. The Apostle John says, "So Jesus came again into Cana of Galilee, where He made water wine." Through this sentence, John is emphasizing the importance of the province of Galilee in Jesus' ministry, as compared to the province of Judea. The signs performed in Cana are presented in the Gospel as the first and the second sign. According to John Chrysostom, the second sign in Cana was mentioned in praise of the Samaritans who had believed in Jesus, while his own people believed in him only after witnessing the sign. Though Jesus considered Jerusalem his own beloved

---

[12]Sheen, *Life of Christ*, 78.

[13]Chrysostom, *John 1–10* (ACCS NT IVa), 88–89; quoted in *A Library of Fathers of the Holy Catholic Church: anterior to the Division of the East and West*, trans. by members of the English Church (Oxford: John Henry Parker, 1800–1881), 88.

[14]Chrysostom, *John 1–10* (ACCS NT IVa), 89.

city, he went to Galilee rather than to Judea, where he was already known.[15] In both instances, Jesus returned to Jerusalem, and Cana was fortunate to witness the transforming and life-giving acts of Jesus. Jesus said, "A prophet is not without honor except in his native place and in his own house" (Mt 13.57; Mk 6.4; Lk 4.24). Yet, this was not why he left Judea and came a second time to Cana in Galilee. Again, John Chrysostom observes, "At first He came, being invited to a marriage; but wherefore now? Methinks to confirm by His presence the faith that had been implanted by His miracle, and to draw them to Him the more by coming to them self-invited, by leaving His own country and by preferring them."[16]

In Jerusalem, the healing of the cripple on the Sabbath day created a controversy. In Galilee a large crowd followed Jesus, and they were miraculously fed. The controversies in Jerusalem led the rulers to decide upon Jesus' death. Pilgrims from Galilee gave Jesus a rousing and triumphant welcome as he entered the city. One can thus see the opposition Jesus faced in Jerusalem while he had a different and welcoming experience in Galilee and other places. Or in other words, "Galilee, held in low esteem in official circles of Judaism, was generally hospitable to Jesus while Jerusalem and Judea were centers of suspicion, rejection, and death."[17]

The first sign took place among the Gentiles (Jn 2.1–12), while those that followed were done as a revelation to Jerusalem (2.13–25); and a sign to the Jews (3.1–36); in praise of the Samaritans (4.1–42); and, now again for the Gentiles (4.43–54). This becomes like a full-circle itinerary in the Gospel.[18] It is interesting to note that Jerusalem and the Jews are portrayed as having a negative attitude, while Cana and the Gentiles are portrayed with a positive one. As the daughters of Jerusalem shed tears during his passion and crucifixion, Jesus admon-

---

[15]Chrysostom, *Homily* 36.1 (NPNF[1] 14:125).

[16]Chrysostom, *Homily* 35, ibid., 123.

[17]Fred B. Craddock, *John: Knox Preaching Guides* (Louisville, KY: Westminster John Knox Press, 1983), 23.

[18]Nadim Paul Tarazi, *The New Testament Introduction: Johannine Writings,* vol. 3, (Crestwood, NY: St Vladimir's Seminary Press, 2004), 159–160.

ished them not to weep for him, but rather for themselves and their children. Here again, Jerusalem was presented as a place of tragedy and sorrow. In Cana, the first sign brought joy and celebration, and the healing of the nobleman's son brought complete cure and great happiness.

The Samaritans had a history of hating the Jews for social and religious reasons, so it was remarkable that after hearing Jesus preach and learning about him from the Samaritan woman, they believed in him even though he was a Jew. "Many of the Samaritans of the city believed in him because of the word of the woman who testified, 'He told me all that I ever did.' So when the Samaritans had come to Him, they urged Him to stay with them; and He stayed there two days. And many more believed because of His word" (Jn 4.39–41). At the very beginning of the Gospel, John writes about the irony and the tragedy of Jesus' "own people," the Jews: "He came to what was his own, but his own people did not accept him" (1.11). It is paradoxical that his own community, who eagerly awaited the Messiah, had failed to recognize and to accept that Jesus was their Messiah. Yet, for many Gentiles, it was much easier to acknowledge as well as to accept him and to believe in him. Even the nobleman, a Gentile whose son Jesus healed, had believed in him long before Jesus healed his son. John writes, "For Jesus himself testified that a prophet has no honor in his native place" (4.44).

Inauguration of the Public Ministry in a Joyous Ceremony of Marriage

The first sign at Cana was performed in the context of a wedding feast. Both the sign and the setting are very important as they reveal the motive, the mission, and the message of the Messiah, the incarnate God. The wedding ceremony has always been a joyful and exciting event in any culture. In Greek literature contemporary to the Gospel, a wedding had great significance, and much of this literature begins with a marriage from where the couple purposefully starts on a difficult and dangerous journey.

> In ancient literature, marriage and death are homologous: elements of one may signify the other. Both begin with purification of the body and libations, the bride and the corpse are both veiled, and both end with a body in a chamber. For the bride, marriage is a death to her former state as a virgin daughter in the household of her father and birth to a new life in the household of her husband, where the death of her virginity makes possible new fruitfulness.[19]

The same is true for the husband. He is also transformed totally, dying to his old self and being born as a new person, in order to become one with his spouse. The ceremony of marriage is a dying to the old (separate) relationship in order to live to the new (united) one.[20]

Jesus Christ initiated his public ministry and began his journey to the cross in the context of a marriage ceremony. However, the mystery of marriage was given special significance and spiritual meaning in the context of Jewish religion and culture, especially at the time when "the Word became flesh." The public ministry of Jesus was inaugurated at a joyous event to reveal that Jesus is the source of joy. He is also the true and unfailing light that replaced the lights illuminating the temple, as he said, "I am the light of the world" (Jn 8.12). During the Feast of Passover in the Jerusalem temple, he spoke about destroying and replacing the temple (Jn 2.19). Through his death, Jesus became not only that altar, but also the sacrificial lamb, as John the Baptist

---

[19]Jo-Ann A. Brant, *John: Commentaries on the New Testament* (Grand Rapids, MI: Baker Publishing Group, 2011), 60.

[20]Kenneth W. Stevenson, *To Join Together: The Rite of Marriage* (New York, NY: Pueblo Publishing Company, 1987), 66. Anointing of the forehead at the time of the betrothal is a part of the Maronite service. For them, anointment at betrothal symbolizes the death of the old self in order to be united with the spouse. The service of the sacrament of marriage in the Coptic Church also includes anointment, related to baptismal and kingship imagery.

addressed him: "Behold, the Lamb of God, who takes away the sin of the world" (1.29). Everything in the past pointed toward the Messiah, and everything was fulfilled in him. His arrival deprived all religious institutions, customs, and feasts of their old meaning.

The gospel is good news because its words are the Word of God. Even the very announcement of the incarnation was good news during Jesus' time. "Do not be afraid; for behold, I proclaim to you good news of great joy that will be for all the people" (Lk 2.10). The message of the resurrected Jesus Christ was, "Peace be with you" (Jn 20.21). The disciples who hid behind closed doors in fear of the Jews and the Roman authorities rejoiced when they saw the resurrected Lord. That joy was a unique sign for them even in the midst of persecution and suffering. While suffering in jail and even facing possible death, St Paul exhorted the Christian community in Philippi, "Rejoice in the Lord always. I shall say it again: rejoice!" (Phil 4.4). He also edified through exhortations the faithful in the city of Corinth who were going through great difficulties, "sorrowful yet always rejoicing" (2 Cor 6.10). The Acts of the Apostles describes the courage, the confidence, and the joy of the Apostles Peter and John in the midst of persecutions and strife, "So they left the presence of the Sanhedrin, rejoicing that they had been found worthy to suffer dishonor for the sake of the name" (5.41). According to writers of that time (both Christian and non-Christian), this was true of the early Church, despite the strong contemporary Gnostic influence that shunned any kind of joy.

The occasion for the Cana sign was a wedding, an extremely joyous occasion. The inauguration of Jesus' public ministry in a marriage setting is itself a symbol of the joy that Jesus is to bring in through his presence and actions. "The emphasis in the incident at Cana of Galilee is on a wedding so as to stress that Jesus sets out on his ministry at a wedding ceremony, to declare himself as a source of joy to humanity, and also to point to his office as Bridegroom for redeemed humanity."[21]

---

[21]Matthew the Poor, "The Wedding in Cana," 16.

The Word and the Voice in the Wilderness: John the Baptist and Jesus Christ

The disciples who were with Jesus Christ at the wedding in Cana had been the disciples of John the Baptist a few days earlier. Though they were few in number at that time, the first place the disciples went with Jesus could have been the wedding in Cana. Following Jesus was an altogether new and different experience for those former disciples of John the Baptist. In a way, attending a marriage ceremony with their master portrays the contrast between John the Baptist and Jesus of Nazareth.

Both John the Baptist and Jesus Christ differed in their mission and vision. There were no similarities in their lifestyle, approach, and attitude. John represents the Old Testament and Jesus the New Testament. The Baptist lived as a strict ascetic, evidenced by his appearance, clothing, and what he ate and drank. "John wore a garment of camel's hair, and a leather girdle around his waist; and his food was locusts and wild honey" (Mt 3.4). It was unlikely that John the Baptist would attend a wedding banquet, especially one where wine was served. His message also revealed his lifestyle, as he preferred the desert, and wine was unthinkable for him.

Jesus was also an ascetic, but he did not run from people or their day-to-day problems. He confronted the burning issues of the times and comforted those who were struggling with religious or secular authorities. Jesus was present at events like weddings where wine was served and regularly attended banquets. He mingled with those who were marginalized in society, like publicans, tax collectors, and Samaritans, as well as with those who were branded by the "pious" and the religious elite as sinners and outcasts. Jesus was in touch with the people's daily lives, sharing in their burdens and joys, successes and failures, anxieties and excitements. Although he did criticize people's accusations and fault-finding with his and John the Baptist's ways, Jesus also spoke about those people and said, "For John came neither eating nor drinking, and they said, 'He is possessed by a demon.' The Son of Man came eating and drinking, and they said, 'Look, he is a glutton and a drunkard, a friend of tax collectors and sinners'" (Mt 11.18–19).

The mission of John the Baptist was to announce the coming of the kingdom of Heaven and to prepare the way for the Lord, the eternal Bridegroom, as well as to identify the One who was to come, the Messiah. When Jesus went to the place where John baptized people, the crowd there remarked, "John did no sign, but everything that John said about this man was true" (Jn 10.40–42). If John the Baptist was the messenger, Jesus Christ was the message. Jesus is the eternal Word, while John was "the voice of one crying in the wilderness" (Mt 3.3). "He was not the Light, but was sent to bear witness of that Light" (Jn 1.8). And Jesus, the Word, "became flesh and made his dwelling among us, and we saw his glory, the glory as of the Father's only Son, full of grace and truth" (Jn 1.14).

John the Baptist baptized people in water for repentance, and the baptism he gave was in anticipation of the coming of the Messiah and a preparation for Jesus' manifestation. Baptism was practiced by the Jewish people, most commonly for repentance and for conversion to Judaism. Jesus also baptized, but his was a baptism in water and in the Holy Spirit. And Jesus performed his first sign on water. If the mission of John the Baptist was to call people to repentance and to prepare them to receive the One whom they awaited, then the purpose of Jesus Christ's coming was to transform and to redeem all of creation. In fact, changing the water into wine in the jars at Cana was the initiation of that transformation process. John the Baptist used water for baptism, and Jesus used it for his first sign. In the transformation process, both made the ultimate sacrifice: John the Baptist was killed and Jesus was crucified.

The Sign and the Encounter of Nicodemus and the Samaritan Woman with Jesus

The beginnings of the second, the third, and the fourth chapters of the Gospel of John are closely related. Jesus' use of water is one of

the main themes in the Cana sign, in the meetings with Nicodemus, and in the conversation with the Samaritan woman. Another
equally important theme in all these events was the aspect of change.
The dialogues between Jesus and the main characters, especially what
Jesus said, were confusing or even paradoxical. This is certainly true
in the context of Jesus' conversation with Nicodemus about rebirth
(as in "from above") being essential for entering the kingdom of God.
The same is true in the context of Jesus' speaking with the Samaritan
woman about his living water as she considered the depth of the well
and his lack of a bucket. If others in the Cana story, along with the
Gospel readers, were confused by Jesus' response to his mother, then
the main characters in the other two dialogues were also unable at first
to comprehend fully what Jesus said to them.

All three episodes were revelations of the divine and mysterious
transformation that was achieved by the coming of the Son of God
and through his actions. If *water* became wine in the Cana sign, then
in the conversation with Nicodemus it was about rebirth through
water and the Spirit; and with the Samaritan woman, it was about
water that provides eternal life. In all these events, it was *water*, as first
created by God, that played an important role and revealed to those
people the re-creation that Jesus Christ came to accomplish.

If the wedding sign symbolizes the transformation of matter
through the incarnation, the dialogue with Nicodemus pointed to
the transformation of individuals through rebirth in Jesus Christ. The
term "mother" is used four times in the Cana sign, where it referred
to the Virgin Mary. During the encounter with Nicodemus, it is used
once (Jn 3.4) to refer to "motherhood." In the Cana story, the disciples
believed in Jesus (2.11), while in the case of Nicodemus, the Jewish
leader did not believe in Jesus, in spite of the long discourse Jesus had
with him about rebirth. Jesus told Nicodemus, "You do not receive
our testimony" (3.11). "In a wider sense the two sequences parallel
each other in their central contention that the old order has passed
away and the new is at hand—the wine of the new dispensation has
replaced the water-purification of the old dispensation, and commit-

ment to Jesus in faith manifested through baptism with and the Spirit has replaced the commitment to God hitherto called for in the old dispensation."[22]

The Cana sign was performed in a community close to Jesus, where his mother and disciples were also present. It is possible that the other participants, including the bride and the bridegroom, were also Jesus' relatives. It was Jesus' conversation that sowed seeds of faith in Nicodemus, a Pharisee and a ruler of the Jews (Jn 3.1), a faith that later grew to its full measure at the time of the burial of Jesus. And it was through his conversation with Nicodemus that Jesus Christ expanded the focus of his mission.

By meeting at the well with someone who was not only a Samaritan, but also a woman, Jesus also expanded the horizon of the revelation and his redemptive work, "For Jews have no dealings with Samaritans" (Jn 4.9). Jesus addressed her as "woman" (4.21), just as he addressed his mother as "woman," and the "water jar" is mentioned on both occasions, but nowhere else in the New Testament.[23] In Cana, the water transformed into wine was in jars. In the Samaritan woman's narrative, there was no need for a jar because Jesus is the "living water." In both these contexts, and as happens often in the Fourth Gospel, a woman represents the community to which she belongs, as the Samaritan woman represents the Samaritan community. Thus, these three events—the Cana sign, the dialogue with Nicodemus, and the meeting with the Samaritan woman—were all occasions of transformation and renewal revealed through the personhood and the actions of Jesus Christ.

The Sign in Relation to Accepting the Word of God

The Cana sign shows the importance of accepting the word of Jesus Christ, who is indeed, the "Word." Obedience to the words of Christ is obedience to the person of Christ. Where there is faith and obedience,

---

[22]Peter F. Ellis, *The Genius of John: A Composition-Critical Commentary on the Fourth Gospel* (Collegeville, MN: Liturgical Press, 1984), 58–59.

[23]Tarazi, *New Testament Introduction: Johannine Writings*, 157.

God can do wonders, and the Cana sign is a visible example of this. Instructed by the Virgin Mary, who is the paragon of obedience to the word and the will of God, the servants at the wedding fully obeyed Jesus' orders. The servants could have asked a thousand questions when asked to fill the pots with water, but they did not, for obeying without question was both their duty and their responsibility.

The condition of true faith is hearing the word of God and keeping it. The words of Jesus Christ are life-giving and are life itself, as they become flesh, a part of one's very self, one's very existence. This can be seen in Jesus' response to the woman who shouted with great joy to him, " 'Blessed is the womb that carried you and the breasts at which you nursed.' Jesus replied, 'Rather, blessed are those who hear the word of God and observe it' " (Lk 11.27–28). And when Jesus was told that his mother and brothers were looking for him, his immediate reply was, "My mother and my brothers are those who hear the Word of God and act on it" (Lk 8.21). It is also important to note that Jesus was not able to perform any miracles in Nazareth, his own native place, for "He was amazed at their lack of faith" (Mk 6.6).

The servants at the wedding fully obeyed Jesus' words, and the result was an amazing sign. "The steward tastes the wine (*pothen estin*), while the servants do. They had drawn the water, and they are aware that the wine is the result of a chain of responses to a series of 'words': the word of the mother concerning the word of her Son (v. 5) and two words from Jesus (vv. 7–8). The importance of the acceptance of the 'word' of Jesus is a crucial theme."[24] The ten lepers whom Jesus healed on his way to Jerusalem are a perfect example of trusting and obeying the word of God. When the lepers approached Jesus expecting to be healed, he told them, "Go and show yourselves to the priests" (Lk 17.14a). When they obeyed, they had not been healed yet, but "as they went they were cleansed" (17.14b). So for them, healing was preceded by obedience, for had they not obeyed, there would have been no healing, no blessings.

[24]Francis J. Maloney, *The Gospel of John*, Sacra Pagina 4, ed. Daniel J. Harrington (Collegeville, MN: Liturgical Press, 1998), 68.

The Cana sign was the result of faith in the Son of God. It began with the faith of the mother of Jesus Christ and continued through the servants who obeyed him. The water that was transformed by Jesus was the result of nature's obedience to its Master. Where there is obedience to God, there are miracles, there are abundant blessings. In this way, the sign at Cana finally paved the way for the disciples of Jesus to believe in him (Jn 2.11). "The sign at Cana thus confirms their initial inclination to follow him because they believe him to be the Messiah."[25]

The Changing of Water into Wine and the Healing of the Nobleman's Son

As narrated in the Fourth Gospel and presented as the first and the second signs (4.54), Jesus changed water into wine and healed the nobleman's son in Cana. John writes in the Gospel that both events took place in "Cana in Galilee." Why did the apostle mention that both took place in Cana? Possibly, or probably, he wanted both the importance of the sign at the wedding and the place where it was performed to be committed to memory by his readers. As mentioned earlier, this sign was not performed in Jerusalem, but in Cana in Galilee, a place distant from Judea and home of many Gentiles.

There are similarities between these two signs, other than the location where both were performed. They were miracles, but mentioned as signs and numbered consecutively as the first and the second sign. It would remind the reader of the water-into-wine sign (Jn 4.46). Jesus performed both signs to resolve difficult situations and thus alleviate the problems of others. Both in the second sign and in the first, the joy obtained through healing and miraculous supply of superb wine was associated not with Jerusalem, but with faraway Cana of Galilee. The nobleman's son was in a grave situation with his disease, and the father likely heard about the sign at the wedding in Cana. That may have been the reason why the nobleman rushed from Capernaum to

[25]Brant, *John*, 59.

Cana, where Jesus was, expecting a miraculous cure for his son. Just as in the wedding scene, where the mother of Jesus informed her Son about something that was needed, and her Son seemed not to respond positively replying with a first rebuff, the nobleman presented his grave predicament about his son, and he, too, did not immediately hear a positive or encouraging response from Jesus. Instead, "Jesus said to him, 'Unless you people see signs and wonders, you will not believe'" (4.48). Jesus was simply stating that the nobleman was after him to get a miracle for his son, but it was very clear from the father's persistence that he had faith in Jesus and that Jesus was the only hope for his dying son. Still, the nobleman immediately "believed the word that Jesus had spoken unto him, and he went his way" (4.50).

The nobleman had not witnessed his son's healing, yet he believed. He responded exactly as the Virgin Mary did in the Cana story. Jesus then told the nobleman, "Go; your son is going to live" (Jn 4.50). Soon after informing Jesus about the problem and after his unusual reply, Mary's words to the servants, "Do whatever he says," were clear proof of her faith in her Son. Both Mary and the nobleman belonged to those of whom Jesus said, "Blessed are those who have not seen and have believed" (Jn. 20.29). The nobleman's servants met him before he got home and told him what had happened to his beloved son. If it was the servants in the sign at Cana who confirmed the transformation, in the second sign, it was also the nobleman's servants who confirmed his son's healing. Leon Morris observes, "The earlier miracle was the changing of water into wine (chapter 2). Perhaps John wants us to notice something of an advance. That was a miracle done on the spot; this one was done at a distance. That was a change in an inanimate substance (water was changed into wine), but this one concerned a living being. That one marked a continuance of social life. This one took a boy as good as dead and gave him life."[26]

Jesus was able to perform the first two signs in Cana, an obscure village in Galilee, as there were people present who believed in him. If

[26]Leon Morris, *Reflections on the Gospel of John* (Peabody, MA: Hendrickson, 2000), 162–163.

in the wedding sign we see his mother believing in Jesus, in the other we see the nobleman, the father of the sick child, also completely believing and trusting him. Even Jerusalem, the cultural and religious center where the sacred temple stood, had failed to produce people of such unquestionable faith.

Conclusion

The Cana sign, through which Jesus Christ inaugurated his public ministry, was thus a prelude to all other miraculous signs in the Fourth Gospel. The transforming power of the Son of God, initially revealed at the wedding in Cana, continued in the signs that followed. Matter created by God is not to be condemned, but transformed. Attending a wedding at this initial stage of revelation itself reveals that joy in this world is not something to be shunned. Cana, an obscure village in Galilee, not Jerusalem, became the stage for the sign and revealed the universal mission of the redemptive work of Jesus Christ. It was in Cana, not in Jerusalem, where the Jewish people expected God's intervention, that the disciples first witnessed the glory of the Son of God, and had their belief in him reinforced.

3
A Village Wedding

Christy was invited

Jesus Christ was invited along with his disciples to be present at the wedding (Jn 2.3). He was requested to be present probably without anyone knowing anything about his supernatural powers or expecting any extraordinary act from him. The disciples who were at the wedding might have witnessed the baptism of Jesus Christ. It was also possible that news about the extraordinary baptism and the words John the Baptist said about Jesus might have made some impact on people who were there. John the Baptist had spoken earlier about Jesus, "Behold! The Lamb of God who takes away the sin of the world" (1.29), and, "He it is, who coming after me is preferred before me, whose sandal's strap I am not worthy to loose" (1.27). Still, no one would have expected anything of a miraculous nature from Jesus at the wedding. John Chrysostom observes, "Assuredly they who invited Him had not formed a proper judgment of Him, nor did they invite Him as some great one, but merely as an ordinary acquaintance; and this the Evangelist has hinted at, when he says, 'The mother of Jesus was there, and His brethren.' Just as they invited her and His brethren, they invited Jesus."[1] Nonetheless, what is important is that Jesus was invited.

When Jesus is invited, an event in this world is transformed into something greater because of the presence of God. The very presence of Jesus Christ made the Cana wedding a unique and miraculous

[1]Chrysostom, *Homily* 21 (NPNF[1] 14:73).

79

event. His presence at the wedding is also the reason we contemplate that sign today. Through his presence, the wedding banquet was transformed into the symbol of the eternal eschatological banquet. As a result of Jesus' being invited and attending, a problem confronting the family that was beyond their resolution at the time was easily resolved, and in a way that was beyond the realm of human ability. This event also became an occasion for revealing the divine glory of the Son of God.

The Sign was performed in a Home

The sign through which Jesus Christ inaugurated his public ministry and manifested his glory was performed in a home, a "miniature church" or, as St Paul calls it, a "household church" (Rom 16.5). It is very important to note that the public ministry of Jesus was inaugurated in an ordinary home, not in the temple of Jerusalem or anywhere else that we would usually label a "sacred place." The home was transformed into a "temple," as the temple is the place where God dwells. The home is a place where people find comfort and consolation, but also face many of their problems. Thus, the presence of Jesus changed the atmosphere of a home from worry and sorrow to joy and happiness. This is exactly what happened when Jesus visited the bereaved Martha and Mary at their home in Bethany. Jesus' presence turned their tears of sorrow over the death of their brother, Lazarus, into tears of joy. It was Jesus' visit to the house of Zacchaeus that effected a complete transformation in his life. Jesus said, "Today salvation has come to this house" (Lk 19.9).

In fact, the "churches" where the faithful assembled in the first century were regular homes. Our Lord had his Last Supper in the home of St Mark, the evangelist. The Holy Spirit descended on the disciples when they were gathered in that same house to pray on Pentecost. Faithful of the early Church gathered in homes on the first day of the week to celebrate the Eucharist ("breaking bread from house to house," Acts 2.46). It is interesting to note that first-century Christians conducted their entire lives—spiritual, social, familial, and so on—in their homes. Their lives were centered in their homes just as their Jewish ancestors did before they had the Jerusalem temple. Once the temple was established, one can see a bifurcation of the sacred and the secular for the Jews, which relocated and limited every sacred activity to the temple. The same attitude continued in communities of Christians, when they moved from their homes to churches to perform their spiritual rites. As a result, people started separating everything into the sacred and the secular: namely, what was done in the church was sacred or spiritual, and everything else was secular or worldly. Piety was often limited within the walls of the church building.

We ought ever to remember that it was in a humble home that Jesus initially manifested forth his glory. The Cana episode reveals that a home is a sacred place where God can manifest his glory. In his commentary on the sign, William Barclay observes very correctly:

> There is a strange paradox in the attitude of so many people to the place that they call home. They would admit at once that there is no more precious place in all the world; and yet, at the same time, they would also have to admit that in it they claim the right to be far more discourteous, far more boorish, far more selfish, and far more impolite than they would dare to be in any society of strangers . . . It is the tragic fact that it is so often strangers who see us at our best and those who live with us who see us our worst. We ought ever to remember that it was in a humble home that Jesus manifested His glory. To Him a home was a place for which nothing but His best was good enough.[2]

Families are established on the foundation of marriage. Historians, such Edward Gibbon (author of *The Decline and Fall of the Roman Empire*), are of the opinion that one of the major reasons for the disintegration of the mighty Roman Empire was an undermining of the unity, the sanctity, and the divinity of the family. The family is the

[2]Barclay, *The Gospel of John*, 86.

basic unit of the society, and any society and culture that ignores the importance of the family will fall apart. When God took flesh and became a man, he became part of a home, just as every other human does. Jesus Christ grew up obeying his parents and doing household chores. He never ignored his responsibilities toward his home, his parents, and his fellow human beings.

It is to be noted also that in the Gospel of John one can see a new kind of lasting and loving family relationship. In the Cana sign we see the role that mother of Jesus played in his presence. In chapter 19, just before Jesus' death on the cross, he entrusted his mother to John the apostle, saying, "This is your mother," and to his mother he said, pointing to the apostle, "This is your son." A family relationship, or the relationship of a mother and her children, is here transformed beyond blood connections. "Both stories point out that Jesus is in the process of creating a new view of family based not on biological connection, but on response to God as manifested in himself and his teachings."[3]

Water was changed into Wine

It was water that Jesus transformed into wine, and the water that was poured by the servants was fresh water, drawn from a well as directed by Jesus. In the Fourth Gospel, water is one of the most important images and is constantly employed throughout that Gospel. The Fourth Gospel begins with John the Baptist and the baptism he performed in water. After the sign of water transformed into wine, the Apostle John narrates Jesus' conversation with Nicodemus, which deals with rebirth through water and the Spirit in order to enter the kingdom of God (chapter 3). In the fourth chapter, Jesus speaks about the water that was drawn (4.7, 11, 15) and the living water that he would give. The man by the pool at Bethsaida, who had been paralyzed for thirty-eight years, anxiously wanted to jump into the healing water of the pool (chapter 5). Here again the Gospel speaks about the

[3] Thurston, *Women in the New Testament*, 82.

gift of living water (7.37–39). At the Last Supper, Jesus took water to wash the feet of his disciples, as a symbol of humility and especially of cleansing (13), alluding to the sacrament of confession. During the crucifixion, blood and water came out of the pierced body of Jesus (19.34), and these allude to the sacraments of baptism and the Eucharist in the Church, the body of Christ.

According to the Genesis account, water was the first creation. It was upon water that God acted to bring into existence all created things. Water was also a symbol of death and destruction. "In ancient Israel, water was symbolic of both good and evil. Water is essential for life in that desert region. But for those who earn their livelihood on the sea, water is also a potential tomb."[4] At the time of the flood, Noah and his family were saved in the ark, while all others drowned. Thus, water became a means of survival and salvation for Noah's family, while for others it paved the way for death and destruction. This was also true for the Israelites and the Egyptians. The Israelites entered the promised land by passing through the Red Sea, while the Egyptians who were pursuing them died in it. As an infant, Moses was saved from the water of the river Nile by the daughter of Pharaoh (Ex 2.5–10). When a person is immersed in water in the sacrament of baptism, the powers of evil forces are destroyed, and the baptized person participates in the death of Christ; when a person emerges from the baptismal font, he is resurrected with the risen Christ. That satanic power was active in water, and Christ crushed its head (Gen 2.15). If water was the first creation, in Cana it was used for the new creation. In baptism, water, which is the sign and symbol of salvation, is also used for the new creation.

One can see in the Bible a link between water and the Holy Spirit. In Genesis we read, "The Spirit of God was hovering over the face of the water" (1.2). After the great flood, Noah came to know through the dove that the waters had receded from earth, "The dove returned to him in the evening, and behold, a freshly plucked olive leaf was in

[4]John Breck, *God with Us: Critical Issues in Christian Life and Faith* (Crestwood, NY: St Vladimir's Seminary Press, 2003), 217.

her mouth" (Gen 8.11). The dove foreshadowed the Holy Spirit. At
Christ's baptism, the Holy Spirit descended from heaven in the likeness of a dove: "When he had been baptized, Jesus came up immediately from the water; and behold, the heavens were opened to him,
and he saw the Spirit of God descending like a dove and alighting
upon him" (Mt 3.16).

Through the fall of Adam and Eve, water was polluted along with
everything else in creation. The same "polluted water," which was part
of the fallen world, was also used for cleansing. Such cleansing could
not bring about purification because the water itself was not clean.
Strangely enough, the water jars at the wedding were empty, but at
Jesus' direction the servants filled them with water. The water in the
pots was changed into wine in the presence of the Lord who created
it. Later on, Jesus shed his own blood for the ultimate sacrifice, thus
for the ultimate cleansing from sin, death, and bondage. Now, wine
is transformed into the blood of Jesus Christ by the Holy Spirit when
the faithful "come together" as the body of Christ, for absolution of
their sins and for life eternal.

Water is extremely important and is considered the great elixir
of the Bible. It is the primordial element. The land of the Bible has
always been a dry area; dry riverbeds and exhausted wells have always
existed. People who live in the Middle East know very well the symbolism of thirst and the importance of water, perhaps more so than in
other places where water is plentiful. David the Psalmist reflected this
very well when he sang, "Like a land parched, lifeless, and without
water. So I look to you in the sanctuary to see your power and glory"
(Ps 63.2–3). Water "appears to man in various forms and hence with
various meanings" and mainly through three sources: spring water,
flowing water (rivers), and the sea.[5] Spring water "from the womb
of the earth" is considered pure, fresh, and a symbol of maternity, of
fruitfulness. Rivers are another great source of flowing water. "A river
is deep, and so embodies danger; descent into the deep can therefore

---

[5]Joseph Ratzinger (Benedict XVI), *Jesus of Nazareth*, trans. Adrian J. Walker (New
York, NY: Doubleday, 2007), 238–239.

signify descent into death, just as ascent from it can signify rebirth."[6]
A vast sea elicits admiration and amazement, and it is the symbol of
salvation, as we see it in the crossing of the Red Sea by the Israelites.

Water has always been one of the least expensive natural resources
in the world. It is one of the life's necessities and, at the same time,
is accessible to almost everyone. From ancient times, it has also been
an important religious symbol. To the people of the ancient world,
water was the symbol of life. One of the first meditations in ancient
days was to recognize water as holy. The Hindu epic, the Rig Veda,
says, "In water there is eternity; water is medicine, thus is the greatness of water" (1.23.19; cf. 10.9.1–9). God created man's body as made
of up to 60 percent water. Thus, water is truly a precondition for life.
Human beings can go without food for a long time, but without
water, they will die very quickly. So we can say that by nature, human
beings are thirsty beings. Without water, cleanliness is impossible;
thus water is also the symbol of cleansing and purity. Water is also a
symbol of power and might, as we see it reflect and, in a way, absorb
the boundless blue sky. All this describes the perception or experience
of water that placed it at the center of religious symbolism. Alexander
Schmemann beautifully expresses the place and the importance of
water in creation:

> It is the natural symbol of life, for there is no life without water,
> but it is also the symbol of destruction and death, and finally, it is
> the symbol of purification, for there is no cleanliness without it. In
> the Book of Genesis creation of life is presented as the liberation of
> the dry land from the water—as a victory of the Spirit of God over
> the waters—the chaos of nonexistence. In a way, then, creation is
> a transformation of water into life.[7]

It is worth mentioning the names of the two of the greatest lumi-
naries in the Old Testament who performed miracles on water. When
Pharaoh's heart was hardened and he refused to let the Israelites go,

[6]Ibid., 239.
[7]Schmemann, *For the Life of the World*, 72.

Moses, by using the rod that was turned into a serpent, miraculously changed the water in the river to blood, and the Egyptians could not drink from there (Ex 7.14–18). When the Israelites were in the desert, they found no water to drink. When they found a place with water, it was bitter. Moses called that place "bitterness" (Ex 15.23). The people complained to Moses about the bitter water, and by casting a piece of wood into the water, Moses transformed it to sweet water (Ex 15.25). Then there is the story of the success of Yahweh over Baal, and Elijah's prayers and sacrifices on Mount Carmel that ended a three-year drought and brought life and fertility back to the barren land (1 Kg 18.30–39). All these miracles on water performed by the great men of the Israelites were leading to the first sign that Jesus performed at the wedding.

"In the beginning," the world came into being through the Holy Spirit brooding over the water, and thus out of chaos he formed the cosmos, which God found to be "good." Just before Jesus' public ministry, he entered into the waters of the River Jordan for his baptism. The Byzantine liturgical text on the day of the Feast of Epiphany has this prayer while blessing the water, "Today the Master has come to sanctify the nature of the water."[8] In the Eastern tradition during the time of the blessing of the water, not only the water that is used for baptism but water everywhere and the nature as a whole are also blessed and sanctified.

Ignatius of Antioch (c. 107) writes in his Letter to the Ephesians that Christ "was born and baptized in order to purify the water by His passion" (18.2).[9] What this apostolic father says is that the purpose of Christ's baptism had the "effect of renewing an element of creation, even creation itself."[10] Cyril of Jerusalem (c. 382) writes, "Water is at the origin of the world, the Jordan is at the origin of the Gospels."[11] So it is not surprising that the initial sign performed by Jesus Christ was

[8]Mother Mary and Archimandrite Kallistos Ware, The Festal Meniaon (London: Faber, 1969), 391.

[9]Quoted by John Breck, God with Us, 166.

[10]Ibid.

[11]A Monk, Orthodox Spirituality, 42.

on water. The Son of God started his cleansing and redeeming activity on water, initiating a new beginning to the already existing world. Through changing water into wine, Jesus revealed the transformation to be attained in humanity and the world. The sign was a prelude to the great offering of his blood on the cross for cleansing the "thirsty world" and for abundant and eternal life for the children of God.

At the time of the baptism of Jesus Christ, his divine identity was revealed by his heavenly Father through water. In the Cana sign, water was the medium for the manifestation of Jesus' *doxa*, glory, and it was through water the disciples witnessed his divine manifestation leading them to their faith in him.

The Servants and the Head Steward

The servants and the head steward, as usual in a banquet, were present in the Cana sign narration. For the head steward the word used is *architriklinos*,[12] one who is "responsible for the seating of the guests and the correct running of the feast."[13] His duties included "arranging the table and the courses of the meal and tasting the food before it could be served to the guests."[14] That was why the head steward at Cana was surprised at the quality of wine that was served last. He might have been a guest[15] selected to run the banquet, whose responsibilities were very similar to those of a master of ceremonies. The role of the head steward, it is also suggested, was that of a chaplain, "to give thanks, and pronounce blessings."[16]

For the success of any celebration, there are many people who work very hard behind the scenes to prepare for it. While servants mostly

[12]The word is translated as "steward of the feast," "head steward," "feast master," "governor of the feast," "chief of the guests," "headwaiter," "master of the feast," etc. in different versions of the Holy Scripture.

[13]Barclay, *The Gospel of John*, 88.

[14]Elmer Towns, *The Gospel of John: Believe and Live* (Westwood, NJ: Fleming H. Revell Company, 1990), 64.

[15]Raymond E. Brown, *The Gospel According to John*, 100.

[16]John Lightfoot, A Commentary on the New Testament from the Talmud and Hebraica: Matthew-1 Corinthians, vol. 3, *Luke & John* (Baker Book House, Grand Rapids, MI, 1979), 255.

work behind the scenes, the head steward has a visible and prominent place. In Cana, the servants possibly worked hard to prepare for and to arrange the celebration. Thus, it was the servants whom the mother of Jesus advised that they do whatever Jesus ordered them. The head steward's responsibility was to make sure there was enough wine to be served to guests. He did fail in his primary responsibility, as he had no clue about the shortage of wine. Without knowing the miracle that had happened there, the steward congratulated the bridegroom for keeping the best wine for last.

The servants filled the jars with water as directed by Jesus, so the mystery of the transformation of water into wine was revealed to them because they believed Jesus Christ's word and obeyed him. They were fully aware that they had not been able to change the water into wine or resolve the problem in any way, but they could fill the jars with water as directed by Jesus. Thus they witnessed how the problem with the wine was resolved. Simply to fill the jars with water must have been difficult, because they already knew there was not enough wine to serve all the guests. To take it to the head steward was probably much more difficult, as they knew what the steward's reaction would be. Yet, because those simple servants believed Jesus Christ, they also believed that the water had been transformed to superb wine. St Paul's definition of faith was true for those servants: "Now faith is being sure of what we hope for and certain of what we do not see" (Heb 11.1).

The key verse, it is said, in the sign is, "When the steward of the feast tasted the water now become wine" (2.9). John McHugh writes, "This verse is the key to the primary message of Cana. This changing of six huge jars of water, each holding twenty to thirty gallons, into the choicest wine—this was but the beginning of the signs which Jesus did."[17] It ends with the greatest sign, the third-day event of the resurrection of Jesus Christ.

The story of the head steward was totally different from that of the servants there. The steward thought that there was more than enough

---

[17]John McHugh, *The Mother of Jesus in the New Testament* (Garden City, NY: Doubleday & Company Inc., 1975), 396.

wine, and then discovered that the wine served last was much better in quality. Yet, he was amazed that the bridegroom had kept the best wine for last, as this was contrary to the common practice of serving the best first and the worst last. "What the feast master does not know is known to the servants, who say nothing at all about their knowledge. The feast master naturally assumes that the newly found wine is the result of crafty planning by 'the bridegroom', whom he contrasts with 'every person.'"[18]

The head steward of the feast was unaware of the mystery that was being unveiled to the many who were gathered there. Lack of knowledge of origins characterizes a number of people in the Fourth Gospel.[19] In the first chapter itself, we read that those who were sent by Pharisees to John the Baptist asked, "Who are you, that we may give an answer to those who sent us?" (1.22). When Jesus met the Samaritan woman, at the beginning of the encounter, she was unaware of whoe it was to whom she was talking. Unlike the apostles, the steward was not able to witness the mysterious glory that was manifested in Jesus. The sign helped the disciples to believe in Jesus Christ, but neither his presence, nor the superior quality of the wine at the end helped the head steward to believe in Jesus Christ. The glory of God was manifested through the sign, prompting the disciples to believe in Jesus. Yet, for the head steward, it was an ordinary event and did not change anything in his life or his vision. Both the mysterious transformation of water into wine and the manifestation of divine glory were hidden from him, despite his being right where these had taken place. Larry Paul Jones observes, "Unlike other unknowing individuals, the steward appears more comic than tragic, but his lack of knowledge underscores for the reader the fact that only the servants find themselves in a position to understand what has happened. This tacitly reveals that those who, like servants, obey Jesus,

[18]Howard-Brook, *Becoming Children of God,* 79.

[19]Larry Paul Jones, *The Symbol of Water in the Gospel of John* Journal for the Study of the New Testament Supplement Series 145 (Sheffield, England: Sheffield Academic Press, 1997), 61.

will find themselves capable of coming to an understanding of what he does and can do."[20]

God can do wonders where there is obedience. Obedience is the result of faith. The servants who filled the pots with water stand as the epitome of obedience. This same quality was revealed throughout the life of the mother of Jesus, as she always remains the paragon of obedience. The head steward was a man of position and power at the celebration, but he did not have the eyes to see a sign that revealed the glory of God, or the faith to believe in the One who provided the superb wine. He was at the right place at the right time, but he missed the great mystery of the divine manifestation that was revealed right there. He left the place unchanged from the way it was when he came there, while the disciples left there with a new vision. It is indeed better to be a servant who obeys God, rather than the head steward who does not have the vision to witness signs and to see the divine manifestation.

[20]Ibid.

4

The Sign of the Messianic Age

The water in the jars at the wedding in Cana was transformed into an exquisite wine. What happened there was a sign indeed—a miraculous act. The Fourth Gospel concludes the account of changing water into wine with a special note: "This, the first of his signs, Jesus did at Cana in Galilee, and manifested his glory; and his disciples began to believe in him" (Jn 2.11). Thus, the sign at the wedding feast is presented in the Gospel not as a miracle story, but as a sign. Signs play a central role in this Gospel, and they are typically and uniquely Johannine.

The author of the Gospel uses the same terminology for the recovery of the nobleman's son (4.54); healing the sick (6.2); the miracle of multiplying bread and fish (6.14); giving sight to the blind man (9.16); and bringing back Lazarus from the dead (12.18). At the end of his Gospel, John presents the very purpose of narrating certain signs and writing the book: "Jesus did many other miraculous signs in the presence of his disciples, which are not recorded in this book. But these are written that you may believe that Jesus is the Christ, the Son of God, and that by believing you may have life in his name" (20.30–31).

In the Jewish prophetic tradition, signs had a long history. Some of the prophets, like Amos and Jeremiah, through symbolic actions of great importance, revealed what was going to happen in the future. It was a call to repentance, directing the people to turn away from their sins and transgressions. The signs also prefigured the reason or cause for the divine actions. "The signs of Jesus both prefigure the future and also reveal what is already present in him . . . Or, to put it more simply, a sign is a parable that hints at a miracle."[1]

Because of the importance given to signs in John's Gospel, it is also known (as already noted) as the "Book of Signs" or the "Gospel of Signs."

> The signs are manifestations to the naked eye of God's power, but at the same time they are symbols of truth that cannot be observed directly. In the miracle at Cana, for example, the wine that Christ miraculously produces from the water is symbolic of the new life that he brings to mankind. It is the new life of the Christian community as contrasted to the old life of Judaism, symbolized by the water jars intended to be used for the ritual purifications required by Jewish law. What the miracle really says is that Jesus is already engaged in the work through which man is purified and is thereby given access to salvation.[2]

Miracles, Wonders, Signs

In the New Testament, three words are used to present miraculous events: miracles *(dynamis),* wonders *(teras)*, and signs *(sēmeion).* The Greek word *dynamis* can mean both "power" and "miracle." On the day of Pentecost, the Apostle Peter used all three words when addressing the people: "Jesus of Nazareth was a man commended to you by God with miracles, wonders, and signs" (Acts 2.22). The first word, *dynamis* (mighty deeds or miracle) is not used in the Gospel, but *teras* (wonders) is used in John 4.48, in the context of healing the son of the nobleman. The third word, *sēmeion* (sign), is used many times. In John's Gospel, the word *sign* is the one that is used. John Phillips defines these words thus: "The word *powers* denotes the manifestations of evident power; the word *wonder* underlines the effect produced on those who witness the mighty work; *signs* emphasize the

[1]Kenneth Grayston, *The Gospel of John* (Philadelphia, PA: Trinity Press International, 1990), 32.

[2]Howard Clark Kee et al., eds., *Understanding the New Testament*, 3rd ed. (Englewood Cliffs, NJ: Prentice-Hall, Inc., 1973), 348.

value or significance of the mighty work."[3] In fact, even though each word has a different shade of meaning, each communicates the mysteries of God's interventions and activities among people.

Jesus himself uses the word sign (*sēmeion*) twice in the Gospel. The first time he uses it is at Cana, interestingly enough not at the wedding scene, but in the context of the healing of the nobleman's son, "Unless you people see signs and wonders you will not believe" (4.48). The second time is at Capernaum, where the crowd gathered after the feeding of the five thousand: "Jesus answered and said to them, 'Amen, amen, I say to you, you are looking for me not because you saw signs but because you ate the loaves and were filled'" (6.26). Nonetheless, in both these instances, Jesus uses the word with a negative connotation. The apostle makes use of the term to relate the words of others, for example, those of Nicodemus in 3.2, and of the crowds in 7.31 and 10.41. The Jews demanded from Jesus a sign to justify his critical words about the temple (2.18). Also in the Gospel, Jesus was the only one who performed signs, and as was clearly written about John the Baptist, "John did no sign" (10.41).

In the Synoptic Gospels, miracles are presented as "mighty works." When repeated in the Fourth Gospel, some of the miracles were not portrayed as miracles, but rather as signs. The best example is the feeding of the multitude. When recounting these signs, John evidently was trying to explain the meaning of the mysteries behind them. In the first three Gospels, we read often that when signs were asked of Jesus, he denied the requests. Some of the scribes and Pharisees asked Jesus to show them a sign. His response was, "An evil and adulterous generation seeks after a sign, and no sign will be given to it except the sign of the prophet Jonah" (Mt 12.39–40). In the Synoptic Gospels, miracles are presented as proof of the coming of the kingdom of God, and to show that the kingdom of God was in midst of the people. In John's Gospel, signs revealed who Jesus was and what his mission was. An in-depth study of the miracles in the first three Gospels and the

[3]John Phillips, *Exploring the Gospels: John* (Neptune, NJ: Loizzeaux Brothers, 1989), 51–52.

signs in the Fourth Gospel allows one to understand clearly that the accounts are not contradictory, but complementary. In the Synoptic Gospels, miracles are signs and symbols for redeeming human beings from the bondage of Satan and sin. Hence there are many exorcisms in the Synoptic Gospels, which are absent in the Fourth Gospel.

John McHugh provides certain noticeable characteristics of the signs in the Gospel of John.[4] All the signs were manifestations of divine power, and they were all either miracles of creation, such as changing water into wine, or bringing someone who was almost dead back to life (the nobleman's son), or someone already dead (Lazarus). Another aspect that is important to note in all these signs is that the situations were beyond solution in the ordinary sense, whether it was a healing, or feeding the multitude, or supplying more wine for the wedding feast. For example, Lazarus was buried and might already have been decaying in the tomb. The ultimate reaction to these signs was either belief or unbelief. Also, in each case there was an inter-locutor who presented the gravity of the situation, as if there were no hope for resolving it. In the Cana sign, it was the mother of Jesus who informed him of a critical situation at Cana (2.3), then in the healing of the nobleman's son, the father himself was the one who told Jesus about the gravity of the situation (4.47, 49). In the account of the rais-ing of Lazarus, it was Mary, the sister of Lazarus, who informed Jesus that even his very presence would not help because he had come too late (11.33). The seriousness of the situation also serves to clarify the symbolism behind each sign.

Miracles are supernatural acts. "A miracle is something that takes place beyond the limits of those familiar laws of nature, something we experience as supernatural rather than natural."[5] There is indeed a difference between signs and miracles in the four Gospels. According to the Fourth Gospel, a sign was something not immediately evident to the naked eye; whereas a mystery or a secret was hidden, but that

---

[4]John McHugh, *The Mother of Jesus*, 398.
[5]Alexander Schmemann, *Celebration of Faith*, vol. 3, *The Virgin Mary* (Crestwood, NY: St Vladimir's Seminary Press, 1995), 16.

mystery was being gradually revealed. Most of the time, the mystery shrouded in the sign was not often revealed to everyone, but only to a specific group of people. For example, in the Cana wedding sign, only a few knew about the real miracle that had taken place there, and they included the mother of our Lord, the servants, and the disciples. Though the steward was able to attest to the fact that the best wine had been kept for last, he was unaware of the miracle that had happened at the wedding or of the source of that best wine that was served last. The same was also true of the many guests who drank that superb wine in the end.

There is truth in the saying that miracles are for children, but signs are for adults. In the Gospels, miracles are for everyone, even though in certain instances faith was essential for performing a miracle. Jesus said to the Canaanite woman, "O woman, great is your faith! Let it be done for you as you wish" (Mt 5.28). So her daughter was healed because of her mother's faith. According to John's Gospel, a sign that revealed a mystery was not for everyone, but only for a believer and all who belonged to a community of believers. On many occasions, outsiders were unable to comprehend the mysteries and the revelations hidden within a sign. Hence, a sign is closely related to faith, the faith of the person who witnesses it or the faith of the community in which it is performed.

In other words, what Jesus did in Cana was an epiphany. To some, the message was revealed, while it was concealed from others. John Knox writes, "Such is the meaning of calling an act a sign: some get the point, some *ooh* and *aah*, others scratch their heads and confer, while others see absolutely nothing at all."[6] In the Cana sign, the head steward had no clue about what had happened at the wedding, even though in his surprise he congratulated the bridegroom for providing the best wine last. Knox continues, "For this writer, seeing, knowing, understanding and believing are joined to commitment and obedience, not to intelligence and proofs. Believers are those who live within understanding distance of God. If any man's will is to

[6]Craddock, *John*, 25.

do his will, he shall know whether the teaching is from God . . ."
(7.17).[7] At the conclusion of the narrative, the Apostle John emphatically proclaims what the sign accomplished: it "manifested his glory;
and his disciples believed in him" (2.11). In presenting the miracle of
the raising of Lazarus, the apostle writes that it was "for the glory of
God" (11.4). In chapter nine, regarding the man who was born blind,
Jesus was asked why the man is blind. His response was, "Neither he
nor his parents sinned; it is so that the works of God might be made
visible through him" (9.3). The author of the Gospel used the sign
to introduce his theology of glory, "And so revealed his glory" (v. 11):
this is the beginning of a magnificent Johannine conception of glory
as being *God's manifested presence.* God glorifies us when he manifests
himself in us; we glorify him when we manifest him to the world. In
this instance at Cana, God's presence is manifested in his Son, his
Revealer."[8] The divine manifestation of the glory of the Son of God
was revealed through the many signs Jesus performed during his public ministry, including the one at the wedding in Cana.

Signs Leading to Glory and Belief

In John 2.11, one can clearly observe a connection between sign, glory,
and belief. The sign revealed the glory of God, which indeed led the
disciples to believe in the Messiah. The relationship between sign,
glory, and belief is important, and in John's Gospel, these three important themes appear constantly in the same sequence. The concluding
sentence in the sign, quoted earlier, combines these three concepts. "In
St. John's Gospel sign proceeds glory and belief, and sign, glory and
belief proceed in the same order always. It is no accident, therefore,
that the climax of the story combines these three concepts."[9] The signs
performed by Jesus led many to have faith in him and, ultimately, the
signs were the revelation of the manifestation of divine glory.

[7]Ibid.
[8]Flanagan, *The Gospel According to John,* 13. It is also good to compare John 1.18
here.
[9]Ellis, *The Genius of John,* 43.

The sign at the wedding scene, as already pointed out, occurred during the initial stage of Jesus' public ministry. It was the time when Jesus was calling his disciples. Among the future group of twelve apostles, only a few had already been called at that time. The sign probably occurred soon after the time that John the Apostle moved from the discipleship of John the Baptist to that of his new Master, Jesus, the teacher from Nazareth. For Andrew, Peter, Philip, and Nathanael, who had also become apostles by that time, the days of apostleship were even shorter than those of John. The incident narrated in the Gospel just before the wedding in Cana is the meeting of Nathanael with Jesus. At that time, Nathanael was promised: "You will see greater things than this" (Jn 1.50). The sign of changing water into wine was one of the first, as well as one of the "greater things" that those disciples were able to witness at the initial stage of their discipleship. Possibly, they had followed Jesus until then based on their expectations and religious traditions. "For with the metamorphosis of water into wine their religious persuasion is radicalized into a vital commitment to his person and work."[10]

The apostles were chosen to be with Jesus Christ. They not only listened to his life-giving words that were at the same time instructive and illuminating, but they also witnessed his wondrous deeds of healing. The apostles were called and appointed to continue the mission of healing and preaching, "to make men divine." But without a strong and sustaining faith in their Master, the disciples would not be able to perform what they were assigned and appointed to do. Of course, if his closest followers were not firmly convinced that he was the one whom the Israelites had been waiting for, neither he nor his disciples would be able to accomplish in a timely manner his mission of establishing the kingdom of God on earth. The few disciples who had already become part of the group of twelve apostles witnessed the sign and believed in their Master. They also witnessed the very water that had been drawn out of the jars and served after being transformed into exquisite wine.

[10]Waetjen, *The Gospel of the Beloved Disciple*, 120.

What happened at the wedding celebration was an instant miracle in entirely two dimensions: the miracle of changing ordinary, drawn water into superb wine. More importantly, by witnessing the miracle, the disciples believed in their Master. Though the immediate purpose of the sign was to save the host family from potential embarrassment, it was also to strengthen the faith of his disciples. Their faith, which had been slowly and steadily growing from that moment, culminated in Simon Peter's public confession, "You are the Messiah, the Son of the living God" (Mt 6.16) and the Apostle Thomas' declaration, "My Lord and my God" (Jn 20.28). The apostles at the Cana sign "beheld his glory, the glory of the only begotten of the Father, full of grace and truth" (Jn 1.14).

It is a point of interest that in the Fourth Gospel, the signs were always performed in the presence of those who believed in Jesus Christ. As noted already, faith is the prerequisite for a sign. The Cana sign was initiated in front of Jesus' mother, who already believed and had absolute faith in him. This is why it was "his mother" who reminded the servants to obey the instructions of her Son, in spite of his reactionary response to her. The same is true in the second sign Jesus did in Cana, healing the nobleman's son who was ill in Capernaum. The nobleman humbly implored Jesus to heal his dying son. Jesus' response was, "Unless you people see signs and wonders, you will by no means believe" (4.48). The sign of healing was performed on the solid foundation of the nobleman's faith. In his raising Lazarus from the dead, the sisters of Lazarus, Mary and Martha, believed in the healing power of their dear friend and master Jesus. The faith of the two sisters was the strong foundation Jesus needed to manifest not only divine glory through the sign of raising Lazarus from the dead, but also to teach them, "I am the resurrection" (11.25).

Just before initiating his public ministry, one of the challenges Jesus received from Satan was to change stones to bread. The devil prompted him by producing a suitable quote from Scripture. Jesus countered and denounced Satan by the same token, by the sword of the Word of God. Christ did not care to turn the stones into bread, because Satan was not going to believe in him even if he succumbed to Satan's suggestions and wishes. The same was true about the other two challenges that Satan put forward while Jesus was in the desert (Mt 4.1–11; Lk 4.1–12). It was futile to attempt to display a sign in order to help Satan and his kind to turn from evil, to believe in Jesus, and to follow him.

The almighty God performs miracles where the soil is fertile with faith. Jesus said, "For assuredly, I say to you, if you have faith as a mustard seed, you will say to this mountain, 'Move from here to there,' and it will move; and nothing will be impossible for you" (Mt 17.20). It was said about Nazareth, Jesus' own village, "He could do nothing due to their unbelief" (Mk 6.5).

The Gospel was written for the faithful to encourage and to exhort them in their faith, as well as for their spiritual nurturing and edification. They believed in the miracle of changing water into wine. They also believed that when they "came together" to celebrate the kingdom, the wine was changed into the blood of Christ, and the bread was changed into his body. The Virgin Mary's life was the best example of this. She was nurtured to grow and to mature in faith. For a young girl her age, the message she received from Gabriel the archangel was not only too much to comprehend, but also to accommodate and to accept. When she yielded and submitted to the divine plan, she also learned of her relative's pregnancy. It was impossible for her relative Elizabeth to carry a child in her womb in the normal way, because she was well past child-bearing age. The very sign of pregnancy for Elizabeth in her old age indeed effectuated Mary's faith, encouraging her to be strong and firm. That was why Mary sang with exuberant joy and thanksgiving:

> My soul magnifies the Lord,
> And my spirit has rejoiced in God my savior.
> For He has regarded the lowly
> State of His maidservant; . . .
> For He who is might has done

Great things for me,
And holy is His name. (Lk 1.46–49)

In short, the apostle was introducing his theology of glory through the very first sign Jesus performed at Cana. He writes, "And so beginning his glory" (2.11). "This is the beginning of a magnificent Johannine conception of glory as being God's *manifested presence*. God glorifies us when he manifests himself in us; we glorify him when we manifest him to the world. In this instance at Cana, God's presence is manifested in his Son, his revealer."[11]

The Coming of the Messiah

Many of the deeds of Jesus Christ, especially in the Fourth Gospel, were symbolic signs. They were signs leading to mysterious and revolutionary revelations of the coming of the kingdom of God. The signs revealed the presence of God in Jesus, prompting the apostles and his other followers to believe in him. These signs indeed helped them have solid faith in Jesus, who they knew would establish the awaited kingdom of God.

In his Gospel, John quotes Jesus (1.51): "Most assuredly, I say to you, hereafter you shall see heaven open, and the angels of God ascending and descending upon the Son of Man." This was an indication of, as well as an invitation to anticipate patiently and prayerfully, more mysterious and miraculous events from the incarnate Son of God in the near future. The wedding miracle was the initial manifestation of the glory of the Son of Man, through which the disciples believed in him. John the Apostle elatedly related that solemn and exhilarating experience within the very first chapter of his Gospel, "We beheld His glory, the glory as of the only begotten of the Father, full of grace and truth" (1.14).

The goal of the Cana sign, and of the subsequent signs in the Gospel, was to reveal to the followers of Jesus that he was the Messiah, the Son of God, who came to introduce the kingdom of God and to offer

---

[11]Flanagan, *The Gospel According to John*, 13.

his life to redeem the world. Though opinions may vary among biblical scholars about the purpose of the sign of changing water into wine, it is clear from the context and the circumstances that the sign was a rare glimpse into the person of Jesus Christ from Nazareth and into his mission. "The primary focus is, as in all Johannine stories, on Jesus as the one sent by the Father to bring salvation to the world. What shines through is his glory, and the only reaction that is emphasized is the belief of the disciples."[12] Flanagan observes:

> The question, as always in John, is: What does the sign mean? In this instance the meaning is multiple, but it is centered on one basic point: the arrival through Jesus of the new Messianic age. What is changed in this incident is not simply water, but water for the Old Testament ceremonial washings. It is changed not simply into wine, but into wine of highest quality and of surprising quantity (six jars, each holding fifteen to twenty-five gallons). Such a superabundance of wine was a frequent prophetic figure of speech for the dawning of the messianic age (Amos 9.13–14; Joel 3.18). The symbol was current also at the time of Jesus, as we read in the almost contemporary 2 Baruch 29: ". . . on each vine there shall be a thousand branches, and each branch shall bear a thousand clusters, and each cluster produce a cor [about 120 gallons] of wine . . . because these are they who have come to the consummation of time."[13]

The changing of water into wine symbolizes the arrival of the messianic age and the inauguration of the kingdom of heaven. It would be the time of the long-expected messianic banquet, and the one who supplies the exquisite wine abundantly at the banquet is the bridegroom, who is Jesus Christ, himself (3.29).

Water was transformed into a large quantity of exquisite wine. The same is true in the sign of the bread and fish to feed the multitude.

[12]G. H. C. MacGregor, *The Gospel of John*, Moffat New Testament Commentary (New York, NY: Harper and Brothers Publishers, 1929), 103–104.

[13]Flanagan, *The Gospel According to John*, 12–13.

A multitude of people was fed with very few loaves and fish, and the leftovers filled twelve baskets. Both signs point to the Jewish manna tradition and the Hellenic wine tradition.[14] Stories of rivers flowing with wine from the god of wine, Dionysus, were popular among the Greeks. According to the eighth-century Prophet Amos, bountiful wine was a symbol of the eschatological banquet:

> Yes, days are coming, says the Lord
> When the plowman shall overtake the reaper,
> And the vintager, him who sows the seed;
> The juice of grapes shall drip down the mountains,
> And all the hills shall run with it
> I will bring about the restoration of my people Israel;
> They shall rebuild and inhabit their ruined cities,
> Plant vineyards and drink the wine,
> Set out gardens and eat the fruits. (9.13–14)

The pre-Maccabean book of First Enoch speaks about the abundance of wine "in those days," the last days. Philo, the Alexandrian Jewish philosopher, "allegorized the Genesis story of Melchizedek" and said, "Let Melchizedek instead of water offer wine, and give to souls strong drink that they may be seized by a divine intoxication, more sober than sobriety itself. For he is a priest, namely Logos, having as his portion him that is, and all his thoughts of God are high, and vast and sublime."[15] In his work *On Dreams*, Philo speaks of the divine Logos in light of the rich red wine. All these were signs of the messianic age.

No event is an occurrence in itself in the Gospel of John. All point to something greater, sacramental or mystical, and messianic. The Gospel specifically tells the story of abundance and "overflowing generosity" that was brought by the Messiah. The Cana sign was the beginning of the messianic replacement. In the first few chapters, the Gospel deals with the replacing of Jewish traditions and institutions.

---

[14]Grayston, *The Gospel of John*, 29.
[15]Ibid., (quoting from Philo), 30.

Later in the Gospel, especially during Jewish feasts, Jesus revealed through discourses the real purpose of the various celebrations. The multiplication of bread to feed the multitude was another major messianic sign of abundance. In the wedding scene, the water used for ceremonial purification was replaced by the best wine. The wine was changed to Jesus' own blood in order to accomplish the final purification and redemption.

No more water for purification was left in the pots. This water had already been used at the wedding feast, and that is why Jesus directed the servants to refill the pots. What was left at the wedding feast in Cana was a wine of choice, the best of its kind, because of the presence of the Messiah and through his personal involvement. Jesus revealed himself as the true source of purification. "When he had by himself purged our sins, he sat down on the right hand of the Majesty on high" (Heb 1.3).

Changing water into wine at the wedding scene was thus a partial revelation of the coming of the messianic age. Those who were born and brought up in the Jewish tradition were well aware of the symbol of marriage as a sign of the messianic kingdom and that there would be an abundance of wine in that time. It was a time of replacing worn-out customs of purification. Even though Jesus was able to save a family from embarrassment by miraculously replenishing the wine with wine of the best quality, through the sign he was introducing the initial stage of the messianic time and also revealing that he is the Messiah whom they eagerly awaited. Thus, the context of the sign, a wedding, and the wine that was transformed in abundance from water all pointed to the messianic age.

The sign also proves that the messianic replacement is always in abundance and beyond human calculation. Not only did Jesus Christ resolve an impending problem, but he also did so with the very best substitute, and with much left over. The same was true in the multiplying of the bread for the multitude in the desert. What God does is always beyond human calculation and estimation. The same theme is emphatically expressed by Paul in his Epistle to the Philippians, "My

God will fully supply whatever you need, in accord with his glorious riches in Christ Jesus" (4.19). "The superabundance of Cana is therefore a sign that God's feast with humanity, his self-giving for man, has begun. The framework of the event, the wedding, thus becomes an image that points beyond itself to the messianic hour: The hour of God's marriage feast with his people has begun in the coming of Jesus. The promise of the last days enters into the Now."[16]

Conclusion

By narrating the sign of changing water into wine at the very beginning of the public ministry of Jesus Christ, especially in the context of a wedding celebration, the Apostle was presenting both that Jesus was the Messiah whom the Jews eagerly awaited and the abundance that the Messiah would bring in. The sign was an occasion for the manifestation of the glory of the Son of God, which encouraged the disciples, including the Apostle John, to believe in Jesus (Jn 2.11). Evidently, it was also the purpose of the Apostle that those who would read the Cana event would also "believe that Jesus is the Messiah, the Son of God, and that through this belief have life in his name" (20.31). Thus, with regard to signs:

> To the believer they describe two planes of reality: physical and spiritual or perhaps better, past and present. On one hand, the miracles acknowledge Jesus, the wonder-worker invested with divine power, who throughout his earthly ministry commanded physical reality. On the other hand, they are epiphanies of the risen Lord, signs anticipating the ultimate truth about Jesus which will only be fully revealed when his hour has been achieved. For John, the miracles further serve to stress the continuity between the earthly and risen Jesus: who he is now revealed as who he was also then, the incarnate Word, full of grace and truth.[17]

[16]Ratzinger, *Jesus of Nazareth*, 253.

[17]John J. Huckle and Paul Visokay, *The Gospel According to St John*, vol. 1, New Testament for Spiritual Reading, vol. 17, ed. John L. McKenzie (New York, NY: Crossroad, 1981), 22.

5
The Marriage Feast
and the "Mother of Jesus"

"A gentle maiden, having lodged God in her womb, asks as its price: peace for the world, salvation for those who lost, and life for the world." —St Peter Chrysologus (*c.* 380–450)

The wedding scene at Cana is colorfully drawn with less than a dozen verses, and this brevity gives a clear, concise, complete and correct picture of the nature, the charisma, and the character of the mother of Jesus. The Virgin Mary is present at the wedding in Cana, at the very beginning of the public ministry of Jesus Christ. She was also present at the completion of his public ministry by remaining at the foot of the cross during his crucifixion. By presenting her at the initial stage of Jesus' public ministry and at the very end of it, in the Fourth Gospel the apostle reveals the symbolic and theological importance of the Virgin Mary in the economy and history of salvation. As usual, her commitment to the will of God at the Cana scene was unparalleled, as was her caring nature. Mary's submission to the divine plan was superb and complete. At the wedding she witnessed her Son's love for others on a small scale just as she would later witness it on a bigger scale, on the cross.

The Cana episode stands out as an embodiment of Mary's absolute faith in her Son. Along with these noble traits of the Virgin Mary's character, her unlimited access to her Son and the power of her intercessory prayer were vividly portrayed in the wedding scene at Cana. Thus, she knew what was lacking at the feast and at the same time how to resolve it, as she was fully aware of her Son's divine nature and eternal powers. She is seen in the Cana sign as the perfect embodiment of the spirit of sublime service, as well as a supreme example of spiritual discernment and determination.

It is indeed interesting to contemplate the important incidents and occasions in the four Gospels where one observes the presence of the Virgin Mary. In their Gospel narratives, both Matthew and Luke give emphasis to the role of the mother of Jesus in the incarnation, and some glimpses into Jesus' childhood. The Apostle John narrates not the human birth, but the eternal origin of Christ, the Word of God, "In the beginning was the Word, and the Word was with God. He was in the beginning with God" (Jn 1.1–2). John was interested in presenting Mary's active role in the manifestation of the glory of Jesus Christ.

The rare appearances of Mary in the Gospels were almost always associated with assisting fellow human beings in their time of critical need. She exceeded her abilities in troubleshooting problems wherever she was or in whatever situation confronted her. Paving the way for the incarnation of the Savior was the supreme example of Mary's total submission to the divine will and of her great dedication to helping others, despite any personal difficulties surrounding such a noble and divine plan.

Since the fall of Adam and Eve, the Creator's desire has been to lift up fallen human beings, to raise and restore them to their destined glory. To achieve this, God Almighty searched for someone, a woman who would completely surrender to the divine economy of the incarnation. "The woman," Mary, did indeed appear on earth in the fullness of time, and it was her positive response and complete cooperation that paved the way for the coming of the Son of God as the Son of Man. When she consented to the unique call she had received by responding "Yes" (Lk 1.38) to the Archangel Gabriel, this marked the solemn and sacred moment of God's condescension to earth and the beginning of man's ascension to heaven. Mary became the medium and the means for such a mysterious and historic meeting. Thus, the first revelation of her innate goodness and greatness was at the time of the Annunciation itself.

The three major events generally for human beings are birth, marriage, and death. We see in the Gospels the presence of Mary in these three situations. Mary's concern and commitment related to a birth, or rather a pregnancy is narrated in Luke's Gospel (1.39–45). Young Mary traveled to the faraway hilly country of Judea to assist a relative in distress. Elizabeth, Mary's aunt,[1] was in pregnancy in her old age. Mary herself was very young and was carrying the baby Jesus in her womb. She journeyed to the hills of Judea trekking the rocky roads to visit Elizabeth in a difficult situation, especially for a young girl who was in the early stages of pregnancy. Elizabeth had been barren during the childbearing years of her life, but became pregnant and was in the sixth month of her pregnancy and experiencing troublesome moments. Mary was not only very young, but was betrothed and waiting to be married while carrying a baby in her womb.

The next important scene in the Gospels where we see the presence of Mary with her Son Jesus Christ is at the wedding celebration at Cana. She was at the wedding "perhaps as a relative of the bride or groom."[2] This is the first time Mary appears in the Fourth Gospel (2.1). Incidentally, she also is the first woman mentioned in this Gospel. Other than birth, the most important event for most people is marriage. The Cana sign is important since this is the only place in the Gospels that Mary asks her Son, directly or indirectly, to act, and especially to perform a miracle. Mary attended the marriage ceremony and the accompanying celebrations in the village of Cana. From the narrative one can surmise, as Barclay suggests, that "Mary held a special place at that feast. She had something to do with the arrangements for she was worried when the wine ran down; and she had authority enough to order the servants to do whatever Jesus told them to do."[3] Her intervention to resolve problems silently and her

---

[1] Some traditions present Elizabeth as Mary's cousin.
[2] Noted in the *Orthodox Study Bible: New Testament & Psalms*, 215.
[3] Barclay, *The Gospel of John*, 80–81.

unwavering faith in her "only begotten Son" are fully revealed in the Cana scene. Unlike in the other Gospels, in the Fourth Gospel, Jesus' public ministry begins neither with teaching, nor with healing, but with attending the wedding. Mary's presence there becomes the catalyst for the inauguration of Jesus' public ministry through the sign.

The final passage in the Gospel where the presence of Mary is mentioned is at the last moment of a person's earthly existence: the death of her beloved Son Jesus Christ (19.25–27). This is also the last reference to Mary in the Fourth Gospel. Jesus was on the cross and about to die. How difficult is it for any mother to watch her child endure pain and suffering? How much more difficult is it to stand by a dying son? One can probably imagine a mother's desperate anguish and agony while watching her only Son being crucified. Accusing him of atrocities, such as treason and blasphemy—the worst kind of transgressions of the time—must have made the mother's agony all the harder to bear. She knew her Son's innocence and innate goodness, and the words of the angel (Lk 1.32–35) were ever fresh in her heart and mind (Lk 2.51).

Multitudes of people often followed the Son of God everywhere before his suffering and crucifixion; but on the cross, Jesus was alone, except two thieves who hung on either side of him, condemned to die with him. The apostles were specially chosen by their Master "to be with Him." Yet, all of them, except John, abandoned him in that very critical moment. According to the Fourth Gospel narrative of the passion, other than the apostle, the only people there were, "his mother, his mother's sister, Mary the wife of Cleopas, and Mary Magdalene" (19.25).

Mary was with Her Son at the Wedding Ceremony

Mary was present with her Son at the wedding scene in Cana. In fact, Jesus was invited to the wedding, but the passage did not reveal that the mother was also an invited guest. Where Christ is, the mother of Jesus and the saints are there, and this is true, physically and spiritually, in the context of the Cana wedding. Mary assisted the family in overcoming a crisis by seeking the mediation of her beloved Son. She tried to resolve the problem actively, yet quietly, quickly, and calmly, staying in the background. The Holy Virgin did not make a scene in that troubled situation, and she did not want anyone to notice her presence or her involvement in solving the crisis. In other words, Mary was at the right place and at the right time, seeking the assistance of the right person who could resolve conflicts and confusion easily, mysteriously, majestically, and peacefully. "In her act of faith and in her prayer, Mary appears as one who represents humanity in difficulty and Judaism in its messianic hope; she is the type of humanity and of Israel which are waiting their deliverance, a mysterious deliverance for humanity, a messianic but still very human deliverance for Israel."[4]

Among all human beings, the Virgin Mary was the first one who had the unique fortune and the unparalleled privilege of enjoying the physical presence of the incarnate Son of God. "In the fullness of time," the Word became flesh, receiving the body and the blood of the Virgin Mother. As the bearer of Jesus Christ from the time of the annunciation, she carried him first in her womb. Later, she held the baby Jesus in her hands and on her lap. Thus, she was physically closer to the Son of God than anyone else in creation. And this is why the woman shouted with great joy to Jesus from the crowd, "Blessed is the womb that carried you and the breasts at which you nursed" (Lk 11.27).

In fact, obeying the Word and doing the will of the heavenly Father allowed Mary to be very close to her Son in a unique way. Paving the way for the incarnation of the Son is the perfect example of Mary's obedience to the divine will and mission. She was willing to cooperate with the Father despite the difficulties that accompanied the divine economy of redemption and salvation. A Christian is one who carries Christ and is always with Christ. In this sense, Mary was the first Christ-bearer, that is, the first Christian who carried Christ. She is the *Theotokos,* the Bearer or Mother of God.

The scripture passage says, "On the third day there was a wedding in Cana in Galilee, and the mother of Jesus was there. Jesus and his

[4]Thurian, *Mary*, 136.

disciples were also invited to the wedding" (Jn 2.1–2). In those days, in a family with close relatives or friends, it was normal for women to arrive a few days before the wedding. They were also the ones who usually prepared food for the banquet, so they had to be there before anyone else. It is not clear in the Gospel narrative whether Mary arrived before Jesus and his disciples or if she followed them to the wedding. Given the custom of that time, it is likely she arrived before they did.[5] Interestingly, this is the only place in the Gospels where Mary's name is mentioned before Jesus' name. She was there with Jesus during the feast, and she informed him about the critical need for more wine, which led to the sign that produced wine of a superior quality. Mary's presence with Jesus turned out to be a blessing for the family as well as for the guests who got the best wine last.

According to the Old Testament, it was the experience of the constant presence of God that encouraged and emboldened the leaders of the Jewish people to guard and to guide them in the midst of uncertainties and difficulties. When given the huge responsibility of leading the Israelites to the promised land, the great prophet Moses asked Yahweh, "You have not let me know whom You will send with me" (Ex 33.12). Yahweh's response was, "My presence will go with you, and I will give you rest" (Ex 33.14). The ever-abiding divine presence gave courage and comfort to Moses in his herculean task of leading the Israelites to the promised land. Indeed, it was this same presence that strengthened the shepherd lad David to challenge the giant Goliath and triumph over him. The presence and the guidance of the almighty God also strengthened David, as king, to successfully lead and guide the Israelites. This was why the psalmist was able to sing with harps and cymbals, "I have set the Lord always before me; because he is at my right hand, I will not be shaken" (Ps 16.8). This is also true for many major characters in Holy Scripture.

Mary believed with certainty that her Son could confront an impending crisis and could resolve the problem easily. In that situation, she was trying, probably with great hesitation, to declare that her

Son is the Messiah and possibly prodding him to reveal his glory. She was certainly sure who her Son is, and she wanted to share the secret revealed her by the angel, which she had been keeping to herself.

Theodore of Mopsuestia (*c.* 350–428) observes, "Perhaps his mother, as mothers do, incited him to perform a miracle, wishing that the greatness of her Son would be revealed—and thinking that the lack of wine offered the right occasion for the miracle."[6] Mary kept everything to herself as, Luke points out: "His mother kept all these things in her heart" (2.51). She thought that the feast at the wedding was an opportune occasion, the moment she eagerly awaited to reveal to the world what she knew about her Son. Was the Virgin Mother aware that revealing her Son as the Messiah, so early in his public ministry would lead him to his passion and the cross? Yet he was sure that his time had not yet come. "She was eager to find an opportunity to share with the whole of Israel what she had known with certitude about the mystery of Christ, the hope of all ages."[7] If that were the case, that would have been, in fact, the beginning of the countdown to the crucifixion. Archbishop Dmitri Royster writes:

> With regard to the presence of the Lord's mother, we may conclude that even if those who invited her did not understand why she should accompany Him, it is important. For she will not only witness His first sign but she will also witness His "hour" or glorification on the cross, in fulfillment of St Simon's prophecy, which he spoke to Mary alone: "Behold, this child is set (*keitai*, from *keimai*, used as a perfect passive of *tithemi*; implying, according to God's plan) for the fall and rising of many in Israel; yea, a sword shall pierce through thy own soul also, that the thoughts of many may be revealed." (Luke 2.34–35)[8]

---

[6]Theodore of Mopsuestia, "Commentary on the Gospel of John 1.2.3," *John 1–10* (ACCS NT IVa), 91.

[7]Matthew the Poor, "The Wedding in Cana," 13.

[8]Archbishop Dmitri Royster, *The Holy Gospel According to Saint John: A Pastoral Commentary* (Yonkers, NY: St Vladimir's Seminary Press, 2015), 46.

The Mother of Jesus is the Mother of All the Faithful

In the wedding scene, the Apostle John writes, "The mother of Jesus was there." The other occasion where we see Mary in the Gospel, as already noted, is in the crucifixion scene. The Gospel narrates that Jesus entrusted his mother to the Apostle John, saying she was "his [John's] mother" (19.26–27). In both places, Mary is not mentioned by her name. Why is she mentioned as "the mother of Jesus" or as "his mother," instead of by name? John is the only one among the evangelists who does so, while Mark mentions Mary by name once, and Matthew five times. Luke mentions her by name thirteen times—twelve in the Gospel, and once in the Acts of the Apostles.

Even though John avoids calling Mary by name in his Gospel, he mentions many other names that often including other persons whose names were Mary, such as, Mary Magdalene, Mary the sister of Martha and Lazarus, and Mary the wife of Cleopas. As George H. Tavard observes, in John's Gospel, the mere name "Mary" is Mary from the village of Bethany, one of the two sisters of Lazarus (chapters 11 and 12).[9] We also see people often mentioned in the Gospel by their names, such as Nicodemus, Jesus' father Joseph, Joseph of Arimathea, and so on. If so many names of various persons are mentioned in the Gospel—those with the name "Mary" also—why was John reluctant to mention Jesus' mother by name? Jo-Ann A. Brant observes, "The omission of the name Mary is puzzling but not necessarily troubling."[10] It seems that the apostle avoided the proper name "Mary," not casually, but rather very cautiously and intentionally. It is also to be noted that, as "Her status comes from her Son, and to refer to her as the 'mother of' is respectable. Moreover, anonymity in this Gospel seems to be a sign of intimacy rather than obscurity."[11]

John the apostle, believed to be the author of the Gospel, is mentioned in the Gospel as the "beloved disciple" (19.26; 21.20) or "the

    [9]George H. Tavard, *The Thousand Faces of the Virgin Mary* (Collegeville, MN: The Liturgical Press, 1992), 12.
    [10]Brant, *John*, 56.
    [11]Ibid.

other disciple" (20.3). His brother, who was one among the twelve and was present at some of the events narrated in the Gospel, also is not mentioned by name but as "sons of Zebedee" (21.2). Leon Morris observes, "If this man was the author of the Gospel and his practice was not to mention the name either of himself or of his brother, he may well have extended this habit to include Mary, who at the time of writing was, or had been, a member of his household."[12]

As was usual in those days, children were known by their fathers' names, for example, Simon Bar Jonah, meaning "Simon son of Jonah," and Barnabas, "son of Nabas" (or "son of encouragement" Acts 4.36), Barabbas, "son of Abbas," and so on. However, mothers were known by their children's names, for example, "the mother of Zebedee's children" in Matthew 20.20. In a difference from our contemporary practice, designating someone as the "mother of so and so" was used instead of saying the name of that person's mother. It was a way of showing more respect to those persons, as well as their mothers. Raymond Brown observes, "Among Arabs today 'the mother of X' is an honorable title for a woman who has been fortunate enough to bear a son."[13] This was perhaps one reason for the apostle's referring to people this way. The purpose of the proper name, especially among the Israelites, was to identify an individual and hence, such a name distinguished them from others. The title "Mother of Jesus" clearly and cleverly indicates the uniqueness of Mary, from whom Jesus was born "not by blood, nor of the will of the flesh, nor of the will of man, but of God" (Jn 1.13). "Her status comes from her Son, and to refer to her as the 'mother of' is respectable."[14] This also signifies that no one could ever duplicate Mary's position and place.

Both the wedding scene and the crucifixion scene, where Mary appears in the Gospel, are correlated with the Genesis story of the fall of Adam and Eve. Eve was the first "woman" in creation. "The man called his wife "Eve," because she became the "mother of all the living"

[12]Morris, *Reflections on the Gospel of John*, 71.
[13]Brown, *The Gospel According to John*, 98.
[14]Brant, *John*, 56.

(Gen 3.20). Eve, the mother in the "first creation" was tempted and fell prey to Satan and ate the forbidden fruit. In turn, she tempted her husband Adam to follow suit. In Cana, the divine Son changed water into wine, and the process of re-creation was inaugurated at the insistence of another "woman," Mary, who becomes the mother of the "new creation." Eve's act was an embarrassment and an act of disobedience to please the devil. Mary's action was to *avoid* an embarrassing situation, and she left the choice of acting in that situation to her Son's divine will. Water was part of the fallen world. Jesus acted upon that water to transform it into wine. Wine is made from the fermented juice extracted from fruits like grapes. The wine Jesus made at the wedding feast was not from grapes or any other fruit, but only from water. In this way, the sign marked the beginning of a new creation or the re-creation of the initial creation. Adam and Eve disobeyed and were banished from the garden of Eden with a curse. God told serpent that the seed of the woman would "bruise his head" (Gen 2.15). In the presence of a "woman," "his mother," Jesus initiated the process of reentry into the paradise lost by Adam and Eve.

Jesus entrusted his mother with an additional responsibility at his crucifixion. By telling John the Apostle, "This is your mother," Mary became not only the mother of John, but also the mother of all the faithful. Jesus did not say, "This is *also* your mother," but only "This is your mother," and with these words, she became the mother of all who believe. If Eve was the mother of all the living, the "woman" Mary, the new Eve, became the mother of the new creation, of all who receive abundant life through Jesus Christ. "Eve, the mother of all living (Genesis 3), that is, of all the human race, is now replaced by the new Eve, and here precisely she becomes the mother of all those who have been born again into the life of Christ, who are represented by the beloved disciple John."[15]

John was the only apostle who remained at the foot of the cross, and his faithfulness to his Master was evident in his presence there during that dangerous event. In fact, of all the apostles, John was

[15]Archbishop Dmitri, *The Miracles of Christ*, 76.

closest to his master and to Mary. "The beloved disciple was looked on as a son given to Mary to replace Jesus who was crucified, even as the old Eve said, 'God has given a son to replace Abel whom Cain killed (Genesis 4.25).'"[16] The Apostle John represents the new faithful children of God, who are willing to risk their lives for her Son, the Master, and his mother becomes the mother of all the people about whom Isaiah prophesied: "Look at me and the children whom the Lord has given me: we are signs and portents in Israel from the Lord of hosts who dwells in mount Zion" (Is 8.18). Quoting Origen, John Behr writes:

> By Christ's own words, his mother is now the mother of the beloved disciple, and this disciple is himself identified with Christ: as Origen points out, Christ does not say, "Woman behold another son for you in my place," but "behold your son," or, as Origen paraphrases it, "this is Jesus whom you bore." Those who stand by the cross, and are not ashamed of it, receive as their mother the one who embodies this fertile, generative faithfulness, and they themselves become sons of God, for they have Christ, the Son of God, living in them.[17]

The Virgin Mary became the mother of Jesus' disciples for they were endowed with eternal life, which is clearly messianic. As a result of his new relationship to Mary as "son," when John the Apostle wrote his Gospel much later, he could have written "my mother" or "Jesus' mother and mine," rather than the "mother of Jesus." That special privilege which Jesus Christ granted Mary to become a mother to John also made John the brother of Jesus. Thus, Jesus became not only John's Lord and Master, but also his brother. Since he was aware of who Jesus was, the apostle didn't want to equate himself to Jesus in relation to Mary's motherhood. Still, one cannot help but wonder

[16]Raymond E. Brown, *The Death of the Messiah,* vol. 2 (New York: ABRL, Doubleday, 1994), 1022.

[17]John Behr, *The Mystery of Christ: Life In Death* (Crestwood, NY: St Vladimir's Seminary Press, 2006), 128.

how the apostle could avoid calling her by name and referred to her instead as "Jesus' mother" or "the mother of Jesus."

Mary was a very common name in the time when she lived. One other hypothesis suggests that the Apostle John avoided calling Mary by name because by mentioning "the mother of Jesus" and "woman" instead of Mary, she would remain unique and would be distinguished from all others named "Mary." The Virgin Mary, the *Theotokos,* was unique among all human beings, "more honorable than the Cherubim, and more glorious than the Seraphim" as she was able to "contain him that nothing can contain." Thus, she who gave birth to Jesus Christ rightly stands separate from all other women, especially those also named Mary, assuring that she would be known for all time not as Mary, but as "the mother of Jesus."

In the Gospel, Jesus is presented at the beginning as the Word who "was in the beginning with God" and "through him all things were made" (Jn 1.2–3). For the apostle, to prefer "the mother of Jesus" to "Mary" conveyed a lot more because she is the mother of "the only begotten Son." McHugh observes:

> In the Fourth Gospel the choice of the phrase "mother of Jesus" in preference to "Mary" is an indication not of her relative unimportance, but of the contrary. It was through her that "the Word became flesh and dwelt among us, that we might see His glory, the glory as of the Only-begotten of the father, full of grace and truth" (cf. John 1.14). Consequently, if we wish to bring out by paraphrase in meaningful English the full content of the Johannine term "mother of Jesus", the only correct equivalent is "mother of the Word Incarnate."[18]

John Marsh suggests, "The figure of Mary, particularly since she is not named, may be intended to refer not only to the Lord's mother, but to Judaism as such, in whose 'womb' Jesus was conceived."[19]

---

[18]McHugh, *The Mother of Jesus,* 362.
[19]Marsh, *Saint John,* 145.

However, it may be too much to posit such an interpretation from the context.

The concept of the "daughter of Zion" was very common in Jewish thought, and we see many references to this in Psalms and in the books of the prophets. It was a reference to the personification of the Jewish people, the Israel from which the Messiah was expected to come. In the New Testament, the Church, the bride of Christ, was referred to as the "daughter of Zion." The Church also viewed Mary, the mother of Jesus, as the new "daughter of Zion" from whom the Messiah would be born, and who would be the "firstborn from the dead" (Col 1.18), and who has the keys of death (Rev 1.18). In the agony of labor and the ecstasy of joy, the new daughter of Zion, Mary, gave birth to a new nation, the new Israel (Jn 6.21; Ez 49.20–22, 54.1, 66.7–11). "A great sign appeared in the sky, a woman clothed with the sun, with the moon under her feet, and on her head a crown of twelve stars. She was with child and wailed aloud in pain as she labored to give birth" (Rev 12.1–2). Those who believe in Jesus Christ receive a new birth. They become brothers and sisters of Jesus Christ and the children of his mother, Mary. At Cana and at Calvary, Mary revealed the role of "woman" in the redemptive history of the world (Rev 12.3–6). In fact, the Virgin Mary is a symbol of the connection between the old Judaism (Mary) and the present Christian community (the "Beloved Disciple").[20] Here, Mary becomes the symbol of the "daughter of Zion" and of the new nation started by the messianic age.

Many of the Fathers of the Church see her not only as the mother of all the faithful but also as the mother of the living, following Genesis 3.20 where Eve is presented as the "mother of all the living." St Ephraim, in his homily *On Our Lord*, explains how Mary became the mother of all the living, "And Eve, who had been mother of all the living, became a fountain of death for all the living. But Mary, the new shoot, sprouted from Eve, the old vine, and new life dwelt in her."[21] St James of Serugh (451–521), a great teacher and poetic writer who

---

[20]Thurston, *Women in the New Testament*, 82.
[21]Quoted by Puthuparambil, *Mariological Thought*, 251.

is called "fruit of the Holy Spirit and harp of the faithful church,"[22] follows upon the same thought and writes,

> In Adam's prophecy, our Lord was prefigured
> Who indeed is life; and his mother was the Virgin Mary,
> He named Eve, *the mother of all life*, and prophesied,
> Because she brings forth to us life—our Lord who is
>   Jesus.[23]

The Virgin Mary, the Symbol of the Church

In the Gospel of John, the Virgin Mary is a symbol, the symbol of the Church as the true and typical representative of the people. The nation of Israel was depicted as a bride in the Old Testament, and the Church was presented as a bride in the New Testament and from second century onwards also as mother. Clement of Alexandria uses the term "Virgin" to refer to the Church. He writes:

> The Lord Jesus, fruit of the Virgin, did not proclaim women's breasts to be blessed, nor did he choose them to give nourishment. But when the Father, full of goodness and love for men, rained down his Word upon the earth, the same Word became the spiritual nourishment for virtuous men. O mysterious marvel! There is one Father for all, there is one Word of all, and the Holy Spirit is one and the same everywhere. There is also one Virgin Mother, whom I love to call the Church. Alone, this mother had no milk because she alone did not become a woman. She is virgin and mother simultaneously, a virgin undefiled and a mother full of love.[24]

One of the images of the Church is "the body of Christ." Jesus received his flesh and blood, that is, his body from his human mother.

---

[22]Jacob of Serug, *On the Mother of God*, trans. Mary Hansbury (Crestwood, NY: St Vladimir's Seminary Press, 1995), 15.

[23]Ibid., *Homily Concerning the Blessed Virgin Mother of God, Mary* 634, 37.

[24]Quoted by Behr, *The Mystery of Christ*, 123.

The presence and the actions of the mother of Jesus at the wedding in Cana reveal Mary mysteriously, but not conspicuously, as the symbol of the Church. The Church brings the needs of others to Christ, just as in Cana, the Virgin Mary brought a need at the banquet to Christ.

While addressing the crowds Jesus clearly gives an answer about who his mother is. "As he spoke these things, a certain woman of the company lifted up her voice and said to him: 'Blessed is the womb that bore you, and the breasts that you sucked.' But he said, 'Blessed rather are those that hear the Word of God and keep it'" (Lk 11.27–28). The same was his response earlier when he was told his mother and brothers were waiting outside to see him, "My mother and my brothers are those who hear the Word of God and do it" (Lk 8.21). Thus, those who hear and obey the Word of God, and those in whom by listening the Word becomes flesh—they are Jesus' mother and brothers. This is exactly what Mary did. The Church venerates her because of her complete obedience to God much more than being the physical mother of Jesus. Valerie A. Karras writes, "The Church's message is clear; the Theotokos is venerated not just because she is Jesus' mother, but because she was attentive to God, which made her appropriate to become God's chosen vessel."[25]

The two instances where Mary the mother of Jesus appears in the Fourth Gospel are important events, and they have many striking similarities. Yet those instances point to Mary far more than just to a woman, a mother, or even the "mother of Jesus." They are also the only two instances where Jesus called his beloved mother "woman." At the wedding scene, Jesus told her that his "time" had not yet come, but it did finally come at the crucifixion. If the first instance paved the way for initiating the redeeming activity of Jesus Christ, the second became the culmination, his hour of glorification. "By reason of its mention of the woman and the hour, which hour is the hour of Jesus' glorification, the Cana incident must be seen in relation to the scene at the foot of the cross. In his portrayal of Jesus' Passion, the evangelist

[25]Aristotle Papanikolaou and Elizabeth H. Prodromou, eds., *Thinking Through Faith* (Crestwood, NY: St Vladimir's Seminary Press, 2008), 151.

is describing the birth of the Church. There the one who had waited in faithful expectation is united to the one who is the faithful disciple *par excellence*, the one whom Jesus loved."[26] Just as the birth of Jesus was through Mary, so it was through her and in her that the Church, the new Israel, came into existence.

Mary is the only woman mentioned in the Cana celebration, but strangely enough or perhaps in a very meaningful sense, she is not called by name, but as "woman." For Mary, the mother of Jesus Christ, "woman" is a common form of address because she is a representative, *the* representative of the Church. If the "woman" Eve represented the "first creation" and the old Israel, the "woman" Mary represents the "new creation" and the new Israel. She is the representative of the saved community, the Church. One cannot consider Mary as just the mother of Jesus, with "the womb that carried him" and "the breasts that suckled him" (Lk 11.27). She is also the image of the Church in which the image of God shines anew and is revealed in all its grandeur. It was through the Virgin Mary that the Son of God became Son of Man, paving the way for the redemption of the world.

Who was the bride at the wedding in Cana? No name is provided in the narrative. The probable reason would be that Mary as the image of the Church represents the "bride." Only when one understands the place of the term "woman" can one understand why the mother of Jesus was the only woman mentioned in the sign at Cana. In connection with the comparison of Mary as the image of the Church, Max Thurian writes:

> Thus Mary, the Mother of the Lord, who has borne the physical body of Christ and is the dwelling of God and the Ark of the Covenant, remains the figure of motherhood for the Church; as a spiritual mother, the Holy Church gives birth to the members of the Body of Christ, the faithful, by her own life, by the Word of God and the Sacraments of His Presence. And they in their turn become temples of the Holy Spirit, and find in Mary the example

[26]Collins, *These Things Have Been Written*, 32.

which encourages them in that purity of heart and of body which, having been redeemed, belong henceforth only to God: they bear God with them and witness to His glory which dwells in them in its fullness.[27]

The same insights were given by St Ephraim the Syrian, "The Virgin Mary is a symbol of the Church, when she receives the first announcement of the Gospel . . . Blessed be God, who filled Mary and the Church with joy. We call the Church by the name of Mary, for she deserves a double name."[28]

The Virgin Mary can be seen thus as the image of the Church, the people of God. Alexander Schmemann writes, "She is the Church as prayer, as joy, as fulfillment. It is this combination of beauty and humility, matter and spirit, time and eternity that is the real experience of the Church and of that experience Mary is the focus and the life."[29] She is the symbol of the Church that gives birth to children through baptism, children who are similar to the "only begotten Son" as they participate, through the experience of baptism, in the death and the resurrection of Christ. It was Mary's vocation to bring Christ to the world, and the Church's vocation is the same. For this reason, Mary is never separated from the Church. In the context of the wedding sign, as well, she was the one who initiated her Son's actions, which ultimately resulted in the manifestation of his glory and the disciples believing in him. From the beginning, this has been the role of the Church, as well.

The Virgin Mary, the True Believer

The Gospels clearly depict Mary as the true believer. She was the one who received the good news, "the gospel," before anyone else, and this was also because of her unquestioning faith. The Cana sign is

[27]Max Thurian, *Mary, Mother of the Lord, Figure of the Church*, trans. B. Neville Cryer (London: The Faith Press, 1963), 55.
[28]Behr, *The Mystery*, 131.
[29]Schmemann, *Celebration of Faith*, vol. 3, *The Virgin Mary*, 67.

another example of where the Apostle John presents the mother of God as a true believer. Her request of her Son and then her instruction to the servants are clear examples of her strong faith. She was sure her request of Jesus would be fulfilled as soon as she made it. Barclay writes, "Even when Mary did not understand what Jesus was going to do, even when it seemed that He had refused her request, Mary still believed in Him so much that she turned to the serving folk and told them to do whatever Jesus told them to do. Mary had the faith which could trust even when it did not understand. She did not know what Jesus was going to do, but she was quite sure that He would do the right thing."[30] In fact, it was Mary's faith that guided her to direct that request to her Son, who instantly performed an amazing miracle.

The Apostle Paul defines faith this way, "Faith is the realization of what is hoped for and the evidence of things not seen" (Heb 11.1). These words were literally true in the life of Mary. She was presented in Scripture as the symbol and the paradigm of a true believer. The unquestioning faith of the Mother of God was eloquently depicted, as already noted, at the time of the Annunciation. If the Gospel of Luke attests to Mary's faith at the Annunciation, the Gospel of John presents her as an embodiment of faith at the beginning of the public ministry of Jesus. The real disciple of Christ is a true believer. As a true believer, the Virgin Mary was a true disciple of Christ as well.

The correct response in the presence of Jesus Christ is to trust in the words of the Word of God, words which are always eternal and life-giving. Mary's telling Jesus "they have no wine" was not a way of merely informing her Son about that situation, but a request imbued with solid faith in his actions. "She trusts unconditionally, indeed even in the face of apparent rejection and rebuke, in the efficacy of the word of Jesus."[31] "A strong faith sees the invisible; believes the incredible; and receives the impossible," is an appropriate saying to summarize the entire life of Mary. In the midst of a problem at the

---

[30]Barclay, *The Gospel of John*, 87.
[31]Maloney, *The Gospel of John*, 68.

wedding scene, she thought of something that others did not think of. For this, she believed the incredible and received the impossible!

Mary's words to the servants, "Do as he says," thoroughly prove her strong faith in Jesus Christ, in spite of his somewhat indifferent response. Metropolitan Anthony Bloom writes, "And Mary instead of answering him, brings the kingdom by showing that what she has pondered in her heart from the beginning has been fruitful, and she sees him for what he is, the word of God. But then conditions are right for the kingdom. God is present because she has given herself to him completely, with total faith. He can act freely, without forcing nature, because he is in his own domain. So he works the first miracle of the Gospel."[32] God acts where there is faith, and the faith of the mother of Jesus, so clearly expressed at Cana, paved the way not only for the sign that was performed, but also for his divine manifestation.

The disciples who were present at Cana believed in Jesus after witnessing the sign (Jn 2.11). The mother of Jesus believed in him before the sign. Nathanael's meeting with Jesus also preceded the Cana sign. It seems that Nathanael believed in Jesus only after Jesus told him about his prior knowledge of Nathanael while he was under the fig tree. This was a kind of a miracle in itself for Nathanael. "Jesus answered and said to him, 'Do you believe because I told you that I saw you under the fig tree? You will see greater things than this'" (Jn 1.50). Thus, one of the "greater things" Nathanael witnessed was the sign. Yet, without any signs or asking for more proof, the mother of Jesus firmly believed that Jesus could do what was needed. She did not leave him after listening to his reply, as she had nowhere else to go other than to God, her Son. This, indeed, is perfect, true, and unshakable faith. "Nathanael is scornful until a minor miracle, hardly a miracle at all, spins him around and makes a believer in him. Mary, on the other hand, who has presumably seen no signs (this being the

---

[32]Metropolitan Anthony Bloom and George LeFebvre, *Courage to Pray* (Crestwood, NY: St Vladimir's Seminary Press, 1995), 55–56.

first), requires none, but believes beforehand that Jesus can do anything necessary and desirable."[33]

When Jesus appeared to Thomas, he said, "Have you come to believe because you have seen me? Blessed are those who have not seen and have believed" (Jn 20.29). Only the Apostle John speaks about believing without seeing. This is exactly what Mary did, and hence, she became the prototype of the saved community, as well as of all the faithful who "believe without seeing." The faith of Mary should be the model for and the basis of the faith of a true disciple. In fact, Mary's presence in the wedding scene and at the foot of the cross also clearly reveals her faith much more than that her position as the mother of Jesus. Of course, she became the mother of God only because of her great faith and her submission to the Word of God.

The sign thus demonstrates not only the strong faith of Mary, but also her divine talent to bring others to believe in the Son of God. In the Cana sign, the disciples believed in Jesus by witnessing a sign with the mother as mediator. Her faith helped the disciples to believe in him. She also enables others to obey the Son of God, which is a true quality in a believer. The obedience of the servants to Jesus Christ also paved the way for the sign. After the sign at Cana, Mary stayed for some time with Jesus and his disciples in Capernaum (Jn 2.12). She was in the community of the faithful, probably helping them sustain and grow in their faith, and served as an example of how to fulfill divine will in their lives. In short, as Francis J. Maloney observes, "At Cana, 'on the third day' a Jewish woman in a Jewish town at a Jewish celebration shows an unconditional trust and commitment to the word of Jesus. Consequently, Jesus manifests his *doxa* (2.11)."[34]

---

[33]L. William Countryman, *The Mystical Way in the Fourth Gospel* (Valley Forge, PA: Trinity Press International, 1995), 29.

[34]Francis J. Maloney, *Belief in the Word: Reading the Fourth Gospel: John 1–4* (Minneapolis, MN: Fortress Press, 2003), 91.

"Do as He Says"

"Do as he says" was the instruction that the mother of Jesus gave to the servants (the "deacons") at the wedding after informing her Son of the critical need. If we ask how to resolve a problem, even if it as serious as the one at the wedding at Cana, Mary's answer is, "Do as my Son says." It was the mother of Jesus, the one who unconditionally obeyed the will of God, who advised the servants to listen to Jesus and to obey him. And it was their obedience that paved the way for the sign. "Her faith and her obedience precede the faith and obedience of both the servants and the disciples; Mary here shares in the spiritual motherhood of the Church which, by the Word of Christ, gives birth to the sons of the Father in heaven by causing them to be born by faith and obedience."[35]

It was during the transfiguration of Jesus Christ, on the Feast of Tabernacles, that the apostles heard these words through a cloud, "This is my beloved Son with whom I am well pleased; listen to Him" (Mt 17.5; Mk 9.7; Lk 9.35). Just as at the baptism of Christ, this was the witness of the heavenly Father about his Son. Such witness by the Father is missing in the Gospel of John. Rather, it is the mother of Jesus telling others to "listen to Jesus," "my beloved Son," at the very beginning of his public ministry. "One of the principal aims of the scene at Cana seems to us to be—as John intended—to show to what extent the *Mother of Jesus* is one in her spirit with the Spirit of the *Father of Jesus*."[36] "Do as he tells you" from the mother and "Listen to him" from the Father both communicate the same message. In fact, what the heavenly Father of Jesus and his human mother are saying to everyone is, "Listen to my beloved Son." In Latin, the word for listen is *obaudire*.[37] It means both to listen and to obey. Obedience should usually follow listening. The commandment of Jesus' Father is not limited to human beings, but it is meant for the entire universe.

[35]Thurian, *Mary*, 143.
[36]Horacio Bojorge, *Image of Mary According to the Evangelists* (New York, NY: The Society of St. Paul, 1978), 48.
[37]Bloom and LeFebvre, *Courage to Pray*, 12.

One can see here a link between the words of the heavenly Father and those of the earthly mother. It is possible that the words of Jesus' mother to the servants were an echo of his Father's voice, which prompted him to advance his time and to perform the sign of transforming water into wine.

In fact, those words have a meaning that is deeply rooted in Scripture. They relate to the beginning of a new covenantal relationship, the relationship between Yahweh and the new community of the "people of God." In the new Israel, which is the community of the New Covenant, the members are those who "do as Jesus says." This is also the essence of Christian discipleship. Mary's words of instruction to the servants foreshadowed the commandment of her Son regarding prayer, "Ask whatever you will and it shall be done for you" (Jn 15.7).

We read in Genesis that the pharaoh directed the Egyptians, "Go to Joseph, and do whatever he tells you" (Gen 41.55). The country was experiencing a great famine, and the people in the land were about to face the dire consequences of that tragic situation. Still, the pharaoh was well aware that Joseph could solve that problem, thus his instructions to the Egyptians to listen to Joseph and to obey him. It was the only way for them to survive. The words of the mother of Jesus reflect almost the same words.

According to Scripture, the relationship between Israel and Yahweh was a special one, and it was based on a covenant. The laws to be kept in that Old Covenant were detailed in the book of Exodus.

> God said to Moses, "Thus shall you say to the house of Jacob; tell the Israelites: 'You have seen for yourselves how I treated the Egyptians and how I bore you up on eagle wings and brought you here to myself. Therefore, if you hearken to my voice and keep my covenant, you shall be my special possession, dearer to me than all other people, though all the earth is mine. You shall be to me a kingdom of priests, a holy nation.' That is what you must tell the Israelites." (19.3–6)

Moses summoned the elders of the people and conveyed to them the message he had received from God. The elders told Moses what the people had answered together: "Everything the Lord has said, we will do" (Ex 19.8). The old covenant was a powerful relationship between God and the Israelites, and it was based on the obedience of the Israelites to God.

In her complete obedience to the will of God, Mary, in fact, became the representative of the new covenant community when she told the servants at the wedding, "Do as he says." St Jacob of Serugh gives Mary the title "the mouth of the Church," in considering her "Yes" to the divine message at the time of the incarnation.[38] She is the "mouth of the Church" by admonishing all her children to do His will, "Do what he says." It is both an advice and a commandment that Mary gives to all her children, all the children of God. According to John 19.26, all believers are her children. Mary is able to tell everyone what she told the servants at Cana, because her own life was a paradigm and a true example of doing God's will. Obedience transforms people into the people of God, and Mary became a model of obedience because she acted according to divine instruction, preparing the way for the incarnation of Jesus Christ.

> By inviting the servants to hear the Word of Christ, and to do the orders of the Messiah whatever they may be, and to abandon themselves to Him in faith and obedience, she ceases to be the human mother of Christ who had power over her Son and becomes the spiritual mother in the community of the Messiah, and gives birth, by faith and obedience, to the servants of the Master. Her faith and her obedience precede the faith and obedience of both the servants and the disciples.[39]

In the place of the Old Covenant, we see a new one initiated here, and complete obedience is once again the foundation for such a relationship. Elisabeth Behr-Sigel writes, "Mary is self-effacement before

[38]Puthuparambil, *Mariological Thought*, 349.
[39]Thurian, *Mary*, 143.

the God who speaks the acquiescence of every part of her being to the Word of God. This is the ontological attitude that constitutes the very vocation of humanity and which also defines, par excellence, the true disciple of Christ, whether man or woman (Mk 3.33–35; Mt 12.47–50; Lk 11.27–28)."[40]

When we obey God there will be new streams of blessing, which will flow abundantly and amazingly. The apostles, who went fishing soon after the resurrection of the Lord, toiled throughout the night. But the result of their earnest efforts was an empty net and an empty basket. That was contrary to the disciples' prior experiences as fishermen. The emptiness and total despair permeated even their moods and words. But when they set the net in accordance with the direction of their master, the disciples were unable to bring the net to the shore because of the weight and the number of fish that were caught in the net. Max Thurian writes, "Mary's faith, which is total abandon to the will and word of Christ ('Whatsoever he says'), communicates itself to the servants (' . . . do it'), and precedes and prepares for the glory of the Messiah which will awaken the faith of the disciples (' . . . and the disciples believed in him'). Mary here fulfills the ministry of communicating the faith, she gives birth to the faith of others, and shares in the motherhood of the Church."[41]

"Do as he says." Bishop Fulton Sheen describes those words as a "magnificent valedictory,"[42] for these were the last words recorded in Scripture as spoken by the Virgin Mary. Sheen observes that though she spoke six other times, as seen in Scripture, she willingly disappeared after the above statement and until the crucifixion, because Jesus had revealed his identity as the Son of God in Cana. Those words of Mary and the servants following her advice resulted in the sign of transforming water into wine and in the resolution of a difficult situation. Above all, what happened at Cana was the divine manifestation, which prompted the disciples to believe in Jesus Christ. Possibly, this

---

[40] *The Ministry of Women in the Church* (Crestwood, NY: St Vladimir's Seminary Press, 1999), 60.

[41] Thurian, *Mary*, 143.

[42] Sheen, *Life of Christ*, 78.

is the only advice the mother of Jesus has to give to all her children, for whom she also continually mediates. "It has often been remarked that Jesus' mother only ever gave one instruction that has been preserved for us: the people should do whatever Jesus told them to do."[43] Mary was able to bring the Son of God into this world by obeying God's will. She has been trying to bring the Son of God to us by asking us to obey him, so that the Son will perform signs and miracles for us, as well.

St Romanus the Melodist (*c.* 490–*c.* 556) writes:

> *Mary tells Jesus they have no wine:*

> When Christ was present at the marriage feast, and the crowd
>   of guests were faring sumptuously,
> The supply of wine failed them, and their joy was turned into
>   distress;
> The bridegroom was upset; the cupbearers muttered
>   unceasingly;
> There was this one sad display of penury,
> And there was no small clamor in the room.
> Recognizing it, the all-holy Mary
> Came at once and said to her son: "They have no wine,
> But I beg you, my son, show that you can do all things,
> Thou who has in wisdom created all things."

> We beg of you, holy Virgin, from what sort of miracles did
>   you know
> How your son would be able to offer wine when He had not
>   harvested the grapes
> And had never before worked wonders, as John, inspired of
>   God wrote?[19]
> Teach us, how, when you had never gazed upon
> And never made trial of His miracles,

> How did you summon Him to this miracle?

[43]Colin G. Kruse, *John,* The Tyndale New Testament Commentaries (Grand Rapids, MI: Eerdmans Publishing, 2003), 93.

For the question now posed to us in this matter is not simple,
As to how you said to your son: "Give them wine,"
He who has in wisdom created all things.

Let us learn the word which the mother of the God of all said
    to us:
"Listen," she said, "my friends, instruct yourselves and know
    the mystery;
I have seen my son working miracles even before this
    miracle. . . .

"For I know that I did not know a husband,
And I bore a son—beyond natural law and reason,
And I know that I remained a virgin as I had been.
Do you, O man, ask for a miracle greater than this birth?
Gabriel came to me saying how this one would be born,
He who has in wisdom created all things.

"After my conception, I myself saw Elizabeth call me Mother
    of God before the actual birth; after the birth, Simeon
    praised me in song;
Anna greeted me with joy; the Magi from Persia hastened to
    the manger,
For a heavenly star proclaimed the birth in advance;
Shepherds with angels heralded joy,
And creation rejoiced with them.
What would I be able to ask for greater than these miracles?
Indeed from them I have faith that it is my son Who has in
    wisdom created all things."[44]

The Creator of time is not subject to time

But Christ seeing His mother saying, "Grant me this request,"

[44]Romanos, "Kontakion on the Marriage at Cana 7.5–9," *John 1–10* (ACCS NT
IVa), 90–91. These are from his metrical sermons. ("These sermons were sung rather than
preached during the liturgy and frequently provide theological insights and Scriptural
connections often unique to Romanus," ibid., 386.)

At once said to her: "What do you wish, woman, my hour has
    not come."
Certain men made use of this saying as a pretext for impiety;
They said that Christ, submitted to necessity,
They said that He was a slave to periods of time. . . .

"Now answer, my child," said the all-holy mother of Christ,
"Thou who dost control with measurement the periods of
    time, how, my son and Lord, dost Thou await a time?
Thou who hast regulated the division of the seasons, how dost
    thou await a season?
Thou who art the creator of the visible and the invisible,
Thou who, as master, dost day and night regulate
The ceaseless revolutions, as Thou dost will them—
Thou who hast defined the years in beautifully ordered
    cycles—
How, then, dost Thou await a time for the miracle which I ask
    of Thee
Who hast in wisdom created all things?"

"I knew before you told me, revered Virgin, that the wine was
    just beginning to give out for them,"
The Ineffable and Merciful straightway answered His holy
    mother.
"I know all the concerns of your heart which you set in motion
    in this matter;
For within yourself you reasoned as follows:
'Necessity now summons my son to a miracle,
And He puts it off under the pretext of "the time." '
Holy mother, learn now the meaning of the delay,
For when you know it, I shall grant you this favor,
I, who in wisdom have created all things."[45]

---

[45]Romanos, "Kontakion on the Marriage at Cana 7.13–16," ibid., 92–93.

6

The Sign's Relation to the Resurrection and the Creation Story

The Apostle John begins his narrative of the marriage in Cana as a third-day event. It is not very clear what the author meant by referring to the third day, and there are various interpretations of this. So this chapter will cover the meaning and usage of the phrase "third day" in the Gospel of John.

For John, every word is extremely important. Within each word are profound, prodigious, and hidden meanings. The mention of the sign as a third-day event is an excellent example of his usage of numbers, words, and phrases with mysterious meanings and scriptural and prophetic insights. About numbers in this Gospel, Wes Howard-Brook writes, "Many numbers are given to describe quantities; each is fraught with symbolic value, as would be expected for a people who found number itself to be a revelatory phenomenon. This first number in the Gospel carries a rich background both in Hebrew scripture and Christian tradition."[1]

Why did the evangelist mention that the marriage in Cana happened on the third day? Was it a casual move on the part of the apostle, or was it calculated to reveal the greatest sign of the Church and an epoch-making event in the life of the incarnate Lord—the resurrection, with the initial sign itself and at the very beginning of his public

[1]Howard-Brook, *Becoming Children of God*, 77.

ministry? Was the eagle-eyed apostle linking the wedding scene and the sign to the great mystery of Jesus Christ's glorious resurrection on the third day?

There is a strong possibility for this. According to the author of the Gospel, the purpose of writing the Gospel was, "that you may come to believe that Jesus is the Messiah, the Son of God," and that through this belief "you may have life in his name" (20.31). The resurrection is the proof that Jesus Christ is the Messiah, the incarnate Son of God. Hence for John, Jesus' first public act was pointing to the resurrection of the Lord on the third day. Apart from the resurrection, the third day was important for the Israelites, as it was on that day the covenantal relationship between Yahweh and Israel was initiated at Mount Sinai.

The sign also has many similarities with the creation story narrated in the book of Genesis. In the very beginning of creation, the Holy Spirit was brooding over water (Gen 1.2) while in the initial sign at Cana the Son of God worked on water to change it into wine. It took seven days for the Creator to complete the creation, and the Cana sign is also presented at the end of a seven-day cycle. In Genesis, it was an initial creation; in John's Gospel, it was re-creation or a renewal of the fallen world and estranged humanity. Jesus Christ initiated his redemptive work of divinization by working on water, the symbol of creation. The Son of God thus started his transforming process from the original creation, water, and culminated it with the crown of creation, human beings.

"On the Third Day there was a Marriage in Cana in Galilee"

In its normal sense, "third day" might mean that Jesus and his few disciples took three days to travel from where John the Baptist was baptizing to the village of Cana in Galilee, the location where the wedding was held. It can also mean as we say "the day after tomorrow."[2]

---

[2] *The Life of the Virgin Mary, the Theotokos* (Buena Vista, CO: The Holy Apostles Convent, 2010), 326.

For example, we read in Luke 13.32, "I do cures today and tomorrow, and the third day I shall be perfected." The "third day" may also plausibly mean the third day from the calling of Philip (1.43) or the third day after Jesus' meeting with Nathanael, the disciple who was from Cana. Nathanael was promised, "You will see greater things than this" (1.50, 51), and an amazing act did take place in Cana. Or was the apostle counting the days to cover the distance for traveling from the place near the River Jordan where John the Baptist was baptizing to the place of the marriage in Cana? This is unlikely. The mention of the "third day" likely refers to the end of the week, which was then concluded with the marriage in Cana. It is to be assumed that the "third day" reference is much more than a chronological reference.

According to Theodore of Mopsuestia (*c.* 350–428) the third was calculated as the third day after the baptism of Jesus.[3] The baptismal scene begins with 1.29–34, which is followed by the first day mentioned in 1.35, and the second in 1.43. Origen (*c.* 200–254), who had the same view, writes, "The third day was now come from Jesus' baptism, and there was a marriage taking place in Cana of Galilee."[4] Caesarius of Arles (*c.* 470–543) linked the third day with the mystery of the Holy Trinity. He writes:

> The third day is the mystery of the Trinity, while the miracles of the nuptials are the mysteries of heavenly joys. It was both a nuptial day and a feast for this reason, because the church after the redemption was joined to the spouse who was coming to the spouse, I say, whom all the ages from the beginning of the world had promised. It is he who came down to earth to invite his beloved to marriage with his highness, giving her for a present the token of his blood and intending to give later the dowry of his kingdom.[5]

[3]Theodore of Mopsuestia, "Commentary on John 1.2.1," in *John 1–10* (ACCS NT IVa), 89. (From Corpus Scriptorum Christianorum Orientalium, vol. 43 [Louvain: Peeters, 1903], 55.)

[4]Ibid. (AEG 2:7; GCS 10(4): 505.)

[5]Ibid. (Quoted from *The Fathers of the Church: A New Translation*, vol. 47 [Washington, DC: Catholic University of America Press, 1947], 402–403.)

Though the "third day" can be interpreted in various ways, in the Johannine style of presentation and in its hidden purpose in writing the Gospel, linking it with the resurrection event is more meaningful. Jesus' reference to the "hour" in the Cana episode also links with his death and resurrection.

In John's Gospel, references to the "third day" are seemingly significant and very frequent. When the early believers "came together," they proclaimed the truth of the great third-day happening of the resurrection of the Lord. Their gathering to celebrate the Lord's Supper was also to celebrate the resurrection, "trampling down death by death" and opening up immortal life. The first sign in the Fourth Gospel was a third-day event. In the same chapter, Jesus spoke about the temple to be destroyed and that he would raise it again in three days (2.19). The importance of three days comes up in that verse, as well. The next sign happened in the same place, the healing of the nobleman's son, and occurred after "two days," also relating to the giving back of life, a symbol of his resurrection (4.46–54). Since the second miracle that too took place at Cana is narrated as having occurred "after two days" (4.43), this means that the healing happened on the third day. There are scholars who suggest, "They are purely symbolic references to the resurrection."[6] The apostle was probably thinking of the prophecy of Hosea, "He will revive us after two days; and on the third day he will raise us up, to live in his presence" (Hos 6.2).

Even in the context of the raising of Lazarus (11.1–44), the sign revealing the power of Jesus over death and him as the one who provides life, John indicated the importance of days and especially of the "third day." After hearing about his friend's death, Jesus stayed in the place where he was for two more days and left for Bethany only on the "third day."

Thus the setting of the marriage of Cana at the end of the week, the new Creation and the mention of the three days which bring to mind for John the resurrection of Christ, set forth this first

[6]Brown, *The Gospel According to John*, 97.

sign of the water changed into wine, and the whole context of the miracle, as a revelation first and foremost of the glory of Christ, a manifestation which will find its fulfillment and its fullness in the last sign to which all the others point: the resurrection on Easter morning.[7]

The faith of the apostles and, above all, the foundation of the very church were built on the solid fact of the greatest "third day" event, the glorious and triumphant resurrection of our Lord. Jesus Christ declared, "I am the resurrection and the life" (Jn 11:25). In the very first part of the narration, during the inauguration of Jesus' public ministry, the reality of the impending resurrection was revealed. John the apostle was fully aware that the resurrection event was concealed in the Cana sign. In fact, the author's purpose of introducing the Cana sign and the narrative of the destruction of the Jerusalem temple in the beginning was possibly to illustrate the meaning of the sacrificial death and the glorious resurrection of Jesus Christ.

John wrote the Gospel mainly to instruct and to illuminate the faithful about the life, the death, the resurrection, and the ascension of Christ, so that their faith in the risen Lord would be strengthened. His Gospel, along with the other Gospels and Epistles, was written to edify the eucharistic community while they gathered for the fellowship of "the breaking of the bread." Since for various reasons the apostles who witnessed the resurrection were not able to be present at all the services of the fledgling and growing Church, the writings of the apostles who witnessed the life, the death, and especially the resurrection of our Lord were written to be read in their place. It was not only to remind worshippers of the redemptive work of Christ, but also as a confession of faith before Communion. We do the same now by reciting the Nicene Creed during the Holy Liturgy and other liturgical services as a confession of faith. To the early Christians for whom the Gospel was written, "the third day" reminded them of the

---

[7] Thurian, *Mary*, 123.

resurrection on which their faith for the present and their hope for the future rested.

The sign also encouraged members of the early Christian community to reflect upon the sufferings and the crucifixion of Christ that preceded his resurrection. Such reflections always lead the faithful to repentance and transformation. There was no time during the incarnation when the mystery of suffering, death, and resurrection was ignored, but rather they were reflected on and hinted at in every action, piece of advice, and admonition of Jesus Christ. The Christ of history, with the cross and the resurrection, is the Christ who is present with us today, and the one who is to come in the future, the Christ of the future *eschaton*.[8] The resurrected Christ of history is to be experienced, not only at Holy Communion or during prayer and meditation, but also at every moment in the lives of true followers of Christ, including in their day-to-day affairs.

According to Jewish customs and practices, especially during the last few centuries before Christ, "a virgin marries on the fourth day of the week, and a widow on the fifth."[9] The usual day for wedding was Wednesday (for a widow it was Thursday).[10] Thus, the "third day" might be a reference to Wednesday, the third day of the week, as the Mishnah specifies regarding the wedding of a virgin.[11] The celebrations associated with marriage usually lasted for seven days, if the bride was a virgin (Jdt 14.12–17; 11.19), and for a widow three days. It could also be prolonged to two weeks (Tob 8.20; 10.17). If the wedding in Cana was on the third day, that is, Wednesday, the other two days mentioned in 1.35 and 1.43 are Monday and Tuesday. In the ancient solar calendar, which the Qumran community used in those days, the week also began on a Wednesday. If so, then the wedding took place at the end of the week and the beginning of the next week (the eighth day).

[8] A Greek word referring to the last days.
[9] Lightfoot, *Commentary on the New Testament: Matthew–1 Corinthians,* 250.
[10] Morris, *Reflections on the Gospel of John,* 178.
[11] Waetjen, *The Gospel of the Beloved Disciple,* 113.

The wedding celebration usually started in the evening and continued for the whole day and the following week. The day starts in the evening for Jews (and in many Eastern Churches, cultures, and religions), not at midnight as it is practiced in the West. The event mentioned in the same chapter of the Gospel after the wedding is the presence of Christ in the temple of Jerusalem. It was the time of the great Jewish feast of Passover. When Jesus entered the temple, he observed what was transpiring in the temple and its sacred premises. He was infuriated and filled with righteous indignation, and he made a whip out of cords and chastised the merchants and the moneychangers who converged in the house of the Lord and converted the holy abode into a commercial market place. Jesus chased them out of the temple vicinity. Then he declared that the temple, which King Solomon built with precision, perfection, and a prolonged period of forty-six years of perseverance and effort, would be destroyed, leaving no stone unturned. Still, that was not the end, because the temple would be built again with no human effort and within a very limited time, on the "third day." Jesus made it crystal clear that he was referring to his own body, which was about to be broken on the cross. Through this statement, he was also declaring that after his death, he would be resurrected, just as the temple on "the third day." It was indeed a reference to his glorious resurrection on the third day.

The greatest third-day event, the resurrection of Christ, occurred after Jesus shared his body and blood with his disciples, which was followed by the breaking of his body and the shedding of his blood on the cross. It was at the time of Passover that Jesus, taking bread in his holy hands and thanking the heavenly Father, said, "This is my body," and, taking the wine, "This is my blood," and he advised the disciples to partake of them. If in the initial third-day event, Jesus transformed ordinary water into extraordinary wine, he has been transforming ordinary wine into his blood, through the Holy Spirit, whenever the faithful gather together in his name. He gives his body and blood as an offering to his heavenly Father. At the same time, the body and the blood are distributed to his children as a gift, a gift of abundant and eternal life, and a gift that can never be matched. The Son of God has been sharing his body and blood with his children and is going to continue the same until his glorious second coming.

There are some biblical scholars who are of the opinion that a few words from the first verse in the sign, "On the third day there was a marriage at Cana in Galilee, and the mother of Jesus was there" (2.1), were part of a creed in the early Church. John Michael Perry writes:

> This statement's first four words are identical to four consecutive words in the early Christian creed quoted by Paul in 1 Corinthians 15.4. There Jesus is confessed as raised by God "on the third day (*te hemera te trite*) according to the Scriptures." These first four words were included in the creed of the Greek-speaking church as a midrashic[12] proof text ("according to the scriptures") taken from the Septuagint version of Hosea 6:2. "After two days he will revive us; on the third day (*en te hemera te trite*) he will raise us up that we may live before him." Hosea 6:2 (LXX)[13]

Mentioning the "third day" in the apostolic period was thus a substitute not only for recollection and affirmation of faith, but also for celebrating the resurrection of the Lord.

In the Gospel of John, allusions to and images of Jesus' birth, death, and resurrection are presented in the very beginning. None of these events could be separated or isolated. The present is in the past, as well as in the future. The Son of God condescended to be born as a child, and he was born in a cave. That cave is usually presented as a tomb in the iconography of the Church. He was wrapped in a winding cloth, foreshadowing the burial shroud, and not in the regular swaddling

---

[12]F. L. Cross, ed., *The Oxford Dictionary of the Christian Church* (London: Oxford University Press, 1958), defines the word "midrashic" thus: "A Jewish method of scriptural exegesis directed to the discovery in the sacred text of a meaning deeper than the literal one." Such a study gives great and careful attention to the meaning of words and phrases. The study was based on the assumption that there are countless meanings behind the words and events that one finds in the Scripture.

[13]John Michael Perry, *Exploring the Evolution of the Lord's Supper in the New Testament* (Kansas City, MO: Sheed & Ward, 1994), 102.

cloth of a newborn. The baby Jesus was laid on an altar of sacrifice rather than in a cradle, symbolizing his forthcoming crucifixion. The passion was very visible even at the joyous event of his birth.

This condescension of Christ continued throughout his passion and death on the cross, but its climax was in his resurrection from the tomb and his ascension into heaven. Jesus came into this world to die, but not to die forever. The concluding chapter of Christ's biography does not end with death, as it does for everyone else. He was resurrected and is alive. Everyone else in this world is born into this world to live, and almost all will do everything at their disposal to extend their earthly existence. Jesus is the only one who came to die. Through his death and resurrection, we live with abundant life now and will continue to live even after our death, because Jesus Christ completely removed from us the burden of death, and we are partakers of his immortal body and blood.

For us, also, the present is linked to the past, as well as to the future. The scope of our salvation or deification is connected to the past, as in the historical event of Christ's resurrection almost two millennia ago. At the same time, it is a present experience as we partake in these events during Holy Liturgy each week, and it is a future hope as to the climax of our salvation in the second coming. Even at our baptism, the birth, the death, and the resurrection of Christ are recollected, "re-membered," and experienced, because the person who is baptized is participating in the same events which Jesus Christ was subjected to during while incarnate. In the words of St Cyril of Jerusalem, the baptismal font represents both the cave and the tomb where we die to sin.[14] It is not only a tomb, but also a womb where we have been born anew as part of the body of Christ in the Holy Spirit, and we are resurrected with Christ for eternal and abundant life. Hence Christians are the people of the resurrection.

---

[14]St Cyril of Jerusalem, "Mystagogical Catecheses 2:4," in Johannes Quasten, Patrology, vol. 3, *The Golden Age of Greek Patristic Literature from the Council of Nicaea to the Council of Chalcedon* (Utrecht, Antwerp: Spectrum Publishers, 1966), 373.

Through holy communion, the faithful participate in the glorified body and blood of Jesus Christ, who was born in the "cave/tomb," and who was resurrected from the tomb on the "third day." The resurrection on the "third day" brings to mind the crucified, resurrected, and glorified Christ, which neither the Church, nor the faithful can ever take lightly.

> This *three day journey* to the marriage feast is designed to remind the disciples of the risen Jesus, who have been baptized "with the Holy Spirit" (1:33; cp. 3:5), that we are empowered to "follow" Jesus (12:26) the "Way" (14:6) through his death and *burial* into his *resurrection* (8:12; 11:25–26). It is by taking this mysterious journey with faith that we will arrive at the marriage feast of Eternal Life.[15]

By narrating the Cana sign that happened at the very beginning of Jesus' ministry and as a third-day event, the author of the Gospel was reminding his readers in advance about the greatest third-day event, the glorious resurrection of our Lord. What happened at the wedding on the third day was only a sign. What is going to happen in the near future on the third day is that the sign will be a reality through Jesus' miraculous resurrection.

The "Third Day" and the Formation of the New People of God

The importance of the "third day" was well known to the Jewish community, and this importance started very early—in fact, at the very beginning of Jewish history. It was on the "third day" that the covenantal relationship between Yahweh and the Israelites was established on Mount Sinai (Ex 19). In the third month of their departure from Egypt, the Israelites reached Mount Sinai. While the people were in the valley there, Moses went up to the Mount to meet the Lord. Then the Lord called to him and said:

[15]Perry, *Exploring the Evolution*, 104.

Thus shall you say to the house of Jacob; tell the Israelites: "You have seen for yourself how I treated the Egyptians and how I bore you up on eagle wings and brought you here to myself. Therefore, if you hearken to my voice and keep my covenant, you shall be my special possession, dearer to me than all other people, though all the earth is mine. You shall be to me a kingdom of priests, a holy nation." This is what you must tell the Israelites. (Ex 19.3–6)

Moses immediately communicated the Lord's message to the people who converged in the valley. They responded with one voice saying, "Everything the Lord has said, we will do" (19.8). For the Israelites, the foundation of the covenantal relationship was obedience. Moses went up to the mountain once again to meet the Lord and delivered the united response of the people.

The Lord directed Moses by giving specific instructions in order to prepare the people thoroughly for the *theophany,* and only then as the Lord had informed would he appear on the "third day." "On the morning of the third day, there were thunders and lightning, and a thick cloud upon the mountain, and a very loud trumpet blast, so that all the people who were in the camp trembled. Then Moses brought the people out of the camp to meet God. And the Lord came down upon Mount Sinai" (Ex 19.16–20). The third-day theophany of the Lord on Mount Sinai was very familiar to the people for whom the Gospel was written.

When we come to the New Testament period, on the "first day," at the baptism of our Lord there was a divine theophany, when "the Holy Spirit descended from the heaven like a dove and abode on Him" (1.32). On the "next day," Jesus chose some of his disciples, including John the evangelist. "On the 'third day,' having gathered a nucleus of human souls, an embryonic church, Jesus and his mother and the disciples attend a marriage."[16] According to the Gospel narrative, at the baptism, John the Baptist announced about Jesus, "Behold the Lamb of God" (1.29), the one to be offered on the cross.

[16]Manley, *The Bible and the Holy Fathers,* 36.

The book of Revelation presents the Church as the "Bride of the Lamb" (Rev 19.7).

The Cana sign took place on the "third day," as it was the beginning of the formation of the new community, the Church. In Cana, the covenantal relationship between the Messiah and the new people of God was initiated, not through blood as in the olden times, but through the wine that was changed from water. In the Old Testament, the relationship between Yahweh and Israel was presented as a marital relationship. In Cana, the relationship also began in the context of marriage. Thus the "third day" points to the New Israel, the Bride of Christ, or the Church.

The Creation Story and the Cana Sign

It is interesting to note the evolution of events preceding the wedding scene. The third-day event at Cana took place at the end of seven days, for before the "third day" in 2.1 there were already four days mentioned in the Gospel of John (1.19, 29, 35, 43). In a way, the total of seven days is similar and is a symbol of the seven days that covered the first week of creation, as narrated in the book of Genesis. It was on the third day of creation that God separated land from water and thus prepared the land for vegetation (Gen 1.6–9). Thus, at the very outset of the public ministry of Jesus Christ, the beginning of a new creation is revealed in a dramatic and dynamic way.

The Apostle John starts the first day with the words, "In the beginning" (1.19), in exactly the same manner in which the book of Genesis started, "In the beginning, when God created the heavens and earth . . ." (Gen 1.1). The first week in the Gospel began with the testimony of John the Baptist about his mission and vision. The following day, the "next day" or day two, the Baptist acknowledged and accepted Jesus, "as the Lamb of God who takes away the sin of the world" (1.29). The "following day" Andrew and Peter, two of the disciples of John the Baptist, left their master and followed a new master, the

Messiah, as Andrew declared to his older brother, Simon Peter, about Jesus, saying, "We have found the Messiah" (1.41).

And they stayed with Jesus two days, bringing the total days to four. The "following day" (1.43) or day five, Jesus called Philip to follow him. Philip, in turn, brought Nathanael, who was from Cana in Nazareth, to Jesus, and he confessed that Jesus was the Son of God, the King of Israel (1.49). There is no mention of the sixth day, but the Cana wedding happened on the "third day," by the inclusive method of calculating days at that time. When we count all these days mentioned before the sign, the Cana event took place at the completion of seven days. Max Thurian summarizes the concept of the "week" thus:

> The priestly author of the first account of the Creation (Gen 1:1–2:3) had constructed his plan on six symbolic days to show the divine origin of the seventh day as a day of rest for God (Gen 2:1–3). St. John in the same way sets the act of the new creation in a week, of which the seventh day coincides with the marriage at Cana when Jesus fulfills a first sign of his messianic status: in a symbolic week, Christ lays the foundation of a new creation of the messianic community, the Church, by calling one by one those who will be the pillars of this new building, the Apostles; and then, the seventh day, the sign of final rest, he shares in the joy of the marriage at Cana which symbolizes and pre-figures the eschatological marriage of God with his people, the messianic banquet of the Kingdom, and he reveals his glory in the first sign of his divine Sonship.[17]

The author of the Gospel is linking the first sign with the beginning of creation out of nothingness. The initial sign through which Jesus inaugurated his public ministry in Cana was on water. Water was the first creation, which also brings to our mind the initial creation story. In another uniquely Johannine way, the apostle connects the creation story to the Gospel through the signs performed by Jesus

[17]Thurian, *Mary*, 120–121.

Christ. There are seven signs in the Gospel, and each sign corresponds to each day of the first creation.

The writers of the Synoptic Gospels, Mathew, Mark, and Luke, also referred to the creation story in their own particular ways. Matthew pointed this out in the beginning of his Gospel with "the book of the genealogy of Jesus Christ." In his presentation of the genealogy, Luke went back to Adam, the first created human being (Lk 3.23–38). By mentioning Jesus with the wild beasts, Mark presumably was comparing Jesus to the first Adam in the garden of Eden (Mk 1.13).

Unlike the Synoptic Gospels, John the evangelist begins his prologue with the words, "In the beginning." As already mentioned, this brings to mind a picture of the first creation of the cosmos. At the same time, John was talking about the eternal origin of the Logos, the one with no beginning or end, who "took flesh and dwelt among us," but in an entirely different way from how it was written in Genesis. "In the beginning was the Word, and the Word was with God, and the Word was God" (1.1). Thus, "in the beginning" in John's Gospel is not bound by time, space, or matter, unlike the creation story in Genesis, which had a beginning. The Genesis story of the first creation and the Gospel mention of "in the beginning" are not related in essence: one is related to mundane existence that has a beginning and an end, while the other is about eternity, without a beginning or an end. Thus in the Gospel, the story of Jesus begins "in the very bosom of God."[18] In the Genesis story, after six days of creation, we read about the "marriage" or God giving Adam a life-long companion. In John's Gospel, the presentation of the wedding in Cana on the seventh day corresponds to the "wedding" in Genesis. In the story about the fall of the first parents, Eve the *woman* had a very important role. The significant role played by the *woman* was well presented in the wedding scene at Cana. The mother of Jesus Christ was the *woman* in the new creation, who was foretold during the fall. Thus, Eve was presented as the *woman* in the Genesis story of creation (3.15). In the

---

[18]Timothy Luke Johnson, *The Writings of the New Testament,* rev. ed. (Fortress Press, MN: 1999), 534.

re-creation process, for the first time at the wedding scene and again while Jesus was on the cross, Mary the mother of Jesus was addressed by him as "woman" (Jn 2.4; 19.26).

The world in the beginning was shapeless and was in chaos and confusion. Through the Creator, the universe of chaos became the cosmos of order. In the Gospel, shapeless and tasteless water was transformed in the presence of and through the work of Jesus Christ to tasteful and powerful wine. The new week of re-creation in the Gospel will refresh us with the reminiscence of the initial week of creation that happened in the very beginning, as narrated in Genesis.

The purpose of the incarnation was to make anew God's creation and especially the crown of creation, the children of God. Water was transformed into wine. The children of God were recreated through the Son of God, so that they can reflect on the marred image, can regain the lost likeness of their Creator, and can re-enter paradise, from which they were shut out through the fall of their first parents. Thus, the sign that Jesus performed in the wedding at Cana points to the process of the new creation that the Son of God initiated and perfected. "By his choice of opening words and by arranging his first narratives in a way that recalls the creation story, he is making the point that he is writing about a new creation. This is not a creation in the physical world, but one in the hearts of men. Jesus does not take sinners as they are and leave them like that. He transforms them. He brings a new power into life and makes them new."[19]

Marriage is a miracle where the bride and the bridegroom are united together as one, and thereby a "new creation" is formed. One of the outcomes of marriage is procreation. Generations pass from one to another through procreation. "The miracle of marriage makes a 'new creation,' not a creation *ex nihilo*, but one that results from the existing conditions of the couple. One offers to God what one has and what one is, while God transforms the existing water into wine."[20] The

---

[19]Morris, *Reflections on the Gospel of John,* 77.

[20]John Chryssavgis, *Love, Sexuality, and the Sacrament of Marriage* (Brookline, MA: Holy Cross Orthodox Press, 1998), 27.

"new creation" formed through marriage participates in the God-given role of procreation.

Thus, the wedding in Cana, a third-day event, was a prelude to the resurrection of the Son of God on the third day. The "third day," the day of the resurrection, became more relevant than the seventh day of creation. John the apostle was a witness to the sign performed by his master at the wedding, where his glory and divinity were revealed. The apostle also witnessed the glory and the divinity of the Lord at the transfiguration. Evidently he also witnessed the empty tomb on the "third day" and also saw with his own eyes the resurrected Lord. The sign happened at the end of a seven-day weekly cycle, linking it to the initial seven-day-creation story narrated in the book of Genesis. Thus the Cana sign marks the end of the first week of the ministry, which was the seventh day and also the beginning of the next week, the eighth day.

7
The Liturgical and Sacramental Significance of the Sign

The sign of changing water into wine during the wedding feast at Cana, a transforming event, sheds important light on the liturgical actions of the Church and alludes directly or indirectly to many of the sacramental mysteries. The materials that were used, like water and wine; symbols, such as jars used for purification; the context in which the sign took place; the transforming effect of the miracle; the words and the roles played by the servants; and, the manifestation of the divine glory, and so on, illuminate different shades of meaning in relation to the holy mysteries of the Church. The goal and the purpose of the liturgy and the sacraments are transformation to divinization. By participating in the holy mysteries, one is raised from the earthly environment and experience to the heavenly realm and thus enters into the kingdom of God, where divine manifestation is being revealed.

Water was initially stored at the wedding feast for ceremonial purification, a religious custom that was in practice, especially among the Jews. The author's very mention of water pots for purification reveals the liturgical and sacramental importance of the sign. There was no more water left in the pots for purification during the feast. The empty water pots not only point to the abrupt end of existing purification laws and systems, but also reveal that Jesus Christ, the Son of God, is the one who fulfills and completes the purification process. It is not by mere water, but through Jesus Christ, who transformed the water-filled jars to ones filled with wine, that real purification is achieved. The polluted water, part of the fallen world, was used for purification until the coming of Christ. Since his coming, Jesus Christ, from whom "flows the spring of water welling up to eternal life," cleanses his people through the shedding of his blood and sharing his life-giving blood and body.

In the chronicle of events detailed in the Gospel of John, the event that followed the wedding in Cana was the presence of Jesus Christ in the temple at Jerusalem. Jesus Christ declared there that the holy temple would be destroyed in three days. Then he made the assertion that he was speaking about his own body, that is, the temple (2.13–25). After feeding the multitude by multiplying a handful of bread and a couple of fish, Jesus taught them about the eternal bread that he would provide by saying, "I am the bread of life" (6.35).

God created Eve from Adam as a companion for him, a spouse. Hence the mystery of marriage was instituted in the garden of Eden immediately after Eve was created. As Jesus says, "They are no longer two, but one flesh. Therefore, what God has joined together, let no one separate" (Mt 19.5–6; cf. Gen 2.24). At the time of his incarnation, the Son of God elevated the union between husband and wife to the superior level of a mystery through his presence and the sign he performed at the wedding scene by transforming ordinary water into a superb wine. Exactly the same thing happens to a man and a woman in marriage. Though they are ordinary people, they are transformed to partake of a higher divine union and relationship that is unique, strong, and lasting.

Thus, the first sign at the Cana wedding was the reversal of what happened in the garden of Eden. Eve misled Adam, and by ignoring the divine instruction, Adam blindly obeyed her, which resulted in the initial fall of mankind. However, in Cana, Jesus listened to his mother, who always unhesitatingly obeyed the will of God, and he acted according to her request. This resulted in God's miraculous work in resolving the predicament of the lack of wine and brought joy to the wedding feast. Adam and Eve had everything to drink and eat in the garden of Eden, but the feast in Cana lacked sufficient wine. Through his divine intervention and manifestation, Jesus not only miraculously resolved this problem, but in excess of what was needed. In his beautiful exposition of the sign, Matthew the Poor writes:

> Whereas attending a wedding was considered a religious service and duty to be observed by every Israelite or every zealous person, for Jesus it was a re-evaluation of the significance of the wedding in the New Covenant; for through the presence of Christ, God attended the wedding. Thus, ever since the wedding in Cana of Galilee and up to the present day, Christian marriage has borne the stamp of the "Divine Mystery"—mystery wherein the sacramental concept of matrimony is linked to a sense of "Christ's presence" which upholds it by making the nuptial bond involve three parties, not two: "What therefore God has joined together, let not man put asunder." (Mt 19:6)[1]

Eve was created for Adam, for his fellowship and salvation, and to avoid loneliness. Through Eve's disobedience, their relationship was broken, replacing love with anger, animosity, and finger-pointing. Through the divine presence of Jesus Christ, marriage again became what it was meant to be: a relationship of love, fellowship, and salvation for both spouses.

Jesus went into the River Jordan to be baptized by John the Baptist. Since he was sinless, cleansing was not the purpose of his baptism, but it was a way of identifying with the fallen human race through baptism. Jesus was also baptized in water and the Holy Spirit, setting an example for everyone. He submitted himself for that sacred ritual not for his sin, but for the sins of the world. Through his entering into water for baptism, he blessed not only the water, but also the entire creation. Baptism is the sacrament of cleansing, and water is essential for baptism. The initial sacrament of the Church includes the blessing of water, which is an important part of the service. When water is blessed during the baptismal liturgy, not only the water is

---

[1]Matthew the Poor, "Wedding in Cana," 12.

transformed, but so is the whole of creation, of which water is a primary element. The same is true for the service of the feast of Christ's baptism on January 6. During the baptismal service the person to be baptized is immersed in the blessed and consecrated water. If Jesus blessed water at the time of his baptism and through it the whole creation, then at Cana he blessed the water and transformed it into wine, a much more powerful substance.

When Jesus died on the cross, "from his side blood and water flowed out" (Jn 19:34). Man cannot live without water. Blood is also extremely essential for survival. Thus these two things, which are essential for the survival of human beings, flowed out from the crucified Jesus Christ. The blood and the water that spouted from Jesus' side were not for the purpose of creating, but for re-creating an already created, but fallen world. According to Jewish thinking, water is always used for cleansing, and blood is especially associated with life.[2] Hence, what Jesus accomplished on the cross was the renewal and the redemption of mankind and the world.

Water was changed into wine, the symbol for the blood of the "Lamb of God who takes away the sins of the world" (1.36) and for the new *Pascha*, the Holy Liturgy. Wine was transformed at the Last Supper, and it became Jesus Christ's blood. Since then, wine is being transformed into the blood of Christ whenever "the people of God," "the body of Christ," "come together" for Holy Communion. "Through its very matter—water and wine—it serves as a prelude to Calvary and already announces the birth of the Church on the Cross, 'out of the pierced side came blood and water.' The symbolism brings together and links the place of the miracle, the wedding, to the Eucharistic reality of the Church."[3]

The Cana sign leads to the sacraments of baptism, marriage, and the Eucharist. It also points indirectly to the sacrament of penance (purification) and the sacerdotal ministry. "It is likely that theological reflection and experience made it possible for the writer to explore

[2]Cf. Gen 9.4; Lev 17.11, 14; Deut 12.13.
[3]Evdokimov, *The Sacrament*, 122.

and explain the deeper significance of the events of the life of our Lord."[4] The sign at the marriage feast lingers in the minds of readers through the words and the symbols used in the narrative of creation, crucifixion, and resurrection.

The Sacrament of Marriage

The Cana sign happened in the context of a marriage. Christ's presence at a wedding, as well as his role in miraculously making the wine needed for the banquet, is very important when one thinks of gnostic and other teachings that devalued many basic things in life, including marriage and marital life, and that were very prevalent in those times. The very presence of Jesus at a wedding in itself shows the importance of marriage and negates heretical teachings.[5] It was the almighty God who united Adam and Eve in paradise. In this initial creation, man and woman were united by the Creator. In Cana, the sign was worked in the context of a marriage, where the bride and the bridegroom were united forever and divine glory was manifested. This is repeated in every sacrament of marriage, and divine glory is revealed.

Throughout almost the whole world, it is not merely wedding vows that are exchanged between a man and a woman, but two different families are also joined and anchored in a formally and publicly recognized legal commitment. This is an enduring and exclusive relationship where the intimacy between the couple is unique and unparalleled. Marriage is a family and a community function in almost every culture and religion.

What then is the difference between a Christian and a non-Christian marriage? Why is a Christian marriage a sacrament and why did St Paul regard it a mystery? John Meyendorff explains it eloquently: "The very notion of marriage as a sacrament presupposes that man is not only a being with physiological, psychological, and social functions, but that he is a citizen of God's Kingdom, i.e., that his entire

---

[4]Archbishop Dmitri (Royster), *Orthodox Christian Teaching: An Introduction to the Orthodox Faith* (Syosset, NY: DRE-OCA, 1983), 77.

[5]At that period Gnostics and some other sects condemned marriage.

life—and especially its most decisive moments—involves *eternal values* and God Himself."[6] According to the Church, the union of two people, a man and a woman, through marriage, is a divine act, and such a union reflects life in the kingdom of God. "It is, in essence, the baptizing and confirming of human love in God by Christ in the Holy Spirit. It is the deification of human love in the divine perfection and unity."[7] Hence the depth and the strength of the divine marital union are beyond human explanations.

The Cana sign, where the public ministry of Jesus was inaugurated at a wedding, was presented, as already noted, in the context of the new creation that took place as a seventh-day event and a concluding one in a cycle of events. Through marriage, the bride and the bridegroom "leave their parents" (Gen 2.24) and are united as husband and wife to become one, a new creation. Procreation is one of the purposes of marriage. New generations come through the marital union, and thus the life of human beings continues in the world.

The presence of Jesus Christ at the wedding in Cana is very significant. Maximus of Turin writes, "The Son of God went to the wedding so that marriage, which had been instituted by his own authority, might be sanctified by his own authority, might be sanctified by his blessed presence."[8] Through his attendance and by his presence, not only water was changed, but also everything that was part of the fallen world. By his presence at the wedding, Jesus transformed marriage to an event of the kingdom of God, a union that happened in this world became otherworldly, divine. Cyril of Alexandria observes the presence of Christ there differently:

> As one who was renewing and refreshing the very nature of humanity for the better, Christ not only imparts his blessing to those already called into being but also prepares grace in advance

[6]Meyendorff, *Marriage*, 10.

[7]Archbishop Dmitri, *Orthodox Christian Teaching*, 42.

[8]Maximus of Turin, "Sermon 23," *John 1–10* (ACCS NT IVa), 90. (Quoted from *Journey with the Fathers: Commentaries on the Sunday Gospels*, ed. Edith Barnecut [New York, NY: New City Press, 1994], 274.)

for those soon to be born and sanctifies their entrance into existence. And yet, there is still another reason why Jesus was at this wedding. God had said to the women . . . "in pain you shall bring forth children." How else could we escape a condemned marriage unless this curse was annulled? This curse too the Savior removes because of his love for mankind. For he who is the delight and joy of all honored marriage with his presence so that he might expel the ancient sadness of childbearing.[9]

Of course, the pain of childbearing was not eliminated after Jesus' presence at the wedding. Everything, including the marital relationship, was tainted and lost its divine foundation through the initial fall of Adam and Eve. Yet, through his presence and participation at the wedding, Christ transformed marriage and elevated it to new heights, to an event of the coming kingdom of God.

It is interesting to note that Holy Scripture opens with a wedding, the union of Adam and Eve. Eve, formed from Adam, was created as his '*ezer*[10] ("companion," "helpmate"; Gen 2.20). Though two persons, by divine command they became one "body" as husband and wife. According to Scripture, this was the Creator's first act after creating man, and it remains as the beginning of the history of mankind. Scripture also concludes with a wedding celebration, the marriage of the Lamb of God, Jesus Christ, to the Church. The Lamb of God is the bridegroom, and the Church is his bride. "The marriage of the Lamb has come and his bride has made herself ready . . . Blessed are those who are invited to the marriage supper of the Lamb" (Rev

---

[9]Cyril of Alexandria, "Commentary on the Gospel of John 2.1," ibid. (Quoted from vol. 43 of A Library of Fathers of the Holy Catholic Church Anterior to the Division of the East and West, 155).

[10]Mordechai Katz, *Understanding Judaism: A Beginner's Guide to Jewish Faith, History, and Practice* (New York, NY: Artscroll Mesorah Publications, 2000), 268. It is a contradictory expression, but the Jewish sages explain about it. One cannot be a good judge of his character. It is the responsibility of a wife to encourage her husband when he does good things and to oppose him in his weaknesses that he might understand his faults and be inspired to improve. "A wife must be both a 'helper' and one 'opposed' to her husband, depending on his tendencies in different areas of his life." Ibid., 268.

19.7–9). The New Jerusalem, that is, the Church or the "wife of the Lamb," "comes down out of heaven as a bride adorned for her husband" (Rev 21.2). The seven angels declared, "Come here, I will show you the bride, the wife of the Lamb" (21.9). Paulos Mar Gregorios writes, "The sanctity of marriage thus has a dual source—the fact that in the beginning God created Adam in His image as man and woman, and the hope of Christians that the final fulfillment is a wedding feast of the crucified and Risen Bridegroom with his bride the Church."[11]

Marriage had great significance in the ancient Hebrew tradition, and this event was always more than social or an occasion for celebrating. The foundation of the Hebrew tradition was based on the union of Adam and Eve initiated by God in the garden of Eden. In the Old Testament, the relationship between the God of Israel and the people of Israel, his chosen people, is described as a sacred and intimate covenant akin to a marital union. The relationship between God and the world was also expressed in terms of marital love and was also considered a mystery, reflecting continued and complete mutual fidelity. Marriage was also considered a sacred institution in the Hebrew tradition, for it is the foundation of the home. The term they used for the marriage ceremony is *kiddushin*, meaning sanctification.[12] The Talmud and other ancient Jewish writings give detailed information about the significance of marriage during the intertestamental period and the time of the New Testament.

According to Genesis 1.27, man is created in the image of God, the image of the Holy Trinity. The man-woman relationship, based on Scripture, is an integral part of the image of God. Thus, in their marital relationship, man and woman bearing the image of God in them should reflect in their own marital relationship the relationship within the Godhead of the Father, the Son, and the Holy Spirit. The Holy Trinity has a relationship of *perichōresis*,[13] a relationship that is pure;

[11]Paulos Mar Gregorios, *Glory and Burden: Ministry and Sacraments of the Church*, (Noida, India: ISPCK & MGF 2006), 212.

[12]Katz, *Understanding Judaism*, 264.

[13]*Perichōresis*, a Greek word meaning "mutual interpenetration," is the concept that each Person of the Trinity is in some way present in the others. So, the Father has the

intimate; and simultaneously without confusion, abuse, authority, or loss of identity. Jesus said, "I and My Father are one" (Jn 10.30). This is the unity expected in every marriage. In the incarnate Jesus Christ, divine nature and human nature united "without separation, division, confusion, or change." In fact, the relationship between husband and wife among the faithful is also to be a reflection of the unity of the divine and human natures in Christ. That mystical and mysterious marital unity cannot be fully explained through words or ideas, but is to be experienced in life.

In St Paul's Epistles, especially in Ephesians, the bride is compared to the Church, and the bridegroom to Jesus Christ (5.25–26). In itself, this proves the importance of the bride and the bridegroom in the very early period of the Church. The same analogy conveys to us a much greater truth about every other bride and bridegroom. There has been only one perfect husband, that is, Jesus Christ. There is only one perfect bride, that is, the Church. One cannot set the same noble and divine standard for other spouses, as they will have at least some imperfections and limitations. It is the responsibility of every bride and bridegroom to be images of the heavenly bride, the Church and of the heavenly bridegroom, Jesus Christ. Both the husband and the wife should reflect the same love, faithfulness, commitment, and sacrifice that the heavenly bride and bridegroom express to each other.

It is the Almighty who unites a man and woman in marriage. Jesus Christ said, "Have you not read that from the beginning the Creator 'made them male and female' and said, 'For this reason a man shall leave his father and mother and be joined to his wife and the two shall become one flesh'? So they are no longer two, but one flesh. Therefore, what God has joined together, no human being must separate" (Mt 19.4–6). John Chrysostom observes, "The two have become one. This is not an empty symbol. They have not become the image of anything on earth, but of God Himself. They come to be made into one body. See the mystery of love! If the two do not become one, they cannot

Son and the Spirit, the Son has the Father and the Spirit, and the Spirit has the Father and the Son (Jn 14.10–11).

increase; they can increase only by decreasing!"[14] It is also to be noted that the climax and the fullness of a couple's physical union as well as their oneness is experienced at the time of the conjugal relationship. Procreation is possible in that sacred act, and thus they are participating in the God-given gift of creation.

Unmatched love and undeterred faithfulness should be in the marital relationship. It is considered as the deepest, closest, most permanent, strongest, and most exclusive relationship. Marriage "is the sacrament of divine love, as the all-embracing mystery of being itself, and it is for this reason that it concerns the whole Church, and—through the Church—the whole world."[15] It is a lasting and loving relationship in which the spouses become one body and thus find unity and togetherness during their earthly existence and beyond.

One cannot choose one's birth parents or siblings. However, every individual has the right to select a spouse. This elevates the choice of a spouse to the level of a binding and permanent commitment, making it one of the most important decisions that a person can make if destined for marital life. Marriage is almost like the sacrament of ordination, where the candidate's total, life-long commitment, faithfulness, and unconditional dedication are expected to be fulfilled. "Once ordained, always ordained" is also true about marriage. Just like the indelible imprint of ordination that remains with the person who received the gift of the Holy Spirit and blessings and grace through "the laying on of hands" (2 Tim 1.6), so the married couple receives divine blessings for their unbroken, binding marital relationship. Paul Evdokimov compares marriage not to the sacrament of ordination, but to monasticism.

> If the monk sublimates duration, time, the Christian couple initiates their transfiguration and their integration into eternity. A chaste marriage protects the heart from the "unclean flux" of temporality and its passions and transforms the unique being of

---

[14]Chrysostom, "Homily XII: On Colossians 4:18," *On Marriage*, 75.
[15]Schmemann, *For the Life of the World*, 82.

the spouses into a shrine for the only Beloved and the point of departure for shared ascents toward the House of the Father . . . The nuptial marriage-priesthood is *ontological*, the new creation that saturates human time with eternity. Like monasticism, marriage is eschatological; it is the mystery of the "eighth day" and the prophetic figure of the Kingdom.[16]

The comparison of marital life to the sacrament of ordination or to a lifetime commitment to monastic vows shows the permanent and deep bond involved in the husband and wife relationship. George Eliot asks, "What greater thing is there for two human souls than to feel that they are joined for life—to strengthen each other in all labor, to rest on each other in all sorrow, to minister to each other in all pain, to be one with each other in silent, unspeakable memories at the moment of the last parting?"[17] In marriage, the sexual relationship is channeled towards an "emotionally and morally constructive end." Pleasure is an inevitable part of sexuality as it gives an impetus for the reproductive process also.

In the mystery of marriage, not only are the bride and the bridegroom transformed, but human love is also elevated to a higher level. In the realm of marriage, love is no longer *eros*, carnal love, but part of celestial love. This is why in the Church marriage is considered a mystery and a holy sacrament. "It is a unique union of two beings in love, two beings who can transcend their own humanity and thus be united not only 'with each other,' but also 'in Christ.'"[18] Father Alexander Elchaninov writes:

Marriage is a revelation and a mystery. We see in it the complete transformation of a human being, the expansion of his personality, fresh vision, a new perception of life, and through it a rebirth into the world in a new plenitude. . . . Marriage, fleshly love, is a very great sacrament and mystery. Through it is accomplished in the

[16]Evdokimov, *The Sacrament*, 47.

[17]Quoted by William J. Bennett in *The Broken Hearth* (Colorado Springs, CO: Doubleday, Water Brook Press, 2001), 186.

[18]Meyendorff, *Marriage*, 16.

most real and at the same time the most mysterious of all possible forms of human relationship. And, qualitatively, marriage enables us to pass beyond all the normal rules of human relationship and to enter a region of the miraculous, the superhuman.[19]

Both marital life and celibate life are equally important, and one is not superior to the other. The Church teaches that to think otherwise is a heresy. St Romanus (*c.* 490–*c.* 556) writes, "For virgins are radiant because of marriage, since they were born in marriage. Indeed the Mother of God, the holy Virgin, even though she remained a pure virgin after childbirth, still it was marriage which brought her forth."[20] At least some tend to glorify celibacy and to place celibate life above marriage. Both the marital and the celibate life require sacrifice and complete dedication, while success in life depends on how one lives his or her life. Jesus said, "Not all can accept this word, but only those to whom that is granted. Some are incapable of marriage because they were born so; some, because they were made so by others; some, because they have renounced marriage for the sake of the kingdom of heaven. Whoever can accept this ought to accept it" (Mt 19.11–12). One must live according to one's calling, whether to the marital or the celibate life.

Marriage is the bonded, self-giving, eternal, and everlasting covenantal relationship with Christ and the Church. That is why St John Chrysostom concludes, "Marriage is an image of His presence in the Church."[21] For this golden-tongued preacher and theologian, every sacrament of marriage is the image of the marriage in Cana and thus the special presence of our Lord at the wedding. According to Cyril of Alexandria, our Lord Jesus Christ is present at every marriage, "to perform the same miracle."[22] It is the miracle of transformation, wonder, and happiness beyond human expectation and expression.

<hr />

[19]Ibid., 96–97; Father Alexander Elchaninov (1881–1934) was a famous Russian priest who lived in France.

[20]Quoted from *The Life of the Virgin Mary*, 325.

[21]Chrysostom, "Homily XII: On Colossians 4:18," *On Marriage*, 79.

[22]Evdokimov, *The Sacrament*, 43.

If Christ is present in the beginning of a marriage, as at the marriage in Cana, it is indeed a good beginning for the husband and the wife and for their marital bliss. There should always be a full effort to keep Christ present throughout a marriage. "Marriage begins in joy, but as at the wedding of Cana, 'the hour has not yet come.'"[23] Ideally, the beauty and the fullness of marital bliss continue to grow throughout married life; and together, both husband and wife are always in the process of growth. Thus marital life is supposed to be an experience of changing water into wine miraculously, every day and even every moment of marital life. With the presence of God in marriage, marital joy is beyond anyone's imagination, and this joy will always grow over the years. The best is reserved for the last, just as the best wine was served at the Cana wedding feast.

Jesus Christ performed the miracle of changing water into wine at the marriage celebration. Marriage is indeed a miracle in which two persons of different backgrounds and from different families are joined together as one. Three persons should be involved in a marriage: the husband, the wife, and Jesus Christ. Only then does it become stable, happy, and blessed.

> The union of the Three Persons in one nature forms a single Subject: God, one and at the same time triune. Likewise, the nuptial union of two persons forms a dyad-monad, at the same time two and one, united in a third person, God. "God made the woman together with the man, not only that thus the mystery of God's sole government might be exhibited, but also that this mutual affection might be greater." It is therefore nuptial man who is in the image of the triune God, and the dogma of the Trinity is his divine archetype, the icon of the nuptial community.[24]

This is very evident when we look at the life of Adam and Eve. They were in paradise, and all of creation was at their disposal. It was a happy and blessed life, as they were experiencing and enjoying the

[23]Ibid., 70.
[24]Ibid., 117.

presence of God. When they started to ignore communion with God and evade his commandments, not only were they exiled from paradise, but also all kinds of problems entered into their relationships and individual and familial lives. "The Christian doctrine of marriage is, indeed, a joyful responsibility; it shows what it means to be truly man; it bestows upon man the ineffable joy of giving life, in the image of his Creator, who gave life to the first man."[25] There is joy and happiness in marital life when the spouses realize the miracle of unity and oneness that takes place through marriage and the awareness of the divine presence in their relationships.

"Marriage itself," writes William J. Bennett, "detached from any objective foundation, is seen by many as possessing little or no intrinsic worth but as being a means to an end; the end, that is, of 'personal happiness' or 'fulfillment.' In the quest for fulfillment, spouses and children are often looked upon not as persons to be loved and valued for their own sake but as objects to be acquired, enjoyed, and discarded."[26] In such a situation, the importance of the marriage feast in Cana and the blessed presence there of Jesus Christ transforming the whole event should help everyone learn about the sacred institution on which the foundation of family, community, and the world are built and raised. "In attending this wedding and performing his first miracle there, Jesus Christ, the Son of God, forever sanctifies marriage."[27]

The Holy Eucharist: The Feast of the Kingdom

In Scripture, both in the Old and New Testament, the kingdom of God is compared to a marriage feast. The marriage feast at the very beginning of the public ministry of Jesus Christ symbolizes the coming of the kingdom of God. The feast of the kingdom is the holy Eucharist, the communion of the body and the blood of Christ. In Cana, water was changed into wine through Jesus, and the wine was

[25]Meyendorff, *Marriage*, 74.
[26]Bennett, *The Broken Hearth*, 11–12.
[27]Noted in the *Orthodox Study Bible: New Testament & Psalms*, 449.

what he miraculously multiplied. Paul Tarazi cites the similarities in the wedding in Cana and in 1 Corinthians 12.17–34, where St Paul speaks about the Lord's table in the context of the eucharistic service:

> Both there and here, the gathering seems to revolve around the meeting of the people who are celebrating, but it is Christ who takes center stage. Paul reminds the Corinthians that although the food is theirs since they brought it, nevertheless, the supper is the Lord's. Here, were it not for Jesus' turning water into wine, the "marriage feast" would have ended in a humiliation for the groom. Also, just as Paul links the church gathering to Christ's sacrificial death, here also, besides the "third day" reference, the wedding celebration immediately precedes the feast of Passover. (Jn 2.13)[28]

The Cana miracle was a prelude to the Lord's Supper, great and holy communion. In the holy Eucharist, wine and bread are transformed into the body and the blood of Christ. In Cana, water was changed into wine. After teaching consecutively for three days, both at the mount and in the valley, Jesus miraculously multiplied bread and fed the multitude (Jn 6.1–15; Mt 14.13–21 and 15.32–39, etc.). In both these instances, Jesus was preparing the apostles and other disciples to understand the great mystery of holy communion. If the followers could witness the changing of water to a superior wine and feeding the multitude by multiplying bread, they would believe that their master could transform bread and wine into his body and blood.

Thus the transformation of water into wine was a sign pointing towards the transformation of wine to Jesus Christ's blood, and that of the bread, to his body. Moses changed the water in the rivers of Egypt to blood (Ex 7.14–24), and that was his first miracle. It was an act of retribution against the pharaoh who kept the Israelites under bondage. To drink from the rivers of Egypt at that time brought death. Jesus, the new Moses, changed water into wine, his first public act, and the wine later to his own blood. To drink this blood, the blood of

[28]Tarazi, *New Testament Introduction: Johannine Writings*, 151.

Christ frees us from bondage of Satan and brings eternal and abundant life.

Dr Rodolph Yanney relates the six jars kept at the Cana wedding scene to the six aspects of the Eucharist: thanksgiving, remembrance, oblation, presence of God, intercession, and communion. He writes, "There are hidden references to these meanings in the miracle of Cana of Galilee where the Lord transformed the six urns of water prepared to purify the Jews (Old Testament) into wine (symbol of the Eucharist), the feast of the New Testament."[29]

The very purpose of the incarnation for Jesus was to give himself as food and drink to the children of God, who were estranged from God through tasting the forbidden fruit. It was through his blood and body that Jesus established his ever-abiding presence with his children. When we consume food and drink, our bodies digest them and they become part of our body and blood. The food and drink we receive enables us to continue our lives, and they provide energy and health for our daily sustenance. In the same way, by sharing with us his own body and blood, Jesus Christ sustains us in our spiritual life, also providing eternal and abundant life. Thus, those who participate in this great communion become partakers of the "divine nature" (2 Pet 1.4).

In the context of the New Testament, feasting always points to the dimension of the heavenly kingdom. Thus, it points beyond perishable food and drink. We experience the fullness of the kingdom of God during the Divine Liturgy. Hence, the celebration of marriage and the marriage feast point to the ultimate celebration of the kingdom of God, where Jesus Christ prepares the banquet table and gives himself to his people as food and drink. He both offers and is offered in holy Eucharist.

At the time of the *anamnesis* (sacrificial, memorial words of commemoration) at the Divine Liturgy, we pray: "Thy death, O Lord, we commemorate; Thy resurrection we confess; and thy second coming

---

[29]Rodolph Yanney, "The Eucharist and its Theological Aspects in Scripture, Liturgy, and Patristic Writings," *Coptic Church Review* 32 (2011): 16.

we look for; May Thy mercy be upon us all."[30] All these are part of Christ's great "hour," and the culmination of the "hour" is at his second coming. The divine "hour" is different from the worldly calculations of time. In the holy Eucharist, we are blessed to participate in his "hour," the hour of the glorification of the Son of God. "Here, [during the Eucharist,] in response to the Church's prayer, the Lord anticipates his return; he comes already now, he celebrates the marriage feast with us here and now. In so doing, he lifts us out of our own time toward the coming 'hour.'"[31] This is why time during the Divine Liturgy is precious, and why through the liturgy we are lifted up to the divine arena and divine time while living in this world's time and space. Time during the Divine Liturgy is time that elevates us to the experience of the eternal banquet.

In his *Mystagogical Lectures*, Cyril of Jerusalem observes, "Jesus once changed water into wine by a word of command at Cana of Galilee. Should we not believe him when he changes wine into blood? It was when he had been invited to an ordinary bodily marriage that he performed the wonderful miracle at Cana. Should we not be much more ready to acknowledge that to 'the sons of the bridal chamber' he has granted the enjoyment of his body and blood?"[32]

> When Christ, as a sign of His Power,
> clearly changed the water into wine
> All the crowd rejoiced, for they considered the taste
>   marvelous.
> Now we all partake at the banquet in the church
> For Christ's blood is changed into wine
> And we drink it with holy joy,
> Praising the great bridegroom,
> For he is the true bridegroom, the Son of Mary,

---

[30] *Service Book of Holy Qurbana*: Malankara Orthodox Church, 19.

[31] Ratzinger, *Jesus of Nazareth*, 252.

[32] Cyril of Jerusalem, "Mystagogical Lectures 4.2," *John 1–10* (ACCS NT IVa), 98. (Quoted from *Documents in Early Christian Thought*, ed. Wiles et al. [London: Cambridge University Press, 1975], 188.)

The Word before all time who took the form of a servant,
He who has in wisdom created all things.[33]

Thus, the marriage feast in Cana was pointing to the heavenly feast of the kingdom. If Jesus Christ there provided wine through transforming water in abundance, at the eternal feast of the kingdom, that is, the holy Eucharist, he gives himself, his own body and blood, for his children for abundant and everlasting life. By participating in a feast at the very beginning of his public ministry, Jesus Christ revealed the very purpose of the incarnation, giving himself as real bread and drink.

The Role of the Servants in the Sign/Miracle

The word used for "servants" in the context of the Cana sign is *diakonoi* in Greek, the original language in which the Gospel was written. In the Syriac translation of the Scripture (Peshitta), the word used is *mshamshone*, which has also the same meaning as "deacon." The usual and the common word for servants in Greek is *doulos*, meaning merely the servants who perform domesticated work, but "deacons" are different in their mission, assignments, and responsibilities. There are five instances (2.5, 9; 12.26; 15.15, 20) where the word "deacon," or in Greek *diakonos*, is used in the Gospel, and "slave" (attendants/maid), or in Greek *doulos*, is used seven times (4.51; 13.16; 18.10, 17, 18, 26, 36). By using the word for deacons rather than the word for slaves, John also shows the sacramental and sacerdotal character of the sign.

It was the deacons/servants who were present at the wedding whom Jesus directed to fill the jars with water. They obeyed him instantly. From an ordinary person's point of view, it would look like a foolish act to follow Jesus' instructions to fill the pots with well water to resolve a lack of wine at the feast. Had they known what was lacking, they would have had the right to question Jesus about how he was

---

[33]Ibid., "Kontakion on the Marriage at Cana 7.20," ibid. (Quoted from Kontakia of Romanos, Byzantine Melodist, 2 vols., eds. Carpenter and Marjorie [Columbia, MO: University of Missouri Press, 1970–1973], vol. 1, p. 74.)

going to resolve the wine problem by filling water pots with water. Yet, they readily and instantly obeyed his instructions. They already had instructions from Jesus' mother to obey her Son. The servants also obeyed a second command from Jesus: "Draw some out now and take it to the headwaiter" (Jn 2.8). To take it to the headwaiter would have been actually more difficult than filling the pots with water because the headwaiter would soon taste and serve the wine. The servants believed that what they brought him was wine, not water. Thus, their total obedience paved the way for the sign.

Diakonia or service was the mission of the twelve apostles. *Diakonoi* is also another word for the apostles in the Gospel. Christ said, "Whoever wishes to be great among you shall be your servant; whoever wishes to be first among you shall be your slave. Just so, the Son of Man did not come to be served but to serve and to give his life as a ransom for many" (Mt 20.27–28). And again, "If any man serve me let him follow me, and where I am there shall also my servant be. If any man serve me him will my Father honor" (Jn 12.26). In fact, service is the mission of the disciples, the apostles. Jesus is the "greatest deacon," not only the one who stands between the Father and the world, but also the one who came to administer the will of his Father who sent him. He served others, even washing the feet of his disciples. *Diakonia* on behalf of the Father and for humankind was the mission behind the incarnation.

The word "servant" or "deacon" denotes a back-and-forth movement from the celebrant to the community of the faithful. "The deacon works in two worlds all the time, and does so both effortlessly and voluntarily. This is reflected in the etymology of the word 'deacon' itself. . . . the word *diakonos*—'deacon'—and *diakonein*—'to serve as a deacon'—are related to the word for 'movement'—*kinesis*. The deacon is the one who moves back and forth between two people or two places."[34] In the Cana sign, the responsibility of the deacons was to

[34]Bishop Basil of Sergievo, "Living in the Future," *Living Orthodoxy in the Modern World*, ed. Andrew Walker and Costa Carras (Crestwood, NY: St Vladimir's Seminary Press, 2000), 31–32.

"go back and forth" between the guests and the master of the feast.
Bishop Basil of Sergievo continues:

> "We are running out of wine, so go and fill those pots with water
> and take them to the master of the feast." This is a completely nat-
> ural movement because this is what the deacons would be doing
> anyway. They would be taking the various dishes and drinks to the
> master of the feast, and then the master would look around the
> room and say: "take them over there—they do not seem to have
> anything to drink," or: "those guests look like they might enjoy
> some of this, carry it over to them." In this way, the master of the
> feast would have the whole feast under his control. But it is the
> deacons who would do the to-ing and fro-ing.[35]

In the Cana celebration, the role of deacons was to act as Jesus
instructed them and then to serve the people as directed by the steward. In other words their roles were obedience and service.

The term "servant" takes us back to the Old Testament and connects us with the covenantal relationship between Yahweh and Israel.
Obedience, or rather total commitment, was the responsibility of
the Israelites, "the people of God." The same kind of obedience was
expected from servants. The deacons were advised by the mother of
Jesus to obey whatever Jesus told them to do. They obeyed exactly,
as did Mary, who was already an excellent example of obedience to
God's will and mission. Throughout her life, one can see total obedience and submission to God's plan and design. So the "deacons"
became disciples through obedience. The servants' unquestioning,
unhesitating, immediate, and willing obedience to the instructions
given by our Lord demonstrated the character and quality of the obedience required of disciples, the obedience that in fact makes one a
true disciple. It is not improbable to suppose that one or more of these
servants may have left his work to become a disciple of Christ, as others of his disciples did upon coming face-to-face with teachings and

[35]Ibid., 32.

mighty acts (e.g., cf. Lk 5.1–11, Jn 1.43–51).[36] This is why they obeyed readily, without any hesitation, and without questioning the instructions given by our Lord. The deacons stood between Jesus Christ, who told them to fill the pots with water and the people who drank the wine that he miraculously made. They easily, readily, and without any hesitation or question believed in Jesus, and they knew that water was changed into wine.

The role of the servants (or deacons) relates to the ministry of deacons who assist at the altar during the Divine Liturgy. The Acts of the Apostles presents the appointment of seven deacons (6.1–6). Their main responsibility was to serve "at the table," the Communion table, and to look after the needs of widows. In ancient times, a servant's responsibility included serving at the table, the Lord's table, as well as serving others, especially widows and the needy. The deacons were assigned the responsibility of resolving complaints within the fellowship of the early Christian church. The seven deacons were men of character and spirituality, "reputable men, filled with spirit and wisdom" (Acts 6.3).

We see a great difference in the sign basically between the steward and the servants. The servants knew what had happened at the feast and were thus "insiders." The steward was unaware that the wine was miraculously made and was thus an "outsider." "There is ironic plea-

---

[36]There is a Coptic tradition that St Mark was one of the servants/deacons at the wedding feast in Cana. Abba Severus of Al-Ashmunein (10th century) writes in his *History of the Patriarchs of the Coptic Church of Alexandria*, Part 1, Chapter 1: "And Mark was one of the Seventy Disciples. And he was among the servants who poured out the water which our Lord turned into wine, at the marriage of Cana in Galilee (http://www.tertullian.org/fathers/severus_hermopolis_hist_alex_patr_01_part1.htm#CHAPTER_I). Pope Shenouda III (20th century) writes in *The Beholder of God Mark the Evangelist, Saint and Maratyr*, p. 11: "It was mentioned that Mark was at the Wedding of Cana of Galilee, where God did His first miracle, changing the water into wine (John 2). He was among those who tasted it." In the footnote to this statement, he cites the following source: http://ixoyc.net/data/Fathers/170.pdf (http://tasbeha.org/content/hh_books/Smark/index.html). Ibn Kabar (14th century) writes in *The Lamp that Lights the Darkness*, p. 77: "Mark was one of the followers (*talaameez*) who drank from the water that was transformed to wine at the wedding in Cana of Galilee." Note that the Arabic word *talaameez* used above is derived from the same root as the Syriac *talmido*, "disciple."

sure when someone who is ostensibly in charge is in the dark and when the servants who are not wedding guests become the insiders."[37] The responsibility of filling the pots was not assigned to the steward. Probably he would not have followed the request by the mother of Jesus. Even though the steward was one among the celebrants and had an important role in the feast, he was unaware of the great mysteries revealed there through Jesus Christ and had no clue about who was there to resolve problems and miraculously to change water into wine. The role the deacons played, silently and staying behind, made a difference at the celebration. The steward had the front seat and possibly claimed credit for the successful conclusion of the feast, even providing the best wine at last!

The deacon faces the people and points to the altar, to Christ. In the Divine Liturgy, for example, he addresses the congregation with these words: "How awful is this hour and how solemn this time, my beloved ones, wherein the Holy Spirit from the topmost heights of heaven takes wing and descends, and broods and rests upon this holy Eucharist set before us and sanctifies it. Stand ye still, with fear and trembling and pray that peace may be with us and all of us may have tranquility."[38] The deacon listens and instructs the congregation to listen. He plays an important role in transforming the faithful into the Church, the body of Christ, just as the servants played a prominent role in the miracle by listening and obeying what was told by Christ in the transformation of water into wine. Herman C. Waetjen observes, "These 'ministers' as the word may also be translated, are those who followed Jesus' instructions, and in their obedience to render service they discover they are insiders who are directly involved in the awesome mystery that has occurred. There is no greater reward for those who minister as servers of the new wine."[39]

Mary foreshadowed the service of the diaconate, as she never pointed to herself. Her disposition was always oriented towards her

[37] Brant, *John*, 58.
[38] *The Service Book of the Holy Qurbana*, Malankara Orthodox Church, 16.
[39] Waetjen, *The Gospel of the Beloved Disciple*, 120.

Son, Jesus Christ. The responsibility of the diaconate is, "Do whatever he tells you to do." This was exactly what the mother of Jesus did. Her response to the angel was, "Behold, I am the handmaid of the Lord. May it be done to me according to your word" (Lk 1.38). The act of service, the mission of the diaconate, was compelling in Mary's character, and it was clearly evident in her visit to her relative, Elizabeth, and in her stay with Elizabeth to help her.

Conclusion

One can easily notice the liturgical and the sacramental consciousness that pervades the entire Fourth Gospel. The sacramental mysteries of the Church are rooted in all the signs narrated in this Gospel. In fact, in one way or other, every sign leads to the sacraments and reveals the significance of the holy mysteries. "The signs and their interpretation, reported in St. John's Gospel, reveal the transforming effect of Christ's presence and then imply that the same transforming presence will be at work in the holy mysteries."[40] The very presentation, as a sign, of the miraculous event of changing water into wine at the wedding in Cana reveals its sacramental and mystical importance.

At the time of the wedding, one can visualize a unique liturgical community in Cana, where the high priest Jesus Christ was present, presiding over the mysterious transformation. Deacons there were at the disposal of the high priest and served what was provided by him to the people. Like the faithful who receive the enriching and heavenly experience through their participation in the holy Eucharist, those who were at the banquet tasted the superb wine and had the exhilarating experience. Saints like the Theotokos (the Mother of God) and the apostles were also present in the liturgical assembly.

The Cana sign is full of symbols and allusions to the sacraments, and its liturgical importance is great. Liturgical experience, including participation in the sacraments, enhances transformation to the divine realm and uplifts one to enjoy the spirit of the kingdom of

[40]Archbishop Dmitri, *The Miracles of Christ*, 77.

God while still living in this world. What happened at Cana was such a transformation. Water as part of the fallen world was transformed. During the "first act" of creation: the Holy Spirit was brooding "over the water." In the process of re-creation, the Son of God worked "on water," which was part of the fallen world, to transform it, and that was his "first act." Water is used for cleansing, regularly for daily cleansing, as well as for ceremonial cleansing. Water is an essential element for baptism. Cleansing, dying, and resurrecting with Christ through water are actualized and experienced in baptism, which is also a rebirth from above. Water also symbolizes the Holy Spirit. At the Last Supper, Jesus transformed wine into his blood and bread into his body. The miracle of feeding the multitude by multiplying bread and the transformation of water into wine are linked to the Divine Liturgy, where the body and the blood of Jesus are consumed. What happened at the wedding was a prelude to transforming wine to his own blood that was shed on Calvary. The Cana sign was thus pointing to both baptism and the Eucharist.

The marriage feast in Scripture is often presented as an image of the heavenly banquet. The faithful Christian participates in this banquet through the holy Eucharist. Also in this context, the sign alludes to the heavenly banquet of the kingdom, where the body and the blood of the Son of God are shared. At the wedding scene, the water of the Old Covenant was transformed into wine, the wine of the New Covenant.

The sign was performed in the context of a marriage. Beyond the sacraments of baptism and the Eucharist, the mystery of marriage is also involved in the great sign at Cana. Through his presence, Jesus blessed the marriage, which was originally initiated at the garden of Eden; in Cana, Jesus elevated the ceremony to its mystical and sacramental heights. Fr Mathew the Poor observes, "It is Christ who in every marriage establishes the promise and guarantees the covenant between the spouses so as to change life from a temporal, ordinary level into an immortal and eternal one, through the mystery of God's presence, being thus analogous to the transformation of the water into wine."[41] Water was mysteriously changed into wine; through marriage the husband and the wife mysteriously form a new paradise, a new heaven on earth.

The presence of the apostles and the role played by the servants (deacons) reminds us of the sacerdotal ministry of the Church. Christ, the new Melchizedek and high priest, was the one who presided, and the deacons obeyed all the master's instructions. The sign was performed amid people, the community of the faithful, who obeyed him, and the intercession of the Virgin Mary paved the way for the miracle.

[41]Matthew the Poor, "Wedding in Cana," 12.

8

The Wedding Feast
and the Empty Jars

I n the Cana sign we read about the six jars that were kept at the wedding scene: "Now there were six stone water-pots there for Jewish ceremonial washings, each holding twenty to thirty gallons" (Jn 2.6). Barclay says of the Fourth Gospel, "There is a simple surface story that anyone can understand and re-tell; but there is also a wealth of deeper meaning for him who has the eagerness to search and the eye to see and the mind to understand."[1] This is very true about the water-pots at the wedding. In Scripture, references about the water-pots[2] are found only in the Fourth Gospel (2.6, 7; 4.28).

The use of jars kept for ceremonial cleansing was transformed completely for more urgent and essential needs. It should also be noted that the jars there were meant for water and not for wine. The author of the Gospel writes that Jesus directed the servants to fill them with water. According to St John Chrysostom, there was a purpose behind the apostle's mentioning this command: "None of the unbelievers might suspect that lees having been left in the vessels, and water having been poured upon and mixed with them, a very weak wine had been made."[3]

---

[1]Barclay, *The Gospel of John*, 80.
[2]Marvin R. Vincent, *Word Studies in the New Testament*, vol. 2, *The Writings of John* (Grand Rapids, MI: Eerdmans Publishing, 1973), 80.
[3]Chrysostom, *Sermon* 22.1 (NPNF[1] 14:77).

The Jews used jars filled with water for two purposes.[4] Water would be used for cleansing the feet while entering a house as Palestine was a dry country where one's feet were covered by dust, and on a wet day they were soiled with mud. Water was also used for the ceremonial washing, a sign and symbol of religious purification. "Palestine is an arid country with few mountains or wells. They used to fill water pots with water so that they would not always have to go to the rivers if they become defiled, but rather could have the means of purification readily at hand."[5]

Jars used for ritual purification were required to be made from stone. The stone jars stood for purity because stone, according to the rabbinical teaching, would not contact ritual impurity. They could also be cleansed even if they happened to be defiled. If jars were earthen ones, they were to be totally destroyed. Moses changed the water in the Egyptian's stone jars (a sign according to Exodus 7.19), probably because of defilement reasons.

Ceremonial cleansing or washing was a prerequisite for Jews before attending religious functions. When Jesus was invited by a Pharisee to dine with him, Jesus did not wash his hands, and the host was astonished by the unusual behavior of the guest. "When the Pharisee saw it, he marveled that Jesus had not first washed before dinner" (Lk 11:38). Instructions were given in the Mishnah,[6] the book that dealt with the traditions, which clearly explained the details of ritual washing, like how much water was to be used and how the washing was to be done. Those details demonstrated how important the ceremonial washing was. They also demonstrated their rigid traditionalism.

In the Cana sign narrative, by mentioning the six empty jars, the problem of the absence of adequate wine was shifted to the Jewish law of ritual purification. In the Fourth Gospel, this was the first instance in which Jesus had to deal with the Law of the Old Testament and the

[4]Barclay, *The Gospel of John*, 84.
[5]Chrysostom, *Sermon* 22.2, *John 1–10* (ACCS NT IVa), 95.
[6]The book is considered Judaism's first major canonical document following the Jewish Bible.

traditions of the Jewish people. Even the word "Jews" in the Gospel denotes not all the Jewish people, according to some commentators. They were the Jewish leaders, probably from Jerusalem, or the Jews who rejected the truth of God, opposed Jesus, and crucified Him.[7]

There Were Six Jars

What is the significance of the six jars? St John, the eagle, as already noted, who rises to lofty heights in whatever he observes, especially in things related to the Son of God, finds mysterious hidden meanings in seemingly minor things including words, numbers, and actions, which for others may appear to be minute or ordinary matters. The apostle was very careful in writing the number of jars kept there at the wedding feast and why they were there. The jars referred to possibly stood in for the six days of the week, one for each day of the week. In the beginning God created everything in six days, one for each day of the initial creation. There was nothing for the seventh day, the day of the Sabbath, which was the day of complete rest. Hence there would not have been an occasion for any kind of pollution or defilement on the Sabbath day.

Purification was an important aspect of rabbinic sanctity. The Mishnah has six books dealing in a very elaborate way with purification. "Thus, it is symbolic that the six water pots represent these six books."[8] Many scholars are of the opinion that, especially in Jewish thought, the number six—one less than seven—is a symbol of imperfection and incompletion.[9] "The number six may signify incompletion or labor. Six is the number of days God works before resting on the Sabbath."[10] They possibly also stand for the imperfections of the Levitical laws. In the book of Revelation, authored by the same apostle, the number six is mentioned with a negative connotation. "The number that is less than seven plays a special role in Revelation

[7] Johnson, *The Writings of the New Testament*, 533.
[8] *The Life of the Virgin Mary*, 333.
[9] Barclay, *The Gospel of John*, 89.
[10] Brant, *John*, 57.

because evil is represented as taking on the appearance of good: the idea here that six is close to seven yet not the real thing. The infamous 666 is three-fold repletion of the 'seeming divine but not really' number six; it may or may not allude to a specific individual, but in any case it represents a paragon of evil masquerading as good."[11] Though it was common to attribute a certain negativity to the number six during those days, there is evidence for the opposite as well. The famous Alexandrian Jew Philo considered six as a number of perfection. His logic was that it was equal to the sum of its factors ($3 \times 2 \times 1 = 6$ and $3 + 2 + 1 = 6$).[12]

According to Jewish numerology seven often denotes perfection, completion, and fulfillment, an idea that continued to prevail in the early Christian traditions and practices. In the Holy Scripture the number seven "has a mystic ring about it."[13] When the three persons in the Trinity and the four sides of the universe are added together, they equal seven. Thus both the Creator and the whole creation are linked in the number seven. This was one way of considering, among some Christian thinkers, the uniqueness to that number. Seven is considered also a divine digit revealing the fullness of divinity. Many ancient traditions and religions also considered seven as a special number and as a symbol of perfection. In the Egyptian tradition seven was a symbol of eternity. The same is true in Hinduism as the number seven appears very frequently in Hindu religious texts. It represents the *saptha-loka* (the seven realms of the universe), thus symbolically representing the world.

Christ did not ask for another jar to make the number seven before the sign. Hence one cannot make much out of the numbers. Still, St John mostly mentions numbers for specific reasons. One possible reason is that in Christ everything is renewed and gets a new beginning. By mentioning the number of empty pots as six, the author of the

---

[11]Tarazi, *New Testament Introduction: Johannine Writings*, 23–24.

[12]Morris, *Reflections on the Gospel of John*, 74.

[13]Rev. Dr V. C. Samuel, *An Orthodox Catechism on the Faith and Life of the Church* (Kottayam, Kerala: MGOCSM Bookshop and Publishing House, 1983), 84.

Gospel was possibly pointing to the imperfections of the existing Jewish rules and regulations. Even the number six, which was a symbol of imperfection, becomes perfect through Christ and in his presence.

The Jars and the Value of Traditions

The place and value of traditions were brought out through the jars also. If in one way the Cana sign reveals the failure of traditions because the jars were empty, it also points to the other side of tradition, the high place it has in the social, cultural, and religious milieu of any society or gathering, whether secular or religious. Jesus could have destroyed them by saying that they failed to fulfill their purpose and hence there was no more need for them. Instead, he raised their goals and aims to a new and higher level, making them worthy and useful. Though empty at the wedding, they stood for certain great truths and pointed to the need for inward and outward purity. In the wedding feast at Cana, what was urgently needed was wine and not water for washing.

Nobody can truly live in the present while ignoring the past and its traditions. For the growth and civilization of the world, the values passed from generation to generation through tradition can never be ignored in either the secular or the religious life. Certain traditions passed down through the Word of God and through the Fathers of the Church must be kept intact. Jaroslav Pelikan correctly stated, "Tradition is the living faith of the dead; traditionalism is the dead faith of the living."[14] The famous saying by our Lord, "The Sabbath is for man and man is not for Sabbath" (Mk 2.27), which has since become a favorite adage, was a new teaching that brought revolution in all the religions, where one gives importance to norms, rules, and regulations while forsaking the spirit of the Law. The idiom has been often quoted in every language and culture and is very valid for every age and every place.

[14]Jaroslav Pelikan, *The Emergence of the Catholic Tradition (100–600): The Christian Tradition* (Chicago: The University of Chicago Press, 1971), 9.

The story of the Good Samaritan brings to mind the picture of the Levite who did not want to lend a helping hand to the wounded and bruised Samaritan. The reason was that it would make him unclean, as he gave importance to fanatical observance of rules and regulations in the name of religion while totally ignoring the greatness of the human beings who are created in the image and likeness of almighty God.

The Empty Jars and Ritual Purification

It is unusual to read about empty pots at a celebration, especially at the beginning or middle of a very joyful event like a wedding. The author of the Gospel did not mention that the jars were empty directly, but it is very clear from his narrative, "Jesus told them, 'Fill the jars with water.' So they filled them to the brim" (2.7). Usually there are a lot of empty jars and bottles after a celebration, but before that it is unusual and is an unwelcome thing. Emptiness in an event is not at all a positive sign, as it only brings shame and disappointment to those who organize it.

The pots at the wedding scene remained empty only for a while. Though they were empty at the beginning, the pots were full when the wine was to be served. There was not only more than enough to drink, but its quality was also superb. Additionally, against the usual practice, where the best was served first and the worst last, at this wedding the best was served last. St John, through the Cana sign, was presenting Jesus Christ as the one who could bring fulfillment and perfection where there was emptiness and want.

If the pots kept at the wedding for washing were empty, the pots failed in performing their responsibility at such an important and joyful event. The empty jars can be interpreted as a metaphor for the emptiness of many of the Jewish ritual practices of the time. The "chosen people of God" were placed among the Gentiles to reveal to the world the will and ways of God and as an example to others. The world was to be redeemed through the community of the then "people of God." They were chosen to be "the light to the nations" and were expected to brighten the world through their very presence; they were to radiate the divine attributes to the peoples around them. The sign, where the empty jars were filled with water and the water was transformed to sublime and first-rate wine, showed the status of the existing religion's failure and was a prelude to the establishment of the kingdom of God by the Messiah.

The common practices at that time were mostly to give more importance to outward cleanliness and purification. The then leaders of the community admonished the followers mostly about observances, which were symbolic, outward, and also outlandish. The rituals, rubrics, and regulations of purification received priority over inward transformation and transparency of character and conduct. The ceremonial outward washing became one of the main means to measure the spiritual status and strength of a person. Even if a person was pure and holy, he was not considered so unless he performed the ceremonial and legalistic duties of purification. It was also true that if a person was a hypocrite and ungodly, a ceremonial washing before the public made him a religious and godly person. The same idea is reflected in many other passages like Mark 7.1–12, where we read the Pharisees complaining to Jesus about his disciples eating without washing their hands.

The laws made many Pharisees hypocrites, especially those who thought that they strictly adhered to the rules and rubrics. Such a lifestyle became part of the fabric of the existing Jewish community. The purpose of the incarnation was to free people from the stale shackles of ceremonial observations which had lost their true meaning. Jesus Christ openly chastised the scribes and Pharisees often and called them names like "hypocrites," "whitewashed sepulchers," etc. "By its purificatory rites Judaism sought to keep God's people in proper relationship with him, and with its closely guarded marriage regulations tried to secure a proper transmission of that relationship. But Judaism has signally failed."[15] This is true about the followers of different religions, in the past as well as present, when they give importance to

[15]Marsh, *Saint John*, 59.

ceremonies, regulations, and rituals without any change within themselves or in their personal behaviors. The sacraments of the Church are meant for the divine transformation of the individual who receives them and at the same time of the community and the world at large.

If the six empty jars allude to the emptiness and uselessness of Jewish purification rituals, it was the same jars that Jesus directed the servants to fill with water. The water was transformed in Jesus Christ's precious presence into wine, the symbol of his blood. The empty jars failed to do the purification ceremonies the Son of God could do through the shedding of his blood, his death, and his resurrection. The failure of existing rules and ways of purification and redemption was the very reason for the incarnation of the Lord and his passion. The whole of humankind and the world were under bondage, and only the sinless "only begotten Son of God" could redeem them through his blood. This was the ultimate act to end all other rituals and actions of purification. Thus, the purification through defiled water came to an end by the offering of the sinless and life-giving blood of Jesus Christ.

The fanatical and perverted religious leaders of the time gave more emphasis to the letter of the Law. They never cared about the content and purpose of the rules and regulations. The original purpose behind the codes and canons of the law was to glorify God as well as to love and serve fellow human beings. While the rules and rubrics are important, the Pharisees and Sadducees of Jesus' time gave priority to the Law's formalities rather than its purpose. In their personal lives they observed these laws according to their convenience and needs. At the same time they went after people, especially the poor and marginalized, who altered, modified, or nullified the existing Jewish rules and regulations; the leaders were very strict and exacting towards them. They tried to condemn them and cast them out of the community on the basis of their lack of adherence to the letter of the rituals and customs.

The transformation and transmutation of water into wine is a sign showing the transcending of the old covenant by the new one. The

Jewish rites of purification were transformed to a "new wine" (Acts 2.13). The Law is fulfilled in the person of Jesus and by his action. "Ritual purification in the end is just ritual, a gesture of hope. It remains 'water,' just as everything man does on his own remains 'water' before God. Ritual purification is in the end never sufficient to make man capable of God, to make him really 'pure' for God. Water becomes wine. Man's own efforts now encounter the gift of God, who gives himself and thereby creates the feast of joy that can only be instituted by the presence of God and his gift."[16] The new act of cleansing is completed through the new wine, which is the blood of Jesus Christ. It is the blood of the new covenant. That blood is shed for the remission of sins of the children of God and for the redemption of the fallen world.

Jesus performed the miracle after water was poured into the same jars. He neither asked to remove the jars nor questioned the purpose of them at the time. It was the water in the jars that was changed to superb wine. Thus, through the miraculous sign and action, he transformed the ultimate purpose of the jars and the contents in them. The author of the Gospel presented the initial sign performed by Jesus to reveal the very purpose of the incarnation.

The Empty Jars Were Kept Outside

The jars for ceremonial purifications were kept outside, as the washing had to be done before the participants' entry into any function. Not only is outward washing not necessary anymore, but there is no need for jars to be kept outside for the purpose of washing. The ceremonial washing came to an end with the coming of Jesus Christ. He came to cleanse the creation with his own precious, life-giving blood and not with water or any other cleaning substance. Since Jesus' coming, what is important is not outward appearance or the symbolic gesture of washing hands, but both inward and outward purity and holiness. One thing that Jesus was never able to tolerate was hypocrisy. He

---

[16]Ratzinger, *Jesus of Nazareth*, 253.

vehemently and with very strong language condemned the leaders of the times like Pharisees, Sadducees, and scribes because of their hypocritical behavior. The inside should be clean, clear, and transparent. For that, humility, holiness, and transparency of character are extremely essential.

The pots were kept outside, and the place for them was always outside. But in the presence of Jesus Christ they did not stay outside anymore but obtained a place, a prominent place, in the banquet. There is something unusual about it. The reason for that was that they were filled with the newly made wine. When the pots were placed inside, they had great use inside. What was in them that saved the host family from shame and sorrow? The purpose of his coming was not to destroy the Jewish Law but to fulfill and carry it out fully. Jesus said, "Do not think that I came to destroy the Law or the Prophets. I did not come to destroy but to fulfill. For assuredly, I say to you, till heaven and earth pass away, one jot or one tittle will by no means pass from the law till all is fulfilled" (Mt 5.17–18). His condescension was to transform the Law to its original purpose of the glorification of God and helping humankind to regain its original glory and destiny. The wine that was served at the banquet saved the family from shame, and those who drank it were surprised by its great taste and its excellent quality.

The jars have enjoyed a prominent place since then. If the water in the jars was transformed to superb wine at the wedding, at the Liturgy the wine in the "cup" is transformed mysteriously and miraculously into the blood of our Lord through the Holy Spirit. The cup provides forgiveness of sin and abundant as well as eternal life for those who participate in it. In the wedding scene it was Jesus' presence that changed water into wine. In the holy mystery of the bread and wine, which become his body and blood, Jesus himself is present, and the same is going to be continued until his second coming. The "jars" thus became the center of the life of the Church and the life of the Christian. It is interesting to note that for Ephraim, the famous Syrian mystic and poet, "these jars symbolized the womb of Virgin Mary in which Jesus had been conceived and that had also witnessed a transformation of nature."[17] In a sense, the body and blood we receive at the time of Holy Communion is the glorified body and blood of our Lord that he received at the time of his incarnation.

"Fill the Jars with Water"

Jesus told the servants (or deacons) present at the wedding celebration to fill the empty stone pots with water. The mother of Jesus already had instructed them to obey whatever her Son would instruct them to do. They obeyed him instantly, filling the vessels with water, paving the way for the miracle.

A wonderful transformation took place in the substance inside the jars in the presence of Jesus Christ. Until then, the purpose of the jars was ceremonial cleansing. Hence, the jars were kept outside. But Jesus transformed the use of the jars from ceremonial goals to the emerging urgent needs of the people. In the presence of Jesus Christ it was no longer the same substance but a new one, more powerful and useful for everybody. Just as what happened to water, the mission of our Lord was in every way to bring the estranged creation, with new life and energy, back into the fold. Through Jesus we are back in the "father's mansion" exactly like the prodigal son in the Gospel of Luke (Lk 15.11–32).

The feast master, after "tasting the water that had become wine, without knowing where it came from" (Jn 2.9), was taken aback and attested the fact of the superiority of the latest wine that was kept until then. It was in a way expressing the superiority of Jesus over the Law of Moses.[18] The water and the pots failed in their responsibilities as they were part of the Law of Moses—though it still paved the way for the new Moses, Jesus Christ. In him everything, including the Mosaic Law, was fulfilled and perfected, and is now beyond failure.

[17]Ephraim, *Commentary on Tatian's Diatessaron 5.6–7, John 1–10* (ACCS NT IVa), 94, 95.

[18]Howard-Brook, *Becoming Children of God*, 80.

9
The Bride and the Bridegroom at the Wedding

The Bride and the Bridegroom

The most important persons in a wedding generally are the bride and the bridegroom, and everything is centered on them. But neither of their names is mentioned in the scriptural narrative of the wedding in Cana, except a casual reference by the steward of the feast about the bridegroom. There is also no indication about which family is the host. The names of the parents of the bride and bridegroom or their relatives in attendance are not given. Many of these seemingly important details about the wedding are missing in the narrative. The details we have are limited to where it happened, what took place in the absence of enough wine, as well as who was present at the scene: Jesus, his mother, and his disciples.

Since there is no definitive name of the bridegroom given, there are some assumptions about him. One opinion is that the bridegroom was Nathanael who was from Cana. In this case Nathanael, who had already known Jesus and had become one of his disciples, extended the invitation to Jesus, his mother, and his disciples. One other specu-lation is that it was the marriage of Alphaeus and Mary who was the sister of the mother of Jesus or one of their sons. They lived in Cana.[1] There is also an apocryphal tradition that Virgin Mary was the aunt of the bridegroom, suggesting Cleopas, one of the two disciples to whom

[1] Foster, *Studies in the Life of Christ*, 352.

the resurrected Lord appeared on the evening of Easter. Another strong suggestion is that Simon the Zealot was the bridegroom,[2] as well as Simon the Canaanite. St Ephraim is of opinion that Simon the Zealot was the bridegroom.[3] In the apocryphal stories, the names of both Lazarus and Nicodemus were suggested as the bridegroom. Strangely enough, there were some who were of opinion that the bridegroom was even John, the apostle and the author of the Fourth Gospel. St John's name came from an old Mohammedan tradition[4] as well as "from an early set of Prefaces to the books of the New Testament called the Monarchian Prefaces."[5] John the apostle was considered from the early days of the Church as the symbol of celibacy and the model of monastic life. Were it John, some allusions would likely have been in the narrative indicating so, such as a reference to the "beloved disciple." It is highly unlikely that John was the bridegroom. St Mark the Evangelist also is mentioned as the bridegroom by some. There is a possibility that either the bride or bridegroom or both of them were relatives of Jesus.

Unlike the many guesses as to who the groom was, there have been no suggestions about who the bride was. It is indeed strange and, at the same time, worth the attention. The only woman mentioned in the Cana marriage celebration was the mother of Jesus, and she stood out as a significant presence and person in the sign. In some liturgical texts the Church is figured as the bride of Cana. The prayer of the Church for Sundays and Feasts (*Penqitho* used by the Syrian and Indian Church) has this prayer for the Sunday of the Wedding in Cana: "O our Savior, the Church Your Bride, the spouse whom You took from the midst of the peoples, is figured by the bride of Cana."[6] At least there is a reference about the bridegroom, but nothing is mentioned about the bride. Since the names of both bride and

---

[2]Noted in the *Orthodox Study Bible: New Testament & Psalms*, 215.

[3]*The Life of the Virgin Mary*, 335. Cited from "Hymns on Virginity."

[4]Foster, *Studies in the Life of Christ*, 352.

[5]Barclay, *The Gospel of John*, 81.

[6]Francis Acharya, *Prayer with the Harp of the Spirit*, vol. 3, *The Crown of the Year*, part II, 30.

bridegroom are missing and because of various other reasons, one can easily surmise that the purpose of the Cana narrative goes beyond an average marriage that Jesus attended with his disciples and it has much more symbolic and mysterious meanings. Larry Paul Jones correctly observes, "The presence of Jesus at the wedding has greater significance than the wedding itself."[7]

What is the place of personal fame and name in the context of the manifestation of the Son of God's divine glory? If the author of the Gospel had tried to write the names and other details of the characters and concerned people, the main story of the revelation of the heavenly mystery and the divine manifestation would have been lost or at least deemphasized. It should also be noted that when the names of brides and bridegrooms published widely and engraved in marble and stone plaques are being forgotten, the bride and the bridegroom in the Cana wedding, whoever they were, are still fondly and prominently recollected.

The same is true about the boy who offered the apostles his lunch containing the five barley loaves and two fishes from which Jesus fed five thousand men (the number of women and children, likely much more in numbers than the men, was not counted). The name of the boy was not given, though the miracle is narrated in all four Gospels and is the only miracle witnessed by all the Evangelists. Yet, he has been known since then more than the many of the boys and the girls with fame and name who came after him. Even the nameless widow who put forth her best for God, a small coin of little value to many, has been better known than others who have contributed millions or even billions for noble causes throughout the centuries.

The Cana wedding event teaches at least one thing. Though it was a wedding, where the bride and bridegroom are the most important persons, in Cana it was centered on Jesus Christ, the eternal bridegroom. The mother of Jesus called upon her Son to act and requested others to follow his directions. The result was the miraculous sign. It was he who also saved the family from shame and sorrow. Above all,

[7]Jones, *The Symbol of Water in the Gospel of John*, 54.

the wedding celebration paved the way for the revelation of the glory of the Son of God.

The Wedding and the Bridegroom

That the first sign Jesus performed was in a wedding scene is very symbolic and very significant. As already mentioned, the bride and bridegroom are the two most important persons in a wedding, and yet there is nothing much about them in the narrative. Possibly the reason is that the Cana sign was pointing to Jesus as the eternal bridegroom. In fact, in each sign presented in the Fourth Gospel a specific role or title of Jesus is presented. If in the initial sign Jesus is the bridegroom, in others he is the Savior, Bread of Life, the Way, the Truth and the Light, the Resurrection, and so on.

Jesus commanded the waiters, after the water in the pots was transformed into wine, "Draw some out now, and take it to the master of the feast" (2.8). When the master of the feast tasted the water that had become wine, he called the bridegroom and said to him, "Everyone serves good wine first, and then when people have drunk freely, an inferior one; but you have kept the good wine until now" (2.10). In fact, the figure of the Bridegroom transformed the whole situation, and the role of the Bridegroom took center stage in the sign, rather than the water changed into wine. Thus, in the Cana sign John presents Jesus Christ obliquely as the bridegroom. The master of the feast likely mysteriously experienced the ubiquitous presence of the bridegroom in Jesus. "For the central issue of this narrative is not the miracle of changing water into wine, if that wonder be isolated from its setting in John's story, but is rather the amazing thing that happens when he who is the bridegroom, the real, the genuine bridegroom, attends the festival of a Jewish wedding, a marriage ceremony among the people of God, and transforms it."[8] Since the bridegroom in the wedding at Cana is not identified, and the role played by Jesus Christ there points to *him* as the bridegroom, he is seen not as a mere bridegroom in the

[8]Marsh, *John*, 142.

sign but the bridegroom who takes center stage and beyond that. In him the long expected bridegroom of the Jews was revealed.

A wedding, in the Old Testament context, was often associated with the messianic time. In early Jewish thought, marriage and the marriage feast, which usually lasted for a week, were a sign and symbol of the final union between God and his people, the people of Israel. The relationship between Israel and Yahweh was presented in the Old Testament as the relationship between a bride and a bridegroom. It is repeated again and again in the Scripture. Matthew the Poor tells us that ten times in Scripture, Yahweh is portrayed as a bridegroom (six times in Song of Songs, three times in Isaiah, and once in Jeremiah) and the people of Israel as his beloved bride.[9] "For your Maker, your Husband—The Lord Almighty is His name" (Is 54.5). Psalm 45, sung in the context of a royal wedding, also beautifully conveys the same message. The people of God is the bride, and God is the bridegroom. The Song of Songs is narrated vividly using the loving relationship between a bride and a bridegroom. The Song of Songs has been interpreted as expressing the tender love in the marital relationship between Yahweh and Israel. It has also been later viewed as the close relationship between Christ and the Church as well as between God and the individual soul.

The wedding has always symbolized the celebration of the joy of the kingdom of God. The prophetic image for the final healing of God's relationship with the people was the wedding. The Prophet Isaiah finds the celebration of marriage as a sign of heavenly blessing, which God sends upon his righteous people in the future (Is 61.10; 62.4–5).

The institution of marriage and its sacredness got much more importance during the post-prophetic days of the Jewish history. According to the details given in Talmud and the other writings dealing with the Jewish rituals, marriage was not considered a merely social event or limited to a contract between two individuals of opposite sexes. It was also not merely the beginning of a loving and lasting

[9]Matthew the Poor, "Wedding in Cana," 11.

relationship between a man and a woman. Marriage was believed to be a mystery where a woman and a man entered into a union with a covenant-like commitment of lasting love that was akin to the relationship between Yahweh and his people.

Austrian rabbi Alfred Edersheim (who later converted to Christianity) reveals in detail and in depth through his writings the Hebrew wedding traditions during the days of Christ, according to the Talmud and other ancient books dealing with Jewish rituals. Matthew the Poor quotes abundantly from the rabbi's writings. The rituals of marriage celebration were initiated with the engagement, which is of great significance in the Jewish tradition. The term for engagement was *arousein qadoshenn*,[10] which means initiation of the couple into holiness. "It meant the solemn pledging of the couple, each to the other, and was so binding that to break it divorce proceedings were necessary. At the conclusion of the betrothal period the marriage took place."[11] Praising the beauty of the bride vividly with romantic descriptions and enumerating her virtues and elaborating on them were part of the extended engagement service.

The wedding took place in the house of the bridegroom. The bride, her friends, and family proceeded to the house of the bridegroom in a procession. Marriage "was considered a point of decision in the life of a young couple who fasted and confessed their sins before the wedding. In the Hebrew tradition, marriage was considered a 'mystery,' so much so that as soon as it was contracted all of the previous sins were automatically forgiven."[12] In the book of Genesis we have an actual representation of this significance. The wife of Esau, whose name before marriage was Bashemath (Gen 36.3), was called after the wedding Mahalath (Gen 28.9), meaning "whose sins have been forgiven."[13]

---

[10]Ibid., 12.

[11]Morris, *The Gospel According to John,* The New International Commentary of the New Testament (Grand Rapids, MI: Zondervan Academic, 1979), 178.

[12]Matthew the Poor, "Wedding in Cana," 11.

[13]Ibid.

Whenever the members of the Jewish community attended a marriage ceremony, it was a time for them to realize the mystical union between God and the people of Israel. The religious leaders participated in the celebration with great awe and, at the same time, with excitement and joy. Hence, it was the responsibility of the community to carefully plan for the marriage and provide for the feast to enjoy the celebration as best as they could. Usually the feast lasted almost a week. The onus of the wedding rituals and celebrations went beyond the family. If the bride and bridegroom were poor and unable to bear the burden of the lavish celebration, the members of the synagogue, especially the rich among them, would provide for the needs and means of enjoyment and excitement. Therefore, the marriage rituals were celebrated with reverence and piety, jubilation and joy.[14] Dancing, moderate drinking, and feasting were part of the extravagant celebration. All those events made the marriage a very important, sacred, and unique celebration.

St John informs his readers in the beginning of his Gospel presentation that Jesus is the bridegroom (a point noted in the other Gospels). Even though the bridegroom's name is missing in the Cana narrative, that of Jesus is mentioned a total of six times—four times Jesus alone and twice in relation to his mother ("the mother of Jesus"). Jesus calls himself the bridegroom in Mark 2.19–20. The same is true in Luke 5.33–35 and Matthew 9.15. In Luke, Jesus responds to Pharisaic question, "Can you make the wedding guests fast while the bridegroom is with them?" (5.34). It was followed by a reference to Jesus' death, "But the days will come, when the bridegroom is taken away from them, then they will fast in those days" (5.35). Matthew links marriage with the kingdom of heaven (22.1–10, 25.1–13). In the parable of the ten virgins in Matthew's Gospel (25.1–13), the bridegroom was none other than Jesus himself. John presents the same theme, quoting the words of the forerunner, John the Baptist, who figured himself as the best man of the bridegroom Jesus. "The one who has the bride is the

[14]Ibid., 12.

bridegroom; the best man, who stands and listens for him, rejoices greatly at the bridegroom's voice" (3.29).

The two most important images of the Church, according to St Paul, are the bride of Christ and the body of Christ. In marriage two individuals, a woman and a man, are united and bonded together in a mysterious way. Through the image of the bride of Christ, the deep, mystical, and inseparable relationship between the Church and Christ is brought out very clearly. This bridegroom is always faithful, and so is the bride. Jesus entered into an unbroken and deep marital relationship with a community of people who did not deserve to enter into such a relationship. In the Epistle to Ephesians, St Paul compares the relationship of Christ with the Church to that of the bride and bridegroom (5.22–32). The image of the bride and bridegroom brings out the disparity and unity between Christ and the Church.

In the image of the Church as the body of Christ and Christ as its head, the strong relationship, the great bond between Christ and the members of the Church, is brought out. In the body there are many parts, small and big, and all of them are strongly connected to one another and all of them are important. When one part of the body suffers, the whole body suffers. No part of the body exists for itself. It is the same blood that runs through the body and as part of Christ's body, the same blood is in Christ and the members of the Church. Thus, through the image of the body of Christ (1 Cor 12.12–28; Eph 1.23; Col 1.18) the members are linked to Christ who is the head of the body. The members of the body include not only those who are here but also those who have departed from their earthly existence as well as also those in future generations.

Jesus was invited to the wedding. He was invited with his disciples. How could one suggest that Jesus was the bridegroom if he was invited to the wedding along with his disciples? Hence, he was only a guest at the wedding and not the bridegroom. Still, there was a paradox as observed by John Marsh: "Jesus was invited with his disciples, and this is the astounding paradox of the story. The true and genuine, the only bridegroom of Israel, is present as an invited guest. And yet he does

not come alone, but with his disciples, the Messiah is no true historical figure without a people of the Messiah; the new Israel, like the old,
consists not in God in awful isolation, nor in a people apart from their
God, but with both conjoined."[15] Possibly one of the purposes of the
Cana sign was also to reveal the presence of the eternal bridegroom
even if he was an invited guest at the wedding.

Oddly enough, usually in a marriage feast, the bridegroom is
not the person responsible for providing wine, especially during the
middle of the feast. All the arrangements would be made in advance
and there would be people in charge of the feast. The bride and the
bridegroom are king and queen and the most important persons on
the wedding day, and they are least bothered about other matters
including things like what is there and what is not there. In the wedding scene at Cana, the headwaiter was addressing and appreciating
the bridegroom for providing the best wine at the end. The headwaiter
assumed that the latest supply of the best wine was the result of the
careful and clever planning of the bridegroom, and he contrasted "the
bridegroom" with "everyone." "But on this occasion of a wedding
among God's people there is present not only the bridegroom who
is to marry his Galilean bride, but the bridegroom who has come to
claim as his true bride all the scattered people of God."[16] Here also
through the headwaiter the author of the Gospel was pointing to Jesus
Christ as the bridegroom.

Jesus Christ made a point of inaugurating his ministry and revealing his glory at a wedding. He was actually making use of the occasion
and the sign to point to the consummation of his ministry when he
invites us all to attend his own wedding, "the marriage supper of the
Lamb" (Rev 19.9), when we shall be the center of the wedding, our
place being that of the bride: "For I betrothed you to Christ to present you as a pure bride to her one husband" (2 Cor 11.2).[17] "Let us
rejoice and be glad and give him glory. For the wedding day of the

[15]Marsh, *John*, 144.
[16]Ibid., 146.
[17]Matthew the Poor, "Wedding in Cana," 12.

Lamb has come, his bride has made herself ready. She was allowed to wear a bright, clean linen garment. Then the angel said to me, 'Write this: Blessed are those who have been called to the wedding feast of the Lamb'" (Rev 19.7–9). Jesus is the bridegroom and we are his "bride." As his bride, we are inseparable from the bridegroom. "Thus the sign at the wedding in Cana of Galilee implicitly draws our attention to the real role of Jesus both at Cana and in our own lives: for he is the true Bridegroom wherever we are as a bride always accompanying her groom. In other words, the wedding in Cana is our own wedding and the bridegroom is our own Bridegroom, and our soul is the bride."[18] Perry writes, "The presence of Jesus at this marriage feast reminds us that Jesus, our bridegroom-Savior, is always present at his supper (14:18–20). His marvelous provision of a prodigious quantity of wine (2:6–9) recalls that he continually pours out the inexhaustible wine of God's love, the Spirit (20:22), for his bride, the church, and all of their children."[19]

For St Augustine, the purpose of Jesus Christ's incarnation was for a wedding, Christ's own wedding. The bridegroom Jesus Christ offered his blood, his life for his bride. Augustine observes:

> The Lord was invited and came to a wedding. Is it any wonder that he who came to that house for a wedding came to this world for wedding? Therefore he has a bride here whom he has given the Holy Spirit as pledge. He wrested her from enslavement to the devil. He died for her sins. He arose again for her justification. Will anyone offer his blood? For if he gives his blood to his bride, he will not be alive to take her as his wife. But the Lord, dying free of anxiety, gave his blood for her in order that when he arose, he might have her whom he had already joined to himself in the womb of the Virgin. For the Word was the bridegroom, and human flesh was the bride. And both are the Son of God and likewise the Son of man. That womb of the Virgin Mary where he

---

[18]Ibid.
[19]Perry, *Evolution of the Lord's Supper*, 105–106.

became the head of the church was his bridal chamber. He came forth from there like the bridegroom from his bridal chamber, as Scripture foretold: "And he, as a bridegroom coming forth from his bridal chamber, has rejoiced as a giant to run the way." He came forth from the bridal chamber like a bridegroom; and having been invited, he came to the wedding.[20]

Thus, Jesus Christ was the true bridegroom who saved his bride from the devil and death through his blood and sacrificial death and still remains as the eternal bridegroom.

The house where the wedding took place, as there Jesus Christ was present along with his disciples and mother, was a symbol of the Church, according to the many of the Fathers of the Church. Evdokimov writes:

At Cana, Christ "manifested His glory" within the confines of a "household Church" (*ecclesia domestica*). In fact, this wedding is the wedding of the spouses to Christ. It is He who presides at the wedding of Cana and, according to the Fathers, at every Christian wedding. It is He who is the one and only Bridegroom whose voice the friend hears and in which he rejoices. This dimension of the mystical betrothal of the soul to Christ, of which marriage is the direct figure, is that of every soul and that of the Church-Bride.[21]

Jesus Christ, the true bridegroom, is present in every marriage uniting the bride and bridegroom as one body, and he accepts the new couple as members of the Church, his body, in their new relationship, thus enabling the newly married to be a reflection of the eternal bridegroom, Jesus Christ and the eternal bride, the Church.

[20]Augustine, "Tractates on the Gospel of John 8.4.1–3," *John 1–10* (ACCS NT IVa), 89–90. (Quoted from *The Fathers of the Church: A New Translation*, vol. 78 [Washington, DC: Catholic University of America Press, 1992], 182–183.)

[21]Evdokimov, *The Sacrament*, 123.

10

"Woman" & "Hour"

The wedding in Cana narrative contains a conversation between Jesus Christ and his mother, the Virgin Mary, as well as Jesus' direction to the servants who were told by the mother of Jesus to follow up on her Son's instructions to them. The response by our Lord to his mother, "Woman, what is it to you and me? My hour has not yet come," is confusing and difficult one to comprehend, and just as it has baffled many in the past, it is still doing the same. Hence, is it not surprising if the ordinary reader finds it confusing. One has to delve deep to understand the mysteries that are hidden in the meaning of words like "woman" and "hour" in this context. The words of our Lord have deep theological and biblical connections and are also greatly related with his redemptive work. There are some even among scholars who use Jesus' words to his mother to ignore or evade the place of Virgin Mary in the Church and her role in salvation history.

"Woman, What is it to you and me?"

The Cana sign contains one of the three conversations between Jesus and his mother recorded in the Gospels. Of the three, two are in the Fourth Gospel, one at Cana, at the very beginning of the public ministry, and the other at the conclusion of his ministry while he was on the cross. The third, and the only one that was earlier than the other two, is in Luke's Gospel. The conversation recounted in Luke happened when Jesus was a twelve-year-old boy, when he was lost and found in the Jerusalem temple. When the grieving mother found

Jesus his response was, "Why did you search for me? Did you not know I had to be in my Father's house?" (Lk 2.49). These were the first recorded words of Jesus in that Gospel. All these responses appear to be enigmatic and confusing, especially to a modern reader, who may understand them as suggesting an austere and possibly unpleasant relationship. They have seemed not to be positive responses and have been interpreted as not the right way for a son to react to his mother.

When the mother of our Lord informed her Son about the absence of enough wine, the first response from him was, "Woman, what is it to you and me?"[1] (It possibly means, "Never mind; don't be worried." Or as Barclay puts it, "Don't worry, you don't quite understand what is going on; leave things to me, and I will settle them in my own way."[2] Such a response has elicited various kinds of interpretations to the extent of negating the unique place of Virgin Mary in salvation

---

[1]In the Syriac Bible it is, "*Athso Mo liu lekhe,*" which means "What is it to you and me?" It is said that the Aramaic as well as Hebrew phrase is difficult to translate exactly into other languages. The Vulgate has, "*Quid mihi et tibi,*" which means "What to me and to thee." It is interesting to read the way it is put in different English translations.

The Orthodox Study Bible: "Woman, what does your concern have to do with Me?"

The New Oxford Annotated Bible (Revised Standard Edition): "O woman, what have you to do with me . . ."

The Harper Collins Study Bible: "Woman, what concern is that to you and to me?"

The Jerusalem Bible: "Why turn to me?"

The Complete Parallel Bible: "Woman! that is no concern of mine."

New American Bible (Catholic Book Publishing Co.): "How does your concern affect me?"

The New American Bible: "Woman, how does this concern of yours involve me?"

The Anchor Bible: "Woman, what has this concern of yours to do with me?"

William Barclay: "Lady, let me handle this in my own way."

New International Version: "Dear woman, why do you involve me?"

New Living Bible: "Dear woman, that is not our problem."

American King James: "Woman, what have I to do with you?"

Knox Bible: "Why dost thou trouble Me with that?"

New International version (2011): "Woman, why do you involve me?"

Phillips Bible: "Is that your concern, or mine?"

New English Bible: "Your concern is not mine."

[2]Barclay, *The Gospel of John*, 83.

history. In fact, it is not easy for others to interpret the way a loving son and mother communicate.

The meaning of words changes according to the context and the way they are expressed. A smile can be interpreted positively or negatively, and it all depends upon the context and the people. It can hurt or heal and make or break friendships and relationships. Conversations between intimates are not held in literary language; phrases half-spoken and looks can convey messages. Even silences are fully understood and stand as substitutes for words. This is especially true when a mother and son communicate. Only the mother and son fully understand the love and concern behind such expressions.

An Unusual Response

At first glance, the response of Jesus to his mother appears to be an impolite and probably inappropriate response. It is all the more difficult to understand when one finds that in Hebrew or in Greek there is no tradition of a son calling the mother "woman."[3] Max Thurian observes, "Normally a Jew spoke of his mother as '*Imma,*' in Aramaic, 'Mother' 'my mother.' It is very strange for a son to speak of his mother as 'Woman' (Aramaic: *Itta*)."[4] In the same Gospel we read Jesus addressing the Samaritan woman (4.21) and Mary Magdalene (20.13) as "woman." In the Gospels, especially in the Fourth Gospel, wherever the term "woman" is mentioned, as already noted, it was a reference to the community to which she belonged.[5] That was true about the above two examples.

In Semitic languages it is a respectable term, especially to address an older person.[6] But that in no way justifies Jesus calling his mother the same way. (The New English Bible has "mother" instead of "woman," "because English has no precise equivalent for the Greek word (*gunai*) used. 'Woman' is too cold; 'lady' too precious; 'madam'

[3]Brown, *Death of the Messiah*, 188.
[4]Thurian, *Mary,* 137.
[5]Tarazi, *New Testament Introduction: Johannine Writings*, 157.
[6]Ibid.

too formal.")[7] Brown points out correctly, "To translate it as 'Mother' would both obscure his possibility and cloak the peculiarity of the address."[8] Certainly the use of the term "woman" is not to negate or devalue the relationship between Jesus and his mother, as the term "mother of Jesus" is repeated twice and "his mother" twice in the sign narrative. Hence, it is clear the term "woman" has symbolic and scriptural importance.

"Woman" in Aramaic, the original language, which was the *lingua franca* of that area at that time and the one Jesus used, is an affectionate and respectable term by which to address women; used in that language and that context, the word does not sound rather rude, as it does or in many of the translations into present-day languages. William Barclay writes, "In Homer it is the title by which Odysseus addresses Penelope, his well-loved wife. It is the title by which Augustus, the Roman Emperor, addressed Cleopatra, the famous Egyptian queen. So far from being a rough and discourteous way of address, it was a title of respect. We have no way of speaking in English which exactly renders it; but it is better to translate it Lady which gives at least the courtesy in it."[9]

The toughness and roughness of the reaction is felt all the more when we realize that the response was from a loving son to his caring mother. It seems to be an unwelcome reaction even if it is from an average son to his uncaring mother. Then how can we comfortably settle with the response of the Son of God who gave the commandment to obey one's father and mother? In fact, the response of Jesus Christ to Mary might divert the attention from the main event. The comment by John J. Kilgallen seems to have some validity. He observes, "It is the dialogue between Jesus and his mother, an exchange which would be strange at any time, but particularly here. One can heighten the problem by suggesting that the story would be very nice, compact miracle story, if one would simply leave out the

---

[7]Hunter, *The Gospel According to John*, 31.
[8]Brown, *The Gospel According to John*, 101.
[9]Barclay, *The Gospel of John*, 83.

famous v. 4: And Jesus said, 'What is this to me and to you, woman? My hour has not come.'"[10]

Some biblical scholars interpreted the verse according to their fanciful imaginations, though many consider it a common conversational phrase of those days. One was that the guests had not exhausted the wine, so there was no need for an immediate action on his part or on hers. But the words of St Mary, "They have no wine," just before Jesus' reply totally excludes such an inference. Another one was that Jesus wanted the master of ceremonies to inform him about the need rather than his mother. That too seems unlikely, according to the context. It is interesting to read the observation made by Neal M. Flanagan. He writes:

> Verse 4, "Woman, how does your concern affect me? My hour has not yet come," is extremely difficult to explain. Cancel the verse out and the story flows with ease. Leave it in, as the text itself demands, and we have the mother asking, Jesus responding negatively, yet the sign taking place. Leave it in, and we must ask: Why does Jesus call his mother "woman"? Why is his verbal response negative but his action positive? Of what "hour" does Jesus speak? Explanations of all this are multiple and extremely divergent. One of the most probable is that verse 4 was not in the original pre-Gospel account, which presented a straightforward story of the incident in which the mother's request was answered by the son's positive response. The evangelist, however, who wished to use the story for his theme of new beginnings, inserted verse 4 to affirm, as do the other Gospels, that during Jesus' public life, until his hour came, his work was determined solely by the Father's will. It is this which is stated by the negative tone of the response and by the use of the impersonal "Woman."[11]

[10]John J. Kilgallen, *A Brief Commentary on the Gospel of John* (New York, NY: Mellen Biblical Press, 1992), 2.

[11]Flanagan, *The Gospel According to John*, 13.

It can mean, "What business is it of ours?" or it can mean simply, "Please, not now." Giovanni Miegge observes, "The least that can be said is that it marks a limit between the one who asks and the one who should reply, and gives to understand that the request is too much or is untimely."[12] This was clear from Jesus' response about time.

Why did Jesus interpret the words from his mother that they had no wine as a request from her for action on his part? There is no clue in the narrative. Though she didn't ask explicitly for action—only a miracle would solve the problem—her words probably seemed nothing less. Even if the response of Jesus appeared to be negative, for his mother it was certainly positive. Or in other words, behind the "No," we assume, she heard "Yes" only. The mother of Jesus could understand her Son better than anybody else.

A thorough understanding of the original language and the context will help us much better to comprehend Jesus' reply. Still it would appear as a reactionary response. The very verse has become unfortunately a favorite one for many who wanted to belittle St Mary in her relationship with her Son and her lofty place in salvation history. To a few, at least among Christians, as already pointed out, the verse has given enough ammunition to establish that Virgin Mary has no special place after she gave birth to Jesus. They compare her to an eggshell and a basket: the eggshell is useless and a waste after what is inside is used, and the basket is valuable only because of its use for keeping things safe.

"What concern is that to you and to me?" is a troublesome question. "Yet the literal meaning, 'What to me and to thee?' rather than separating them, binds them together in purpose, especially in view of His explaining 'for mine hour is not yet come.'"[13] Mary, at that moment, is not sure how and when Jesus' glory will be revealed. In this conversation possibly the mother and the Son were speaking to each other with two different perspectives.[14] It also invites her to

[12]Giovanni Miegge, *The Virgin Mary: The Roman Catholic Marian Doctrine,* trans. Waldo Smith (Philadelphia, PA: Westminster Press, 1955), 26.

[13]Archbishop Dmitri, *The Holy Gospel According to Saint John,* 48.

[14]Waetjen, *The Gospel of the Beloved Disciple,* 117.

adopt the outlook of her Son and to abandon her own initiative in order to follow his. It is clear that the Cana event is an important milestone on the way of "Mary's conversion, for she is made to understand that her role henceforth is to lead servants to her Son and to listen to his word and obey it fully."[15] In spite of the reactionary response of Jesus to Mary, whether it is a rebuke or not, she believed in her Son completely and unconditionally. To summarize, "Because the mother of Jesus, despite the rebuke that her Son directed toward her, trusted completely in the efficacy of the word of Jesus, the disciples have come to see the sign, the *doxa*, and they have come to faith."[16]

"Woman" in Biblical Language

The term "woman" has deep biblical roots and is a word with great theological connotations.[17] It was through Eve, the first woman, that the fall occurred and paradise was lost. Eve is called in the Genesis story "the woman" who instigated Adam to disobey God. It is wrong to interpret that Jesus was signaling to her that he was not going to misuse his power at her request. (Of course, her Son performed the miracle and revealed his glory). It was also said at the time of the fall that the offspring of the woman would destroy the head of the dragon that had prompted and drawn Adam and Eve to the fall. Jesus is that offspring of the "woman" who came to demolish the demonic

---

[15]Alain Blancy, Maurice Jourjon, and the Dombes Group, *Mary in the Plan of God and in the Communion of Saints* (Mahwah, NJ: Paulist Press, 2002), 67.

[16]Maloney, *Belief in the Word*, 91–92.

[17]James Puthuparambil notes the four references in the Scripture which refer Mary as "woman" thus: "In the Book of Genesis, Mary is spoken of as 'woman' whose Son will bruise the head of the serpent (Gen 3:15). The second reference is at the marriage at Cana where Jesus speaks of Mary, His mother as 'woman.' And the third is in Calvary Jesus turns to His mother and says, 'Woman, behold, your son!' (Jn 19:26). The fourth text in which Mary is called woman is in the book of Revelations. John saw a portent in heaven: 'a woman clothed with the sun, with the moon under her feet, and on her head a crown of twelve stars [. . .]' (Rev 12:1). We admit that only Cana incident refers directly to Mary, all the others can be attributed to Mary only because of the meaning they have in the context." *Mariological Thought*, 233.

domains. On the cross, while Jesus Christ was destroying the head of the serpent, Mary was called once again "the woman" (19.26).

> The passion and death of Jesus is seen in the Fourth Gospel as the triumph of Jesus over the Prince of this World (12:31; 14:30); and at the very moment of his triumph Mary is brought back on the scene, addressed as "woman," and brought within the family of discipleship. In other words, the two Johannine scenes in which Mary is addressed as "woman" may be seen as a reenactment of the Eve motif with a happier ending.[18]

Early Fathers like Justin Martyr[19] in the mid-second century, and a little later Irenaeus[20] and Tertullian, compared St Mary to Eve, the new Eve. The process of the destruction of the demonic powers was initiated during the wedding feast at Cana where Jesus inaugurated his public ministry. The Son of "the woman" was the one who would do it. That "woman" was the one for whom the whole creation had been anxiously waiting. It was in the presence of the Virgin Mary that the ministry of Jesus was consummated at Calvary. Here also Jesus uses the term "woman" to address his mother. "She is addressed in this manner to alert us that we should understand her as the New Eve for whom the archetypal 'woman' in Genesis is the midrashic[21] prototype. The maternal role of the New Eve is indicated when the dying Jesus recommends her to the beloved disciple (who signifies ideal discipleship) as that disciple's 'mother' (19:27)."[22]

There is another characteristic also to identify Mary as the New Eve. Perry writes:

> We should recall that the Old Eve was taken as helpmate from the side of the Old Adam when God caused him to fall asleep in

---

[18]Brown, *The Death of the Messiah*, 189–190.

[19]Justin Martyr, *A Homily Concerning the Faith* (11) 12:8, in Richardson, *The Early Christian Fathers*, 224.

[20]Irenaeus, *Against Heresies* 19:95; ibid., 390 and 126.

[21]A Jewish method of scriptural exegesis.

[22]Perry, *Exploring the Evolution of the Lord's Supper*, 108.

the garden of Paradise (Genesis 2:21–22; see John 19:41; 20:15b). Correspondingly, the Fourth Evangelist midrashically alludes to Jesus as the New Adam who has "fallen asleep" in death (19:33; see also 11:11–14) on the new tree of the cross. From the pierced side of Jesus (19:34), God is beginning to bring forth the New Eve, symbolized by Mary standing below (19:25). (The Greek word which the Fourth Evangelist uses for the pierced "side" (*pleura*) of Jesus is the same word used in the Greek Septuagint for one of the "ribs" (*pleuron*) taken from Adam's side to form Eve.)[23]

The first time Jesus addressed her as "woman," he advised her—or rather admonished her—that his "time" had not yet come. When he called her "woman" the last time, the "time" had already arrived. If Jesus revealed his glory at the wedding scene right in front of his mother before the arrival of his "time," he perfected and culminated it on the cross in her presence at the fullness of his "time." In both places Mary was associated with the disciples. The Cana event took place during the time of the calling of the disciples. One can notice a parallel between Jesus' performing the miracle at the request of his mother on water to make wine at the wedding and Adam eating the forbidden fruit as directed by Eve at the garden of Eden.

Addressing Mary as "woman" can be seen and interpreted in an entirely different sense, as the divine Son of God addressing his human mother. Fr. Matthew the Poor observes, "In order to clear away the mystery which envelops the way the Lord addresses her ('O woman') we should understand that Christ speaks here as God, for he is about to work a miracle of supernatural creation. In other words, the Son of God is here addressing his human mother."[24] Many Fathers including John Chrysostom and Augustine are of the same opinion. Ammonius of Alexandria (fifth century) writes, "He chides his mother for having importunely reminded God, who has no need to be reminded of anything. It is as if he had said, 'Do not regard me only as a man but also as God. Not yet has the time of my manifestation come. Not as yet it

[23]Ibid.
[24]Matthew the Poor, "Wedding in Cana," 13.

is known who I am.'"[25] Jesus Christ is perfect God and perfect man. Hence, it is not good to separate his actions and words as one related to his humanity and another one to divinity. Still, in everything he did, the purpose was to please his heavenly Father much more than anybody else, including his beloved mother.

The same is true of Jesus' response when Mary and Joseph had lost him in the temple. Matthew the Poor continues, "Thus Christ is eloquently indicating to the Virgin that he has come into his divine sphere to begin his supreme ministry which by no means admits the counsel of a woman or any human being. At the age of twelve he had once told her, 'Did you not know that I must be in my Father's house?' (Lk 2:49). But now he has entered forever into his mystic relation with the Father, where the only counsel is from the Father and from no one else."[26] Jesus' response to those who told him about the presence of his mother and brothers was, "Here are my mother and my brothers. For whoever does the will of God is my brother and sister and mother" (Mk 3.34–35). The mother of Jesus is not only his mother but also the mother of all believers, the symbol of the Church, as already noted. Was she representing all the faithful right there while asking for a miracle? Probably so.

"What is it to me and you," is a biblical idiom (a Semiticism) that we see in many passages in the Old Testament. "But the king replied: 'What business is it of mine or of yours, sons of Zeruiah, that he curses'" (2 Sam 16.10). Or "David replied: 'What has come between you and me, sons of Zeruiah . . .'" (2 Sam 19.23). It has two shades of meaning as suggested by Raymond E. Brown.[27] The context for one occurs when a person unreasonably bothers another, and the one who is bothered may say, "What is it to me and to you?" meaning, "Why you do it to me since I did not do anything against you to deserve it" (see also Jud 11.12; 2 Chr 35.21; 1 Kg 17.18). In the other context, a person is forced to do something that he feels is not his business, and

[25]Ammonius, "Fragments on John 57," *John 1-10* (ACCS NT IVa), 91.

[26]Matthew the Poor, "Wedding in Cana," 13.

[27]Brown, *The Gospel According to John*, 99.

so his reaction may be to say to the other person, "What is it to me and to you?" with the meaning, "That is your business, why involve me?" (see Kg 3.13; Hos 14.8). Thus, Jesus was using a phrase at the wedding which was possibly very familiar to the people at that time, especially for both Jesus and his mother, who were well aware of those scriptural passages.

It is worthwhile to note that one of the reasons as presented by St John Chrysostom for Jesus' response, "What have I to do with you?" was "It was that His miracles might not be suspected. The request ought to have come from those who needed, not from His mother. And why so? Because what is done at the request of one's friends, great though it be, often causes offense to the spectators; but when they make the request who have the need, the miracle is free from suspicion, the praise unmixed, the benefit great."[28] Blessed Theophylact has the same view. " 'If there is no more wine,' He says, 'let the host approach Me and ask for help, not you—because you are my mother.' If a man performs a miracle at the request of a family member, the bystanders who witness the miracle might suspect that it had been pre-arranged. But when the one in need of help makes the request, there is less cause for suspicion."[29] Jesus performed the miracle not for the sake of publicity but to resolve a problem. Hence, suspicion doesn't seem to have much place in that context.

The creation story says that God did not want Adam to be alone, and that was why he fashioned Eve as Adam's mate and companion. It is also true that Eve was created from Adam's bone. Hence, without Eve, Adam was in a way incomplete. It was totally and completely true in another sense in the case of Mary. It was her cooperation and willingness that paved the way for the incarnation of our Lord. In the wedding scene at Cana, the men and women who worked behind the scene must have noticed the absence of adequate wine for the feast. But it was a woman, not any woman, but Mary, who noticed what

---

[28]Chrysostom, *Homily 21* (NPNF[1] 14:74).

[29]Blessed Theophylact, *The Explanation of The Holy Gospel According to John* (House Springs, MO: Chrysostom Press, 2007), 39.

was lacking at the feast and tried to intercede on behalf of the family and resolve the problem.

In fact, the response from Jesus Christ is not easy to understand, because of the different shades of meanings attached to it. It is not easy for human beings to comprehend fully the words of our Lord. In order to resolve the problem at hand, the Son had to act; he had to advance his "hour." It was through Eve, the "woman" that the troubles started which led to the incarnation. In Cana, God's glory was about to be manifested through the sign, and there the "woman," the new Eve, the Virgin Mary, was the one who took the initiative for such a divine manifestation. If the first woman disobeyed and acted without God, "the new woman" wanted God to act. Archimandrite Theodor Micka writes, "Mary, knowing His mind and His mission—though dimly—but knowing also the slowness of the human understanding and its need for signs and patient teaching over a long period of time, nudged Him on to start His work in this way. He, knowing that her bidding in her humanness was a presumption, said, 'Woman, what have I to do with you?' yet, respecting her, He took action."[30] The Son of Man who is the Son of God might have thought of the difference between the first woman whose disobedience resulted in man's alienation from God and finally God's incarnation, and, at Cana, the "woman," his mother, who was seeking God's operation and cooperation. In conclusion, "While John the evangelist calls Mary the 'Mother of Jesus,' it is Jesus who reveals and assigns her vocation to her when he calls her 'woman' and appoints her to be the mother of the beloved disciple while she is at the foot of the cross."[31] By calling Mary "woman," Jesus was revealing her role beyond mere physical motherhood.

---

[30]Manley, *The Bible And The Holy Fathers*, 37–38.
[31]Blancy and Jourjon, *Mary*, 66–67.

"My hour has not yet come"

Strangely enough, Jesus' words, "Woman, what is it to you and me? My time has not yet come," can, in Greek, be interpreted as a statement as well as a question. It is interesting to read Dostoyevsky's observation about the passage. In *The Brothers Karamazov*, he writes about Jesus' response thus: "'Mine hour is not yet come,' He said, with a soft smile (He must have smiled gently to her). And indeed was it to make wine abundant at poor weddings that He had come down to earth? And yet He went and did as she asked Him . . ." (This chapter was entitled "Cana of Galilee").[32]

What is the meaning of "my hour," which also means time? There are a few other references to "time" or "hour" in the Fourth Gospel. "Therefore they sought to take Him; but no one laid a hand on Him, because His hour had not yet come" (7.30). "He spoke these words while teaching in the temple courts near the place where the offerings were put. Yet, no one seized Him, because His Hour had not yet come" (8.20). "The hour has come that the Son of Man should be glorified" (12.23). "Father, save me from this hour" (12.27). "Now before the Feast of the Passover, when Jesus knew that His hour had come that He should depart from this world to the Father . . ." (13.1). "Indeed the hour is coming, yes, has now come, that you will be scattered . . ." (16.32). "Father, the hour has come. Glorify Your Son, that Your Son also may glorify You" (17.1). It has been interpreted in various ways, such as: (1) the hour of the crucifixion; (2) the hour of the exaltation (the crucifixion and resurrection together); (3) the hour of the manifestation through signs and miracles; (4) the hour of Jesus' revelation as Messiah; (5) the time of his actions, not by his choice but as directed by the Father.[33]

One can see almost the same kind of response from Jesus to his brothers, "My time has not yet come, but your time is always ready" (7.6). In that particular context the difference was that his mother

[32]Fyodor Dostoyevsky, *The Brothers Karamazov* (New York, NY: New American Library, Division of Penguin Books, 1999), 347.

[33]McHugh, *The Mother of Jesus*, 366.

believed in Him but not His brothers (7.5). In essence Jesus was informing his brothers that the "old time" was theirs. That was not exactly Jesus' response to his mother. He was certain that he would act not according to human direction but in accordance with the heavenly Father's will, which he came down from heaven to do. Or in other words, providing wine at the banquet was not his main concern at that time. His mission was to bring the cosmos and Creator back together. "Jesus is present at a human celebration not in order to satisfy needs felt there but to manifest his glory and inspire faith. It is this latter purpose that he makes known in advance by performing the sign."[34]

Based on the Scripture, there are different attitudes towards time. There is ordinary time and sacred time. Sebastian Brock defines them thus:

> Ordinary time, is linear and each point in time knows a "before" and an "after." Sacred time, on the other hand, knows no "before" and "after," only the "eternal now": what is important for sacred time is its content, and not a particular place in the sequence of linear time. This means that events situated at different points in historical time, which participates in the *same* salvific content— such as Christ's nativity, baptism, crucifixion, descent into Sheol, and resurrection—all run together in sacred time, with the result that their total salvific content can be focused at will on any single one of these successive points in linear time.[35]

Time is holy and good. God became man at a specific time and in a specific place. He died, rose from the dead, and ascended to heaven at particular times in history. The Genesis story of creation says, "God divided the light from the darkness. And God called the light Day, and the darkness he called Night. And the evening and the morning were the first day" (1.4). He promised Noah that while the earth

[34]Blancy and Jourjon, *Mary*, 67.
[35]Sebastian Brock, *The Luminous Eye: The Spiritual World Vision of Saint Ephraim the Syrian* (Kalamazoo, MI: Cistercian Publications), 16. Cited by James Puthuparambil, *Mariological Thought*, 280–281.

remains, seedtime and harvest, and cold and heat, and summer and wind, and day and night should not cease (Gen 8.22). Yet, "my hour" is a very mysterious and meaningful phrase in the New Testament, and it usually does not connote the usual fraction of time especially in relation to Jesus Christ. "Hour" or "time" stands for the Son of God's suffering, crucifixion, and death. In the high priestly prayer Jesus said, "Father, the hour has come" (17.1). "We observe that his first reference to his 'hour' was to his mother; the last was to his Father."[36]

Jesus Christ possibly wanted to inform his mother that he had his own time, which would be decided by his Father. That hour or time had not yet come, even though he was in a pilgrimage towards the end. But, listening to his mother and obeying her request, he knew he was about to start the journey towards his "time," his death. His mother also was aware of that "hour," because she was the one who kept everything in her heart from the very beginning—although she did not understand it in its fullness. At that time she might have even thought of Simeon's words to her when Jesus was presented in the temple, "A sword will pierce your own soul too" (Lk 2.35). For Jesus, even if the day of his death was imminent as a result of his revealing himself, it was all right, and he was willing to accept the request of his mother, provided it would be in accordance with his Father's will. That was what happened at the wedding, in spite of the apparently indifferent response.

The almighty God acts, at times, at the insistent requests of his children. The parable of our Lord about the persistent widow and the inconsiderate judge (Lk 18.1–8) tells us that if we keep on asking, keep on seeking, and keep on knocking we will be answered positively. The judge who "neither feared God nor respected any human being" decided not to give any consideration to the widow's petition. But her consistent and persistent request changed the mind of the indifferent judge, which prompted him to act favorably on her petition. To the confident and constant request, the loving and caring God changes his divine plans.

[36]Phillips, *Exploring the Gospel*, 54.

"The hour" is the coming of the kingdom and eternal life. As Anthony Bloom writes, "Or 'Has everything that you learned from the angel, everything that you kept in your heart and pondered in the course of your life, revealed to you that 'I am here,' a presence which makes this human marriage unfold to the dimensions of the Wedding of the Lamb? If you are speaking to me because you are my mother according to the flesh, my hour has not yet come."[37] Jesus did leave the question hanging. The request Mary made was not because she was the mother and the mother had the right to ask her Son what she needed. It was an expression of her solid faith in her Son and at the same time to avoid a tragic and troublesome situation.

The Holy Virgin did not respond: "Am I not your mother? Do you not know how much faith I have in you?" She only answered him with a gesture, but it was much more convincing than all the words and phrases she could have uttered. Her words to the servants clearly showed her complete faith in her Son. She made a total, integral, unlimited act of faith, faith on which the Annunciation was founded; the faith that she bore witness to in being the mother of the Child-God now came to light in all its fullness. Because Mary believed in a perfect way, she established at this instant, in the village wedding, the kingdom of God.

> The holy Virgin, by this act of faith, established the conditions of the Kingdom and opened to God the doors of this village wedding. So it turns out that the hour of the Lord has come: it is the hour of the Kingdom, where everything is in harmony with God because man has believed. He blesses the exhausted waters, the useless waters, the waters soiled by washing, and transforms them into the wine of the Kingdom, into a revelation of something greater, which makes this wedding that had begun as a human event unfold to the measure of the Kingdom of God.[38]

[37]Metropolitan Anthony of Sourozh, *God And Man* (Crestwood, NY: St Vladimir's Seminary Press, 1983), 100–101.
[38]Ibid., 101.

John's Gospel structures three elements: "Mary-as-Mother-of-Jesus, Mary-as-woman, and Mary-as-mother-of-the-disciples, in a theological gradation: starting with 'Mary Mother of Jesus,' it proceeds by way of Mary as 'woman' to Mary 'mother of the disciples' with a new kind of motherhood that is of an order different from the first and that the church professes with him."[39] St Mary's role at Cana is very active and supremely important. Her thoughtful and discreet presence and actions changes a delicate and embarrassing situation to a pleasant one. Her role is subordinate and at the same time indispensable. The mother of God takes the initiative and speaks about the deficiency of wine that affects the festivities. "She was the intermediary between Jesus and the bridegroom and bypassing the chief steward, the waiters."[40]

[39]Blancy and Jourjon, *Mary,* 68.
[40]Michael O'Carroll, *Theotokos: A Theological Encyclopedia of the Blessed Virgin Mary* (Wilmington, DE: Michael Glazier, Inc., 1988), 97.

11

Water Became Wine

Once Blessed by Jesus, There is More than Enough

How did the water change into wine at the wedding scene? There was the great and urgent need. The mother of our Lord informed her Son and interceded before him about the problem. The servants obeyed what Mary told them. The culmination of all these was in the submission of the Son to the will of the heavenly Father. These things made the difference at the wedding and led to the mysterious miracle.

There was more than enough wine once the lack of wine was presented to Jesus through Mary's intercession, and through his divine intervention. At the request of the mother, Jesus transformed the ordinary water that filled the jars into a scintillating, colorful, and powerful wine. "In this miracle Jesus achieved instantly what God's power, plus man's labor, ordinarily brings about through a long process."[1] The almighty Lord acts with simple and ordinary events, things and persons and transforms them to a superior and sublime level. In the prayers (Penkitho) for the Sunday of the Wedding in Cana it is said, "His creative will turned to the water pots. He poured into them a pure essence, not coming from the grape. He performed a sacred sign upon the plain water which they contained, changing it into good wine."[2]

---

[1] Foster, *Studies in the Life of Christ*, 357.
[2] Acharya, *Prayer with the Harp of the Spirit*, vol. 3, *The Crown of the Year*, part II, 31.

Jesus pictures himself as the vine in the same Gospel (chapter 15) and the grapes are the product of the vine. In the sign, Jesus instantly makes wine of superior quality, avoiding the lengthy process of wine-making, and thus revealing his divine authority over nature and creation. It was a prelude to what would happen to wine in the coming together of the Church also. Close to Jesus' death, he blessed the wine and gave it to his disciples telling them that it is his blood of the New Covenant. The one who transformed water into wine in the wedding ceremony is transforming wine into his blood and the bread into his own body. Thus, Jesus started his ministry in this world with the miraculous sign involving "good wine" and ended his ministry with another incident involving wine, transforming it to his own blood.

Wine, Symbol of Joy and Happiness

Wine represents joy and feasting. In Latin there is a saying, "*In vino veritas*" ("In wine there is truth"). Probably it means that people are more likely to tell the truth when they drink wine or are under its influence. The absence of an adequate supply of wine is an important theme in the narrative of the wedding sign. Though the names of the bride and bridegroom are not mentioned in the sign, "wine" is mentioned five times and that itself proves the point. Wine, from a religious point of view, is a traditional symbol for prosperity, abundance, and happiness. For the Jewish religion and faith it was very true:

> It gives man a taste of the glory of creation. In this sense, it forms part of the rituals of the Sabbath, of Passover, of marriage feasts. And it allows [one] to glimpse something of the definitive feast God will celebrate with man, the goal of all Israel's expectations; "On this mountain the Lord of hosts will make for all peoples a feast of fat things, a feast of wine on the lees, of fat things full of marrow, of wine on the lees well refined." (Is 25.6)[3]

---

[3]Ratzinger, *Jesus of Nazareth*, 249.

Even in the book of Genesis we see the importance of wine as an offering to God. Melchizedek, king of Salem and priest of God, offered bread and wine to the Almighty (14.18). During the time of the prophets, wine symbolized messianic blessings (Amos 9.13; Hos 2.24; Joel 4.18; Is 25.6; Jer 31.5). Wine was considered by many Jews in the Old Testament times as a gift from the Messiah who was to come. In the Jewish meal (including the *chaburah*[4] supper) the food was blessed by the host or leader in the name of all present. But when wine was served, especially when it was refilled, each person also blessed when it was served. "By an exception, if wine were served at the meal each person blessed his own wine-cup for himself every time it was refilled, with the blessing, 'Blessed art Thou, O Lord our God, eternal King, Who create the fruit of the vine.'"[5] It shows the special place that they gave to wine in their meals.

The best wine was served last at the wedding in Cana. Usually what happens in a banquet is the opposite. What our Lord provides is always the best. There is another symbolic meaning to it. Until the coming of Christ, what was revealed to the Jewish community and the world at large was only partial, as "the fullness of time" had not yet arrived. "In the past God spoke to our ancestors through the prophets at many times and in various ways, but in these last days he has spoken to us by his Son, whom he appointed heir of all things, and through whom also he made the universe. The Son is the radiance of God's glory and the exact representation of his being, sustaining all things by his powerful word" (Heb 1.1–3). Bishop Sheen observes, "Truly the best wine was kept. Up until then in the unfolding of relation, the poor wine had been the prophets, judges, and kings. Abraham, Isaac, Jacob, Moses, Joshua—all were like the water awaiting the miracle of the Expected of the Nations."[6] Irenaeus of Lyons was of the opinion that the wine served in the beginning represents the time before

---

[4]It is a ritual meal for the Jewish people.

[5]Dom Gregory Dix, *The Shape of the Liturgy* (London: Dacre Press, Adam & Charles Black, 1964), 52.

[6]Sheen, *Life of Christ*, 78.

Christ. It was not of the best quality and was inadequate. The one that was served last, the one that was mysteriously made by Christ, represents the new time, the time of Christ.[7] Hence, it was superb in quality and was in abundance.

It is a custom in many cultures that the bride and bridegroom drink wine at the time of the wedding. Wine is a must for a Jewish wedding. There are two cups for the bride and bridegroom symbolizing the happiness and sorrow they may face in their journey together. The bride and bridegroom drink from both cups in order to show their willingness to face difficulties together and as equal partners. Wine is shared by the bride and bridegroom during the time of the engagement and at the time of the actual wedding ceremony, whether both ceremonies are conducted at different times or at the same time.[8] One of the prayers for the occasion as used by the Jewish Reformed liturgy brings out the symbolism of the wine:

> This cup of wine is symbolic of the cup of life. As you share the one cup of wine, you undertake to share all that the future may bring. All the sweetness life's cup may hold for you should be sweeter because you drink it together; whatever drops of bitterness it may contain should be less bitter because you share them. As I recite the blessing over the wine, we pray that God will bestow fullness of joy upon you.[9]

Wine was seen as a symbol of life and also as the symbol of evolution of the soul. Wine, because of its connection with the soul and afterlife, was one of the items offered to the deities in many ancient cultures. Grapes are to be completely annihilated to make wine. In the same way, only by annihilating one's self can immortality be attained. At the Last Supper, when Jesus blessed the wine, he told his disciples that it was his blood, meaning his very life. Even now during the Holy

[7]Cyril C. Richardson, *Early Christian Fathers* (New York, NY: Touchstone, 1996), 380.

[8]Kotatch, J Alfred, *The Jewish Book of Why* (New York, NY: Penguin Compass, 2003), 29.

[9]Ibid.

Liturgy, wine is transformed to the blood of Christ, and thereby those who receive it attain eternal life. Wine thus becomes life-giving as well as refreshing.

Wine was also considered as a powerful medicine. In the parable of the Good Samaritan, it is written, "He approached the victim, poured oil and wine over his wounds and bandaged him" (Lk 10.34). St Paul advises Timothy, "No longer drink only water, but use a little wine for your stomach's sake and your frequent infirmities" (1Tim 5.23). This medicinal value of wine is mentioned in other places in Scripture.

Wine, in another sense, is something that is supposed to bring flavor, joy, and happiness. The Psalmist says that wine, "Gladdens the heart of man" (103.15 LXX). One of the prayers of the Armenian Apostolic Church says, "The juice of the grape makes the wine which dispels sadness and creates gladness, as the Holy Bible states: 'Wine that makes glad the heart of man.'"[10] It was considered as a symbol of beauty also. Wine represents the exuberant side of life. In the wedding feast at Cana there was enough wine in the beginning. Hence there was plenty of joy and happiness. But that situation was changed later because the supply of wine was not sufficient for the gathering. In the absence of adequate wine, the celebratory moods and movements slowly disappeared, especially for the people who were responsible for the feast.

Wine Represents the Material Things of the World

Wine is a favorite drink for many. Though it is an exciting and enjoyable drink, the pleasure and joy it imparts is not lasting. The same was true at the wedding scene. One cannot depend upon worldly things. There is an urge, an insatiable longing in almost everyone for material things. But that urge in the end often leads to frustrations and disappointments. The reason is the limitations of material things, and the fact that man is created with an urge for things beyond and above this world. Our Lord told the Samaritan woman, "Everyone who drinks

[10]Prayer over the grapes on the day of the feast of the Dormition of the *Theotokos*.

this water will be thirsty again; but whoever drinks the water I shall give will never thirst; the water I shall give will become in him a spring of water welling up to eternal life" (Jn 4.13–14). Things of this world are not everlasting. That is why Jesus told the multitude, who after the multiplication of the bread and fish to feed them followed him for the satisfying of their hunger for bread forever, "Do not labor for the food which perishes, but for the food which endures to everlasting life" (Jn 6.27).

There was not enough wine. That was a very meaningful signal. Wine stands for worldly enjoyments, and these can be exhausted at any time, which is what happened at the wedding scene in the Gospel. The host probably thought that he had kept more than enough of a supply for all the guests. But at the crucial moment of serving the wine, there was not enough for the feast. While analyzing the Cana sign, John Chrysostom writes, "There are those who give their minds to the fleeting things of this present life, who despise not this world's luxury, who are lovers of glory and dominion; for all these things are flowing waters, never stable, but ever rushing violently down the steep."[11] It is a warning to married people: in marital life do not depend on the material part alone, as it can be exhausted at any time. And this warning is not limited to spouses alone. Whether one is single, monastic, married, or widowed, a life dependent mainly upon material things and worldly pleasures will ultimately fail.

Only when there is super-substantial wine from the Lord is there peace and harmony in oneself and at home. Only then can the spouses enjoy the blessings of marital bliss. Evdokimov writes,

> Through its action, the water of the natural passions is changed into "the fruit of the vine," the noble wine that signifies the transmutation into "the new love," a charismatic love springing forth to the Kingdom. This is why the *Theotokos*, like the Guardian Angel, bends over the world in distress: "They have no more wine," she says. The Virgin means to say that the chastity of old, considered

[11]Chrysostom, *Homily* 12 (NPNF[1] 14:78).

the integrity of being, has ceased. Nothing is left but the impasse of masculinity and femininity. The jars destined for the "ablutions among the Jews" are hardly sufficient; but "ancient forms have passed away"; the purification of the ablutions becomes baptism, "the bath of eternity," in order to grant access to the Eucharistic Banquet of the one and only Bridegroom.[12]

The transformation Jesus brings is the transformation of the kingdom of God, which is beyond the human and worldly standards. About wine, we read in the book of Proverbs:

Those who linger over wine, who go to sample bowls of mixed wine. Do not gaze at wine when it is red, when it sparkles in the cup, when it goes down smoothly! In the end it bites like a snake and poisons like a viper. Your eyes will see strange sights, and your mind will imagine confusing things. You will be like one sleeping on the high seas, lying on top of the rigging. (23.30–34)

If this is so, why did Jesus attend a marriage where wine was served? Why did he transform water into wine, an alcoholic drink? Why did he perform the miracle of having an abundance of wine? Why was the wine he made out of ordinary water of superior quality, making it strong and powerful? All these questions may baffle many. For many alcoholics, the wedding in Cana and the miracle of making wine from water unfortunately is the justification for using alcohol and is the theological and biblical basis for drinking.

In those days there were two main beverages, water and wine. Water was often polluted "through animal usage, washing, sewage, and plain dirt. This included water that had been collected in a cistern. For this reason wine was a staple drink."[13] In Palestine, where vineyards were common and grapes were one of the main crops, wine was a common drink. To mark pleasant and important events like weddings, wine was served. During those times wine mostly was diluted with water and was served not as an alcoholic beverage in

---

[12]Evdokimov, *The Sacrament*, 122.
[13]*The Life of the Virgin Mary, the Theotokos*, 305.

the Middle East. "Wine was diluted with water in the ancient world; the Jews diluted it in a proportion of one part wine into three parts water, to discourage drunkenness."[14] The minimum alcohol contents in the wine served as a natural antibacterial; such a drink was healthier than plain drinking water, which was often contaminated. "It is well known that the Jews were remarkable for their moderation in drinking wine, which in Palestine was a common drink usually mixed with water; to become drunk was considered completely inappropriate."[15] The rabbis were highly critical of drunkenness. Wine mixed with water, and thus without much alcoholic content, was the drink of the day, especially during celebrations, including marriages. The proportion of one part wine to three parts water was the Jewish custom of serving at celebrations and thus avoided excessive drunkenness during joyous celebrations. In the Gospel narrative of the wedding there is no drunkenness recorded. Foster observes, "The Greek word *oinos* (wine) does not necessarily mean intoxicating wine."[16] The wedding scene and the miracle are not excuses for alcoholic abuse.

Everybody Serves the Best in the Beginning

After tasting the wine that was miraculously made, the headwaiter was surprised and affirmed, "Everyone serves good wine first, and then when people have drunk freely, an inferior one; but you have kept the good wine until now" (Jn 2.10). Some scholars are of the opinion that the saying was a proverb, the first of a few in the Gospel, though there are no clear proofs in the extra-biblical literature that this is so.[17] Through the mouth of the steward a great truth has been revealed. "Now" is the time of the Messiah, the time of the coming of the kingdom of God. One enjoys the best through Christ and in

---

[14]Noted in the *Orthodox Study Bible: New Testament & Psalms*, 215.

[15]Archbishop Averky (Taushev), *The Four Gospels: Commentary on the Holy Scriptures of New Testament*, vol. 1, trans. Nicholas Kotar (Jordanville, NY: Holy Trinity Seminary Press, 2015), 33.

[16]Foster, *Studies in the Life of Christ*, 358.

[17]Collins, *These Things Have Been Written*, 137.

Christ only. It is in him that the fullness is revealed. Until then it was the poor wine that was served, whether it was patriarchs, fathers like Abraham, Isaac, Jacob, or prophets. "The world generally gives its best pleasures first; afterward come the dregs and the bitterness. But Christ reversed the order and gave us the feast after the fast, the resurrection after the Crucifixion, the joy of Easter Sunday after the sorrow of Good Friday."[18]

None other than the head steward attests the superb quality of the wine. Why the steward and not the servants who brought the pots to the steward or the guests who had drunk the wine? Nobody would believe the servants if they verified the quality of the wine. The other reason, suggested by John Chrysostom, was that Jesus did not want the miracle to be known instantly as he himself was not fully revealed.[19] For the guests, anybody could say that they were not sober. Chrysostom says, "For he does not say that the guests gave their opinion on the matter, but 'the ruler of the feast,' who was sober, and had not as yet tasted anything. For of course you are aware, that those who are entrusted with the management of such banquets are the most sober, as having this one to dispose all things in order and regularity."[20]

In the context of marital life, how true is that statement! At the time of the betrothal and especially at the time of marriage, the experience of the marital bliss is only initiated. It has just begun to be nurtured and matured. Hence, the best is yet to come. The emotional and worldly joy of the nuptial cup might soon be exhausted. If the relationship is not transformed to a spiritual level the relationship may easily and slowly begin to disintegrate. But in Christ marriage has been transformed, and in the wedding that Christ attended the order of the natural world was reversed and transformed. "The 'now' is the moment of Christ; it knows no passing. The more the spouses are united in Christ the more their common cup, the measure of

---

[18]Sheen, *Life of Christ*, 79.
[19]Chrysostom, *Homily* 22.2 (NPNF[1] 14:78).
[20]Ibid.

their life, is filled with the wine of Cana and becomes miraculous."[21]
In the mysterious transformation of water into wine, the nature and
character of the kingdom of heaven are revealed:

> The wine at Cana is the sign of the new world which Christ had
> just created during this first week of the new creation. The good
> wine of the new creation succeeds the less good of the old world;
> the new Covenant succeeds the old which has perished; the King-
> dom of God will succeed the time of the Church according to the
> words of the last Supper: "Truly I tell you I will not drink of the
> fruit of the vine until the day that I shall drink the new wine in
> the Kingdom of God." (Mark 14.25)[22]

One cannot consider heavenly joy and blessings through worldly
concepts. Usually, in every banquet the best is served first and the
worst last, though at Cana the best was served at the end, as attested
by the feast master. In the new world order established by the Messiah,
it is different. There is no difference between beginning, middle, and
end, and it is always going to be the same, as the kingdom of heaven
belongs to God Almighty, who is beyond change. Still, the climax of
the experience of the kingdom of God is at the end, which is to be
enjoyed in the eternal kingdom where time and space have no place.
The best of the kingdom of God is yet to be realized fully, not in this
world but in the world to come.

Those who drank the superb wine miraculously made, were not
aware of its origin. The mystery was hidden from them. Also, they did
not believe in Jesus also. They enjoyed the wine but were unable to go
beyond the superb flavor, taste, and quality of the drink. They were
not aware of the person who made it or the circumstances in which
it was made. We enjoy the world, all the material things provided by
God. But we often forget the one who gives all these to us.

---

[21]Evdokimov, *The Sacrament*, 123.
[22]Thurian, *Mary,* 126.

The Power of Man

Human beings, who have the image of God and divine likeness, are dynamic beings endowed with magnificent talents. The Psalmist says, "Yet you have them little less than a god, crowned them with glory and honor" (8.6). Children of God, men and women have the capacity to change water into wine. Even petty things that we encounter in our everyday lives can be transformed to noble and powerful moments if there is love and if almighty God is with us.

The problem the family in Cana confronted was an inadequate supply of wine to serve. The joy of the hour was lost. What should be done? To get it from outside was impossible at that place and time. When Mary looked at the face of Christ, she believed that her Son could convert the water in the well and would give them what they needed. They did not have to go outside. It was right there. If they went outside they would not have got what they wanted or whatever they might have gotten would not be the best one like that mysteriously and miraculously provided by Jesus Christ.

The power of a human being is fully exerted and experienced when he seeks the guidance of his divine Master and acts according to his will. Mary quietly used her power to resolve a serious situation. She was sure that by her letting her Son know about the problem, he would bring it to a happy ending. Others at the wedding who were aware of the impending situation were probably brooding over the difficulties they were about to confront. The mother of Jesus was optimistic as she knew very well, given the divine power of her Son as well as her own power as a human being, how to face such situations both positively and optimistically.

12

"They have No Wine"

Wine was the drink at the wedding banquet, just as at any other feast in those times. While the feast was going on, the supply of wine ran out. It was indeed a huge problem for the hosts. How could this be solved? When the "mother of Jesus" found out that the wine was soon to be exhausted, she conveyed to her Son, "They have no wine." It can also mean "They have no *more* wine."[1] The Greek word used there, *hystesantos,* implies two possibilities: there was not enough wine to be served as well as the wine there was of poor quality.[2] The first one is more suitable, but the response from the master of the feast about the best wine served last, fits the second possibility. These words from his mother prompted Jesus to perform the sign-miracle. The Virgin Mary's words served as catalyst for Jesus' action.

The words of the mother, "They have no wine," are thought by some to be similar to the desperate response to Jesus by the apostles during the miracle of the feeding of the multitude, "How can one feed these men with bread here in the desert" (Mk 8.4). Even though

---

[1] This verse has been translated differently though the common one is, "They have no wine" (The Orthodox Study Bible; it is the same way in the King James Bible also).

"They have no more wine" NIV Study Bible (The same is in some other Bible translations also).

"When the wine ran out . . ." The New International Version

"The wine supply ran out . . ." New Living Bible

"When they wanted wine . . ." American King James

"When the wine failed . . ." American Standard

"They have no wine left." Ronald A. Knox Translation

[2] Brant, *John,* 56.

running out of wine would create a difficult situation at the wedding, and the mother of Jesus was very much concerned about it, there was nothing in the narrative to indicate that she was desperate like the disciples in the situation just mentioned. Others surmise that she was informing her Son and his followers to leave the scene so that they could save the family from the embarrassment of the shortage of wine: there would be enough for the remaining guests. Even if the presence of the followers of Jesus was unexpected at the gathering, it is too much to assume that Mary's words to her Son were an indication to them to leave, as she had long been well aware of who her Son was. It was the practice of the time for the guests to bring provisions to the wedding celebrations, which lasted for a week. Bonnie Thurston suggests, "When the wine gives out, Mary, as Jesus' mother, has every right to ask him to provide more. As a guest, he was obliged to bring a present."[3]

It can easily be conjectured that the words of his mother were not limited to her Son's obligations as a guest, but possibly they meant much more than that. The provisions for the celebration were the responsibilities also of the participants. Since Jesus and his disciples were poor, some surmise, they had failed to bring the supply of wine and caused the shortage, and the mother was informing her Son of the reason for the shortage. It is also suggested that Mary was desperately asking her Son to do something, even to the extent of getting out and buying more wine. They forget the fact that it would have been impossible to do so in that rustic and remote area in those days. As already mentioned, there was nothing to show that Mary was desperate, other than her concern for the desperate family and her faith in her Son.

In those ancient times, when there were not so many celebrations or festivals as in modern days, marriage was a great and rare occasion for the families and the community to come together to make merry and entertain. In the Aramaic language, "the word for 'wedding feast' has the same roots as the word 'drink,' a sign that it was time

---

[3]Thurston, *Women in the New Testament*, 81.

of great revelry and rejoicing."[4] It was important that everything be done properly and in order. There was a kind of reciprocity involved in the marriage, in the sense that one who provided such and such quantity and quality of wine was entitled to an equivalent when his invitee's son was married, and expected it. This was even considered a legal obligation. Morris quotes J. Duncan M. Derrett:

> In the ancient Near East there was a strong element of reciprocity about weddings, and that, for example, it was possible to take legal action in certain circumstances against a man who had failed to provide the appropriate wedding gift . . . But it means that when the supply of wine failed more than social embarrassment was involved. The bridegroom and his family may well have become involved in a pecuniary liability.[5]

If there was not enough wine to serve everybody present, it was a serious matter with cultural, social, legal, and other ramifications.

Another opinion, which was supported by John Calvin, the Protestant Reformation leader, and some others, is that Mary was informing Jesus "to offer some religious exhortation, for fear the company might be wearied, and also courteously to cover the shame of the bridegroom."[6] In no way would an exhortation help to resolve the situation; nothing would suffice other than to supply what was needed at the wedding. Leslie D. Weatherhead, in his book *It Happened in Palestine,* writes on the sign thus: "The wine runs out. Water is served. Why, that's the best joke of all! They lift their wine-cups, as we do in fun when we shout, 'Adam's ale is the best of all.' The bridegroom is congratulated by the master of ceremonies, who carries the joke farther still. 'Why you've kept the best wine until now.' It requires only a servant going through the room into kitchen for a wonderful rumor to start."[7] It is strange and indeed petty to relegate a sign that

---

[4]Jean Vanier, *Drawn into the Mystery of Jesus through the Gospel of John* (Mahwah, NJ: Paulist Press, 2004), 51.

[5]Quoted in Morris, *Reflections on the Gospel of John,* 17.

[6]Towns, *The Gospel of John,* 622.

[7]Quoted in Morris, *The Gospel According to John,* 175.

manifested the glory of the Lord and edified the disciples to believe in him to the level of a mere joke. Hence, it is better to consider such a suggestion a joke rather than an opinion worth considering.

An Excellent Example of Communication

What Mary told her son will always remain an excellent example of communication, not only to God but also to our fellow human beings. The success of the life of a person depends, to a certain extent, on his or her communication skills. What we say and how we say it is very important. "The word is a self-manifestation, a revelation, a presence, a power, a mode of communion and union between hearer and speaker."[8] The words we use can harm others and hence the proverb, "Words are stronger than bullets." Or, they can also comfort and console. The Canaanite woman in the Gospels is an excellent example of good communication skills in the midst of troublesome and difficult circumstances. She earnestly approached Jesus Christ on behalf of her sick daughter despite the many heavy barriers that were in existence at the time (Mt 15.21–28). Through her gentle words and pleasant and positive attitude, she was able to get what she wanted even though the disciples considered her a nuisance when she approached Jesus and he was reluctant to grant her wish in the beginning. It was the tone of the Canaanite woman's words and her attitude that made the difference. Mary communicated to her Son the need of and urgency for his involvement through her simple words.

Words can affect one's self-esteem and people may have to live bearing the scars caused by biting and wounding words. St James writes, "So the tongue is a little mentor and boasts of great things. Consider how a small fire can set a huge forest ablaze. The tongue is also a fire. It exists among our members as a world of malice, defiling the whole body and setting the entire course of our lives on fire, itself set on fire by Gehenna" (3.5–6).

---

[8]Thomas Hopko, *All the Fullness of God* (Crestwood, NY: St Vladimir's Press, 1982), 61.

Just like words, a look can either hurt or heal us. It can confuse us, correct us, or comfort us. That is very true of all of our actions, reactions, and movements. On the eve of Jesus' passion, he "turned and looked at Peter" after the apostle's denial (Lk 22.61). That caring look had a strong and lasting effect on the apostle. It was a look that led to him to tears and remorse. Jesus' simple but significant look became the turning point for Peter's life. Peter once was scared to death in front of a servant girl at the palace. But he was completely changed, and later he confronted the emperor to his face, standing for the truth. It was the powerful and meaningful look of our Lord that brought about a total transformation in the fallen and fearful apostle. Jesus also communicated more through silence while he was in the chamber of Pontius Pilate. Those silences conveyed more than his words. In fact, Pilate was stunned, saddened, and above all totally confused by that silence.

The mother of God was able to communicate with a few simple words the impending difficult situation. The contents of her words conveyed the urgency of the need for action on her Son's part as well as her care and concern for those who were about to face the problem. It was presented in such a way that the problem would be resolved. Mary stands in the sign as an effective and excellent communicator.

A Model Prayer

"They have no wine." In the narrative, these were the words communicated by Mary to her Son about the situation at the celebration, and at the same time it turned out to be an exceptionally great model prayer. It remains an example of how our prayer ought to be, a paradigm for all prayers. Mary addressed the need of the hour in an extremely matter-of-fact way with great confidence and clarity, and in a concise manner. Nobody could attribute any selfish or egotistic goals to her humble and simple request. It was clear expression of her confidence in her Son, and of her concern for the members of the family who were unexpectedly going through a great crisis.

For any human being, prayer should be like breathing, but most of the time one fails to pray properly. Even the apostles were ignorant of it, and therefore Jesus taught them how to pray with the Lord's Prayer. St Paul says that everyone needs the assistance of the Holy Spirit to pray properly and with the right perspective. Sometimes prayers become a cacophony of language or words, often of words "signifying nothing." For many, prayer has become an exercise in repeating mundane jargons, and for others it has become a shouting match, full of thunderous yelling of nonsensical, trivial utterances, as if the Almighty were deaf and dumb. Some are concerned only about style and content, while some others about sound and music. A few of the extemporaneous prayers appear like excellent essays, because often the purpose of such utterances is not to please heaven but to please people and a congregation or audience. When we give importance to those things our prayers become "sounding brass or a clanging cymbal" (1 Cor 13.1). Often such prayer is mechanical and an exercise without much faith, thought, or intensity, but cloaked with expressions of emotion. Above all, what is lacking is the guidance of the Holy Spirit.

We see the essence of a successful prayer in Mary's request to her Son. It is a prayer, so plain and simple, one of the shortest and best prayers recorded in Scripture. But the prayer remains one of the most confident and assuredly faithful prayers of all time. Her supplication was a very realistic presentation of the situation.

Mary informed her Son, "Son, they have no wine." The response from Jesus was somewhat of a refusal. It was indeed a refusal even before any request was made: "What is that to me and to you? My hour is not yet come." The reaction and the response seem to be Jesus' way of telling her that the problem the family was going through was none of their business. She did not ask him to do anything through words or language, the usual and most common way of communication. But the response from the Son was in the affirmative followed by immediate action. It was a positive gesture even though his words did not appear to be. That was why she advised the attendants to follow whatever her Son would tell them to do. If it were totally negative, she would not have given such an instruction.

There is not much left in the narrative for the outside world to understand the communications between the mother and the son. They were not adequately expressed in the common form of speech, i.e., in words. We see in the result the power and effect of the mother's prayer at Cana. Thus, the words of the mother of Jesus to her Son, "They have no wine," will remain as a perfect example of prayer.

The Power of Intercession

St Mary was presented in the very beginning of Christ's public ministry, at the very first sign, as a great intercessor and mediator. Mary's powerful mediation with her Son on behalf of others, along with the positive effects of that mediation, is vividly brought out in the wedding celebration. At the moment of crisis, though there were many people at the wedding and possibly some among them were aware of the impending problem, they failed to get involved and to resolve it. How could it be solved at that time in that place? Humanly it was impossible. But the mother of Jesus, the *Theotokos*, had an answer and a solution to resolve the crisis by seeking the assistance of the almighty Lord. It was Mary who utilized that great resource, and it was through her intercession to her Son that the impending problem was easily resolved.

As John 2.1 suggests, Mary possibly had already been at the home before Jesus and his disciples. She was not simply an invited guest at the wedding but was also greatly involved and had access to the place where food and drink were stored. The Virgin Mother had such freedom inside to infer in advance, "They have not enough wine." Thus, she was fully aware of almost all the things connected with the wedding banquet, along with what was going to be exhausted. Her keen sense of observation, concern, and care were evident at the sign. On the other hand, Mary was well aware who her Son was. She knew more than anyone else about the divine power vested in Jesus Christ.

She had firsthand knowledge about her Son from the angel at the time of conception. In the context of the family's return from the temple of Jerusalem, St Luke writes, "His mother kept all these things in her heart" (2.51). She was certainly sure that her Son was the Messiah. She was not only aware of the words of John the Baptist about her Son, but she also knew many of the Baptist's disciples had already left him to follow her Son. Jesus Christ was thirty years old at the time of the Cana wedding, and she thought it was the time for him to act. Hence, the Virgin Mother presented the matter with humble excitement and great expectation before him.

What Mary did at the feast in Cana is exactly the way saints act. Nobody told Mary to get involved to resolve the impending problem. She presented the problem before her Son without any request or remainder. The saints, like Mary, know the needs and necessities of the world and the people, and they constantly present them before God. It is always good that we seek their mediation, but we should also be aware that they act and pray for us even without our request and intercession. The wedding in Cana and the mother's actions there clearly prove that great truth.

Intercession is not reminding the Almighty of something he is not aware of or has forgotten. It is putting the intercessor in the mood and mindset of the troubled situation. Metropolitan Anthony Bloom beautifully presents what intercession is: "The word in Latin means to take a step which puts us at the heart of a situation, like a man who stands between two people about to fight."[9] The true intercessor, in many instances, must know very well the one to whom that person intercedes and the one for whom he intercedes or on whose behalf he intercedes. Only then will the intercession be powerful and effective. In all these matters, the intercession of Mary at the wedding scene stands as a superb paradigm.

How silently and effectively Mary interceded. She stayed behind and was invisible in her action. The right kind of intercession is always

[9]Bloom and LeFebvre, *Courage to Pray*, 55.

like that. Matthew the Poor links intercession in the Orthodox Church with the intercession of the Virgin Mother:

> In Orthodoxy, intercession raises us to the level of the intercessor, bringing us into the presence of Christ, then the mediator disappears. This is to say that intercession is a communion with Christ by grace; the Virgin grants us all the powers granted to her so that we might come before Christ. We then stand before Him as the Virgin, that is, in the spirit and grace of purity and holiness granted to us in her. This is what Paul did with all his might: "I betrothed you to Christ to present you as a pure bride to her one husband" (2 Cor 11.2). This speaks, in the first place, for the correctness of the Orthodox concept of intercession because in the last analysis it cancels out the distinction between the intercessor, that is the Virgin, and those who intercede with her. We take from the Virgin the courage that derives from her motherhood and her unique love for Christ. All these things are considered granted to her for our sake, and she, in her great confidence before God, is able to transfer them to us, just as a stronger member in the body grants its strength to a weaker one. Second, this kind of intercession removes all the barriers between us and Christ. We approach Him unhindered and unimpeded by our weakness, to take from Him help or ask for a particular request or healing or repentance. It is only this that can truly be called intercession. The interceding servant must be prepared to put himself in the place or situation of the servant for whom he intercedes, and must even be prepared to give all he has to make up for the deficiency of his fellow servant.[10]

During intercession, one takes up the pain, pressures, and needs of others and presents everything before God as if they were one's own personal problems and necessities. The one who offers intercession is completely empathetic with the person on whose behalf he intercedes. Intercession is always an uplifting action where one gives priority to

[10]Matthew the Poor, *The Communion of Love* (Crestwood, NY: St Vladimir's Press, 1984), 212.

the needs of the other rather than one's own. When it is done properly, it is a joyful, vicarious experience.

Only a person who is not self-centered can seek intercession properly. Mary was not self-centered and did only what was the will of God. She continuously intercedes for us, mainly to enable us in our life situations to seek and do the will of God. Of course, anyone who does the will of God, or in other words obeys his commandments, becomes the mother of Jesus, and his brothers and sisters. "And looking around at those who were seated in the circle he said, 'Here are my mother and brothers. For whoever does the will of God is my brother and sister and mother'" (Mk 3.34–35). The intercession of Mary is more powerful than all else, not because she was the one who carried Jesus in her womb for nine months and fed him when he was a child, but because of her closeness with her Son and above all throughout her life as she tried to do the will of God. Her intercession to her Son is never a long-distance call but a very close one. It is indeed a direct and straight call, a call that is always connected and considered and, hence, it is always answered.

The Virgin Mary's intercession was very strong and at the same time simple. She did not claim the recognition or acclamation from others for the miracle. Here one sees the right kind of intercession. Matthew the Poor refutes the disparaging critiques of seeking intercession from Mary by stating (as we noted earlier):

> When the Virgin intercedes for our aid, healing, or repentance, she draws us into the realm of her relationship with Christ. In Orthodoxy, intercession raises us to the level of the intercessor, bringing us into the presence of Christ, then the mediator disappears. This is to say that intercession is a communion with Christ by grace; the Virgin grants us all the powers granted to her so that we might come before Christ. We then stand before Him as the Virgin, that is, in the spirit and grace of purity and holiness granted to us in her.[11]

[11]Ibid.

The intercession of the Virgin Mary, according to the Cana wedding event, is for two things: for our shortcomings (2.3) and for our obedience to Christ (2.5). She brings before the Lord our burdens and problems even before we seek her intercession. She is certainly aware of her children's needs and shortcomings. She also knows to whom those ought to be submitted: to her own dear Son, "Jesus the mediator of the new covenant" (Heb 12.24). She pleads on our behalf so that we will be able to obey the Lord and avoid shortcomings.

The intercession of Mary is vital for us. That is why in our intercessory prayer, the *Hail Mary*, we say, "pray for us now and always, especially at the time of our death." The time of death is a crucial moment for all human beings and everyone needs spiritual strength to face death with courage, calmness, and confidence. All the disciples except one, left Jesus Christ at the time of his crucifixion and went into hiding, seeking their safety and security. But the mother of Jesus was right there at the foot of the cross. It is indeed a terrible and very sad sight, especially for a mother. She had the divine courage and strength to face such a painful situation. That is why we seek her mediation every day and in the intercessory prayer we request her prayers, especially at the time of our death.

Let us imagine that we are at the wedding feast at Cana. Try to listen to what Mary says to her Son, "They have no wine." Try to visualize that she is not speaking about what is lacking at the wedding feast at Cana in Galilee. She is not speaking to the bride, the bridegroom, or anyone else there. She is looking at us. Imagine that she is pointing out problems in our day-to-day lives, and the status of our spiritual life. She is communicating to our Lord where we stand and what we lack. A mother's concern is always for her children. Mothers are easily upset when their children fall behind their expectations. How much more we can expect from Mary, who is the beloved mother of all believers and the mother of our Lord. If we are married, this may be true about our marital life. If we are single and lonely, she is speaking about our loneliness. It may be about our jobs, career, or relationships. The wine has run out. The joy in our life has disappeared. Goals in our life have gone or changed for the worse. She is interceding on our behalf constantly. In our own lives we often have no time for self-reflection. There are arid areas that need to be filled. This may be true about our relationships, both towards heaven and towards our fellow beings. The same can be said about our activities at home and outside. Mary is pleading before her Son for all of us because she is our mother and we are her children. The mother of Jesus "surrounds us with a silent tenderness, always attentive to our needs, compassionately interceding for us. A trusting and loving intimacy with her brings into our life refreshment, calmness, and hopes."[12]

After Mary informed her Son about the situation at the wedding, and after the actions that Jesus instantly took, her instructions to the servants were clear proof of her powerful mediation and intercession. In spite of Jesus' initial response, which appeared to be neither positive nor encouraging, Mary proceeded to instruct the servants to obey whatever her Son told them to do. The servants did exactly what they were told, and Jesus Christ performed the amazing sign of changing water into wine. In short, at Cana Mary requests nothing of her Son, but she reveals what is happening there and then addresses the servants. She is the one who makes known the impending deficiency that is going to affect the celebration. "That is the way in which she intercedes with her Son. Here she already shows by her intervention how believers should listen to their fellow human beings and make known their needs so that Jesus may come to their aid."[13]

Conclusion

The words of Mary to her Son, "They have no wine" or "They have no more wine," informing him about the predicament the family was about to face at the wedding celebration, were very simple at a glance, but at the same time it was a profound statement with various important shades of meaning. Even though Jesus' response to his mother in

[12]A Monk of the Eastern Church [Lev Gillet], *Serve the Lord with Gladness, Our Life in the Liturgy: Be My Priest* (Crestwood, NY: St Vladimir's Seminary Press, 1990), 54.

[13]Blancy and Jourjon, *Mary,* 67.

the very beginning seemed to be not positive, as his time had not yet arrived, he advanced it in order to fulfill his beloved mother's request. For him, his "hour" or "time" was the time of glorification through his passion. His acting at his mother's request at the scene, even by advancing his time, reveals his bond and profound relationship with his mother.

As the Cana wedding happened at the very beginning of the public ministry of the Lord, his mother's request prompted him to intervene in order to rescue a family from shame. But that very act, the sign, was a revelation, a manifestation of divine glory through which Jesus' disciples believed in him. Hence, Mary's statement to her Son paved the way for a two-dimensional act, manifestation of the divine glory, leading his followers to believe in him, as well as relieving the pain and shame of a distressed family. Mary's statement, "They have no wine," reveals her personality and character. If her care and concern for others are very visible in those words, they also show how calmly and quietly she approaches difficult circumstances and transforms them into successful events and occasions for divine action. Her very simple words communicated to her Son the need and the urgency of the situation. They remain as a model prayer and an excellent example of intercession. Those who strongly believe in the power of her intercession look at the Cana sign by believing that her mediation on behalf of others is never going to be unanswered by her Son.

It was Mary's confidence in her Son that led her to him with the request. She knew who her Son was from the beginning, as she "kept all these things, reflecting on them in her heart" (Lk 2.19). For any sign to be performed by the Son of God, according to St John's Gospel, the prerequisite is faith. All the signs in the Gospel were done in the presence of people who had faith, and the signs also led the people to strengthen their faith. It was Mary's faith that stood as the foundation for the initial sign of her Son. For signs and miracles the Almighty is looking forward to the cooperation of human beings. In Cana, that was exactly what had happened at the initiation of the Virgin Mary.

13

"Water Saw Its Master and Blushed"

The famous English poet Lord Byron participated in an essay competition about the wedding in Cana while he was a young school student. All the participants except Byron in the contest wrote page after page detailing the sign. With a very simple but uniquely eloquent sentence, the young boy, the future great poet, went away with the top prize. He scribbled, "The water saw its master and blushed."[1]

If the young poet was able to elucidate and dramatically summarize the event in a small sentence of marvelous and picturesque language capturing the beauty, majesty, and the mystery of the sign, St John the apostle, who narrated the event in his Gospel, succinctly summarized the scope of the incarnation along with the vision and mission of Jesus Christ in his brief narrative of the Cana sign. The sign is unique in many ways. It is stated in the narrative as the first, chronologically, of Jesus' signs in the Fourth Gospel (2.11), but it can also mean, as mentioned earlier, the first in the sense that the most important one of all the signs in the Gospel. Jesus Christ attended a wedding, an ordinary but religiously and culturally significant event, in a remote and rustic village where the hosts were poor and simple folk who could not

---

[1]The same is assigned to many English writers, including Walter Scott, Alexander Pope, and Dryden. It is also ascribed to the English poet Richard Crashaw (1613–1649), with slight variation, "The conscious water saw its God, and blushed." In Latin it is, "Nympha pudica Deum vidit, et erubuit."

adequately provide the drink, wine, to all the invited guests while the banquet was going on. Jesus transformed water into wine of superior quality at the request of his mother, in order to resolve the impending problem. Thus the wedding became an occasion for Jesus not only to help those who were in dire need but also to reveal the glory of God. It paved the way for the disciples, who had just started to follow him, to believe in him at the very beginning of his public ministry.

The wedding sign is filled with symbolism: symbols of past events and symbols to be fulfilled through the incarnate Lord. The references such as the third day, wedding, Cana, sign, water, wine, washing, purification, and hour, convey much more than what they really are in the ordinary sense. They are symbols with great meanings of eternal dimensions revealing the transforming and life-giving acts of the Son of God. Where the wedding sign took place also is very significant. It was performed in Cana, a small village in Galilee, known for its gentile inhabitants, and not in Jerusalem in Judea, the center of Jewish religion, life, and culture, in order to teach the universality of Jesus' mission as its goes beyond "the lost one of Israel."

The narrative of the Cana sign is presented as a "third-day" event. Though the reference to the "third day" can mean many things according to the context, the primary purpose seems to be to reveal to the followers of Jesus the glorious resurrection of our Lord on the third day, at the very beginning of Jesus' public ministry. The resurrection of our Lord is the foundation of the Christian faith and the central theme of the apostles' preaching. St John wrote the Gospel to instruct the followers in the faith and edify the Christian communities he was shepherding. He, an apostle who saw the resurrected Lord, was not able to be present and was not able to witness personally to the resurrection at places where the breaking of the bread, the celebration of Christ's coming, death, resurrection, and second coming was recollected and remembered. Those communities of catechumens and communicants of the eucharistic fellowship consisted mainly of recent followers of the "new way." At the fellowship they celebrated the great "third-day" event. When they read about the Cana event, it would help them to remember and to celebrate the resurrection of our Lord. It was considered as part of the confession of faith in those communities.

The "third day" was very important in the Hebraic tradition also as it was on that day that the covenantal relationship between Yahweh and Israel was initiated at Mount Sinai under the leadership of Moses. Sharing the body and blood of the Son of God is the symbol of the new covenantal relationship which was primarily based on the greatest "third-day" event.

The wedding in Cana was a miracle on water, which is part of nature as well as the first creation. If the initial creation in Genesis is narrated as a seven-day-cycle event, the Cana sign—where the re-creation process was initiated—was presented at the end of a seven-day cycle. The Cana sign is thus pointing to the end of the first week of creation, which is the seventh day and the beginning of a new week with a new day, the eighth day. The resurrected Lord appeared to the apostles, including Thomas, who missed the earlier appearance, on "the eighth day," according to the Fourth Gospel (20.26). The eighth day also became the day of the celebration of the resurrection of the Lord, and thus it became the first day of the week. It is the "Day of the Lord" or "the Lord's Day."

By changing water into wine, our Lord initiated the transformation process with nature. It leads to the re-creation process of the estranged creation. The transformation started thus with the creation, the fallen nature, before the transformation of human beings, the crown of creation that carries the image and likeness of the almighty God.

Water in the pots became what it should be in the presence of Christ, or in other words, the colorless and odorless substance of water became superb wine, with sparkling color, exotic taste, and powerful flavor. Ordinary water was completely changed into extraordinary wine in the presence of Jesus Christ. It was a revealing moment as later at the Last Supper giving bread to his disciples he said, "This is my body" and giving wine he said, "This is my blood."

In Cana, if water was transformed into superb wine as a prelude, wine could become Jesus Christ's own blood. Thus, what happened at Cana was a transforming event of eternal dimension as wine would be changed, through the Holy Spirit, into Christ's life-giving blood in the Eucharist in the Church, the body of Christ. The Cana event was a prelude to the experience of the presence of the kingdom of heaven in this world through the Holy Communion.

In the Bible, on many occasions wine is presented as a symbol for the Holy Spirit. One can see many similarities in the narration of the Cana sign with the day of Pentecost detailed in the second chapter of the Acts of the Apostles. On the day of Pentecost those who were waiting for the coming of the Holy Spirit were filled with the Spirit just as the jars at the wedding feast were filled to the brim with the best wine. Those who were filled with the Holy Spirit were accused of having too much wine: "Some, however, made fun of them and said, 'They have had too much wine'" (Acts 2.13). The transformation of water into wine that filled the water jars to the brim, alluded to the coming of the Holy Spirit to the faithful so that they would be filled, guided, and rejuvenated by the Spirit. The words of Mary to her Son, "There is no more wine," were also interpreted by many Fathers and scholars as the absence of the Holy Spirit in the wedding gathering, meaning there was no joy of the Spirit in them.

The sign happened in a home. The almighty God, who, in the very beginning of creation, united Adam and Eve as husband and wife to form a family, was again, through his very presence and personal involvement, blessing the marriage at Cana, a joyous event for two individuals, a man and a woman, for two families, and for the communities to which they both belonged. Marriage is a transforming event, just as ordinary water was transformed into superb wine. In marriage human passions are transformed to creative, comfortable, and pleasant experiences for both spouses, uniting them as "one body" in its full sense. The bride and bridegroom are transformed through the mystery of marriage to partake of a higher divine union of unique and lasting relationship. It transforms not only two individuals—husband and wife—but also two families and communities.

True marital life brings abundance of joy, similar to the superb wine that was filled to the brim. Still, the best is yet to come, just as the best wine was served at the banquet not in the beginning but at the end. The love, dedication, commitment, and sacrificial submission are increased as months and years pass by, just as the quality of the wine improves as months and years pass by.

It is through marriage, the sacrament of love and the mystery of life, that new generations come to be and human beings participate in the divine energies of creation, and new generations of "the image and likeness of God" thus are brought forth into the world. The sign took place in a home, and thus the experience of paradise at home, which was forfeited and forgone by the first family, was regained once again for humankind. The home was thus reinstated as a "paradise on earth" and a "miniature heaven." St Paul has this in his mind when he writes, "the church that meets in their house (*kat' oikon autōn ekklēsian*)" (Rom 16.5).

Unlike the other signs and miracles Jesus performed, he seemed surprisingly reluctant to act at the wedding upon the request of his mother. His response to his mother, "Woman, what is it to you and me? My time has not yet come" was a clear expression of this. Though the water in six stone jars was transformed into superb wine, no one was aware of the source of the new wine except possibly the servants who poured water into the jars, and the mother of Jesus who gave direction to the servants to follow whatever her Son advised them to do. In a way, there was not much need for such a miraculous action as nobody was in a dangerous situation and no one was asking for a resolution of a tragic situation, as was the case in many other miracles Jesus performed. No responsible person at the wedding other than his mother informed him about the needful situation. Above all, nobody properly appreciated Jesus for what he had done there, though the bridegroom was congratulated by the feast-master for keeping the best wine to be served last.

The initial sign at the wedding performed by our Lord was a revelation—a revelation of what was about to be manifested in his presence. The divine presence of Jesus completely and instantly changes any given situation. Ordinary water became superb wine, and its quantity was beyond everyone's expectation. His presence can completely transform individuals as well as marital unions. That was also the personal experience of the author of the Gospel, who, along with his brother James, was once known as a "son of thunder." He became "the apostle of love" through experiencing the love and warmth of his Master. "The episode at the marriage in Cana is the frontispiece to the Gospel, summing up pictorially what is to come; how unbelievably he suffices in every difficulty: and above all how he enriches things for us. What water is to wine, what that embarrassing insufficiency was to the relief he wrought for his host, so is any other life compared to the fullness, the color, the adventure, the achievement that he gives."[2]

In the gathering at Cana, "the mother of Jesus" and the disciples were present, though the number of the disciples may not have reached twelve at the time. Mary brought to her Son's attention the problem of the absence of adequate wine for the feast. It was her request that ultimately resolved the problem. The place and power of the intercession of the *Theotokos* was very visible in the sign. It was a unique intercession from the mother to the Son as she was fully aware that her beloved Son would never delay or deny her request. St Mary's words to her Son, "They have no wine," remain as a simple yet superb and exceptionally great paradigm for all prayers. It is indeed one of the shortest and best recorded prayers in Holy Scripture.

At Cana Jesus proceeded to advance his time at the request of his mother, though he had already warned his mother, "My hour has not yet come" (Jn 2.1). At the same time he positively responded to his mother's request, and dramatically and miraculously saved a distraught family from disgrace. For Jesus the "hour" was his hour of crucifixion, and that was the time of his glorification also.

---

[2]George Arthur Buttrick, et al., eds., *The Interpreter's Bible: The Holy Scriptures,* vol. 8 (Nashville, TN: Abingdon Press), 491.

As the mother of all believers, St Mary's advice to the servants, whose role prefigured the diaconal ministry in the Church, is her advice to all her children, "Do whatever he says" (Jn 2.5). It was for Jesus an echo of his heavenly Father's voice. Hence we see both the heavenly Father and the earthly mother witness the uniqueness of Jesus Christ, and the advice of the heavenly Father to everyone is to listen to his Son, and the advice of the earthly mother is to do what her Son says. To do what he says one has to listen to him. In fact, to listen to Jesus Christ means to obey him. It is interesting to note, as already mentioned, that the meaning of the Latin word *obaudire* is both "to listen" and "to obey." That was exactly what the servants did at Cana. They, like Mary, listened to Jesus, obeyed him, and followed him. Barclay writes, "This story is John saying to us: 'If you want the new exhilaration, become a follower of Jesus Christ, and then there will come a change in your life which will be like water turning into wine.' "[3]

St Mary's request was more than enough for Jesus to change his mind and thereby to change the water into wine. How could he, who taught others to obey their parents, refuse his beloved mother's wish? The Cana event shows Jesus' close relationship with his mother, though many interpret the passage to prove the opposite. Her Son advanced his time, i.e. the time of his death on the cross, to fulfill his mother's request. It was another revelation of the true Eve—the woman who listened to the Lord and obeyed him despite the difficulties. It was unlike the first Eve, who listened to Satan and followed upon his directions in the midst of plenty and in spite of the pleasant and joyful atmosphere.

The servants in the Cana sign, just like Mary, will always remain great paradigms of faith, as it is defined in the Letter to the Hebrews, "Faith is the realization of what is hoped for and evidence of things not seen" (11.1). At the time of the incarnation, the Virgin Mary was the one who made it possible for the Son of God to be the Son of Man. In Cana, she was the one who made the circumstances fer-

[3]Barclay, *The Gospel of John*, 91.

tile and suitable for Jesus to act and reveal himself, as she was the
embodiment of faith. It was her timely intercession that prompted
the disciples to believe in Jesus. At the same time, the failure of the
feast-master, whose responsibility was to make sure that there was
enough for every one of the guests, and the unawareness of all the
mysterious things that had happened is the picture of modern man,
who ignores the abiding presence of the Almighty and his amazing
activities in the world at every moment. The feast-master did not have
the inner eye to witness and believe the mysteries that had unfolded
right before his eyes.

The liturgical and sacramental importance of the sign is evident
throughout the narrative. The very naming of the event as a sign by
the apostle, the context of the sign, a wedding, the transformation
that happened to the water through the presence of Christ, and the
role of the deacons (or servants) all point to the sacramental mysteries of the Church. In the use of water, the initial creation at the very
beginning, the re-creation process was inaugurated. Water is used for
baptism, the regeneration of human beings.

The Bible opens with a marriage, the one between Adam and Eve,
and it concludes with a marriage as well, in the book of Revelation,
the marriage of the Lamb. At the time of the inauguration of the
public ministry of our Lord, the first thing he did was to attend a
marriage and transform that occasion to manifest the divine glory. If
the empty water pots were symbols of the failure of existing purification rituals, the presence of Christ and his transforming power bring
true purification. It is Jesus who sanctifies, not through water but by
his life-giving blood.

Through the presence of the Virgin Mary—the "mother of Jesus"—
and the apostles, the divine communion of the saints with the Lord
is fully revealed. Jesus said, "Where two or three are gathered in my
name, I will be there." The Cana wedding sign is a unique example for
the divine fellowship. "Name" according to biblical language means
presence, and Jesus was physically present there. In such a fellowship
what happens is divine manifestation and active transformation.

It is the same thing that is happening even today where two or three are gathered in his "name." The wine and the bread are being changed through his presence and through the Holy Spirit to Christ's blood and body to provide abundant and eternal life. They are meant for those who "do what he says." The result will also be overflowing with superb wine, "the Holy Spirit," the "peace that passes understanding," excitement beyond human imagination and calculation, and—above all—the manifestation of the divine glory. Still "the best is yet to be," which will be at his second coming, the time of "the wedding banquet of the Lamb."

Bibliography

Scripture

The Anchor Bible. Garden City, NY: Doubleday & Company Inc., 1966.

The Complete Parallel Bible. New York, NY: Oxford University Press, 1993.

The Greek New Testament. 4th revised edition. Philadelphia, PA: American Bible Society, 2004.

The Harper Collins Study Bible. London: Harper Collins Publishers, 1998.

The Jerusalem Bible. Garden City, NY: Doubleday & Company Inc., 1966.

Jewish New Testament. Trans. David H. Stern. Jerusalem: Lederer Messianic Publications, 1989.

The Orthodox Study Bible: New Testament & Psalms. Nashville, TN: Thomas Nelson Publishers, 1997.

The New Oxford Annotated Bible with the Apocrypha, Expanded Edition, An Ecumenical Study Bible: Revised Standard Version. New York, NY: Oxford University Press, 1977.

The NIV Study Bible: The International Version. Grand Rapids, MI: Zondervan Bible Publishers, 1985.

The New International Living Bible: The New Laymen's Parallel Bible. Grand Rapids, MI: Zondervan Bible Publishers, 1987.

Knox Bible (Ronald A Knox translation). Old City, PA: Baronius Press, 1950.

The New American Bible. New York, NY: Collier-Macmillan Ltd., 1970.

New American Bible: St. Joseph Edition. Totowa, NJ: Catholic Book Publishing Co., 1971.

The New Living Bible. Carol Stream, IL: Tyndale House Publishers, 1971.

The Syriac New Testament (Peshitta).

Other Sources

A Monk of the Eastern Church [Lev Gillet]. *The Year of Grace of the Lord.* Crestwood, NY: St Vladimir's Seminary Press, 1992.

A Monk of the Eastern Church [Lev Gillet]. *Orthodox Spirituality: An Outline of the Orthodox Ascetical and Mystical Tradition.* Crestwood, NY: St Vladimir's Seminary Press, 1987.

Antony of Sourozh, Metropolitan. *God and Man.* Crestwood, NY: St Vladimir's Seminary Press, 1983.

Acharya, Francis, translator and editor. *Prayer with the Harp of the Spirit, Volume iii, The Crown of the Year – Part ii* (Translation from the original Syriac of the Penqitho). Kurisumala Ashram, Vagamon, India, 1985.

Athanasius, *On the Incarnation*, translated and edited by John Behr. Popular Patristics Series 44B. Yonkers, NY: St Vladimir's Seminary Press, 2011.

Aus, Roger. *Water into Wine and Beheading of John the Baptist.* Atlanta, GA: Scholars Press, 1988.

Averky (Taushev), Archbishop, translated by Nicholas Kotar. *The Four Gospels: Commentary on the Holy Scriptures of New Testament,* vol. 1. Jordanville, NY: Holy Trinity Seminary Press, 2015.

Barclay, William. *The Gospel of John,* vol. 1 of The Daily Study Bible. Edinburgh: The Saint Andrew Press, 1964.

Basil of Sergievo, Bishop. "Living in the Future." In *Living Orthodoxy in the Modern World,* 23–36. Edited by Andrew Walker and Costa Carras. Crestwood, NY: St Vladimir's Seminary Press, 2000.

Behr, John. *The Mystery of Christ: Life in Death.* Crestwood, NY: St Vladimir's Seminary Press, 2006.

Behr-Sigel, Elisabeth, translated by Fr. Steven Bigham. *The Ministry of Women in the Church.* Crestwood, NY: St Vladimir's Seminary Press, 1999.

Bennett, William J. *The Broken Hearth: Reversing the Moral Collapse of the American Family.* New York, NY: Broadway Books, 2001.

Blancy, Alain, Maurice Joujon, and the Dombes Group. *Mary in the Plan of God and in the Communion of Saints.* Mahwah, NJ: Paulist Press, 1999.

Bloom, Metropolitan Anthony and George Lefebvre. *Courage to Pray.* Crestwood, NY: St Vladimir's Seminary Press, 1995.

Bojorge, Horacio. *Image of Mary According to the Evangelists.* New York, NY: The Society of St. Paul, 1978.

Brant, Jo-Ann A. *John: Commentaries on the New Testament.* Grand Rapids, MI: Baker Publishing Group, 2011.

Breck, John. *God With Us: Critical Issues in Christian Life and Faith.* Crestwood, NY: St Vladimir's Seminary Press, 2003.

Brock, Sebastian. *The Bible in the Syriac Tradition.* Piscataway, NJ: Gorgias Press, 2006.

Brock, Sebastian P. *Studies in Syriac Spirituality.* Bangalore: Dharmaram Publishers, National Printing Press, 2008.

Brook, Wes Howard. *Becoming Children of God: John's Gospel and Radical Discipleship.* Maryknoll, NY: Orbis Books, 1994.

Brown, Raymond E. *The Death of the Messiah*, vol. 2. New York, NY: A.B.R.L., Doubleday, 1994.

_____. *The Gospel According to John I-XII: The Anchor Bible.* Garden City, NY: Doubleday & Company, 1966.

_____, ed. *Mary in the New Testament.* Philadelphia, PA: Fortress Press, 1978.

_____, ed. *The Jerome Biblical Commentary.* Englewood Cliffs, NJ: Prentice-Hall, 1968.

Buttrick, George Arthur, ed. *The Interpreter's Bible*, vol. 8. Nashville, TN: Abingdon Press, 1952.

Chrryssavgis, John. *Love, Sexuality, and the Sacrament of Marriage.* Brookline, MA: Holy Cross Orthodox Press, 1998.

Collins, Raymond F. *These Things Have Been Written.* Louvain: Peeters Press, 1990.

Crank, George. *The Message of the Bible.* Crestwood, NY: St Vladimir's Seminary Press, 1982.

Cross, F. L., ed. *The Oxford Dictionary of the Christian Church.* London: Oxford University Press, 1958.

Countryman, L. William. *The Mystical Way in the Fourth Gospel.* Valley Forge, PA: Trinity Press International, 1995.

Craddock, Fred B. *John: Knox Preaching Guides.* Atlanta, GA: John Knox Press, 1983.

Dmitri (Royster), Archbishop. *The Miracles of Christ.* Crestwood, NY: St Vladimir's Seminary Press, 1992.

_____. *Orthodox Christian Teaching.* Syosset, NY: DRE-OCA, 1983.

_____. *The Holy Gospel According to Saint John: A Pastoral Commentary.* Crestwood, NY: St Vladimir's Seminary Press, 2015.

Dix, Gregory. *The Shape of the Liturgy.* London: Dacre Press, Adam & Charles Black, 1964.

Dostoyevsky, Fyodor. *The Brothers Karamazov.* New York, NY: New American Library, Division of Penguin Books, 1999.

Ellis, Peter F. *The Genius of John.* Collegeville, MN: Liturgical Press, 1984.

Elowsky, Joel C., ed. *John 1–10.* Ancient Christian Commentary on Scripture, New Testament, vol. IVa. Downers Grove, IL: Inter Varsity Press, 2006.

Etheridge, John Wesley. *The Syrian Churches: Their Early History, Liturgies and Literature.* London: Elibron Classics, 2005. Reprint of London: Longman, Green, Brown, and Longmans, 1846.

Evdokimov, Paul. *The Sacrament of Love.* Crestwood, NY: St Vladimir's Seminary Press, 1995.

Flanagan, Neal M. *The Gospel According to John and the Johannine Epistles.* Collegeville, MN: Liturgical Press, 1983.

Forest, Jim. *The Ladder of the Beatitudes.* Maryknoll, NY: Orbis Books, 1999.

Foster, R. C. *Studies in the Life of Christ.* Grand Rapids, MI: Baker Book House, 1971.

Grassi, Joseph A. "The Wedding at Cana (John II 1–11): A Pentecostal Meditation?" In *The Composition of John's Gospel,* edited by David E. Orton, 123–128. Leiden: Brill, 1999.

Grayston, Kenneth. *The Gospel of John.* Philadelphia, PA: Trinity Press International, 1990.

Harrington, J. Daniel. *John's Thought and Theology.* Wilmington, DE: Michael Glazier, Inc., 1990.

Holy Apostles Convent. *The Life of the Virgin Mary, The Theotokos.* Buena Vista, CO: Holy Apostles Convent Publications, 2010.

Hopko, Thomas. *All the Fulness of God: Essays on Orthodoxy, Ecumenism, and Society.* Crestwood, NY: St Vladimir's Seminary Press, 1982.

_____. *The Lenten Spring.* Crestwood, NY: St Vladimir's Seminary Press, 1998.

Huckle, John J. and Paul Visokay, edited by John L. Mckenzie. *The Gospel According to St. John,* vol. 1. New Testament for Spiritual Reading 17. New York, NY: Crossroad Publishing, 1981.

Hunter, A. M. *The Gospel According to John*, The Cambridge Bible Commentary. London: Cambridge University Press, 1965.

Jacob of Serug, translated by Mary Hansbury. *On the Mother of God*. Crestwood, NY: St Vladimir's Seminary Press, 1995.

Johnson, Luke Timothy. *The Writings of the New Testament*, rev. ed. Minneapolis, MN: Fortress Press, 1999.

Jones, Larry Paul. "The Symbol of Water in the Gospel of John." *Journal for the Study of the New Testament Supplement Series* 145. Sheffield Academic Press, 1997.

Katz, Mordechai. *Understanding Judaism: A Beginner's Guide to Jewish Faith, History, and Practice*. New York, NY: Artscroll Mesorah Publications, 2000.

Kee, Howard Clark. *Understanding the New Testament*, 3rd ed. Englewood Cliffs, NJ: Prentice-Hall, 1973.

Kesich, Vaselin and Lydia W. Kesich. *Treasures of the Holy Land*. Crestwood, NY: St Vladimir's Seminary Press, 1985.

Kilgallen, John J. *A Brief Commentary on the Gospel of John*. New York, NY: Mellen Biblical Press, 1992.

Koester, Craig R. *Symbolism in the Fourth Gospel: Meaning, Mystery, Communication*. Minneapolis, MN: Fortress Press, 1995.

Kostenberger, Andreas J. *New Testament II*. Ancient Christian Commentary on Scripture. New York, NY: Oxford University Press, 1993.

Kotatch, J. Alfred. *The Jewish Book of Why*. New York, NY: Penguin Compass, 2003.

Krempa, S. Joseph. *Captured Fire: The Sunday Homilies, Cycle C*. New York, NY: St. Pauls, 2005.

Kruse, Colin G. *John*. The Tyndale New Testament Commentaries. Grand Rapids, MI: Eerdmans Publishing, 2003.

Lewis, C. S. *Miracles: A Preliminary Study*. New York, NY: Harper San Francisco, 2001.

Lightfoot, John A. *A Commentary on the New Testament from the Talmud and Hebraica*, vol. III. Grand Rapids, MI: Baker Book House, 1979. Originally printed 1958.

MacGregor, G. H. C. *The Gospel of John*, Moffat New Testament Commentary. New York, NY: Harper and Brothers Publishers, 1929.

Manley, Johanna, editor. *The Bible and the Holy Fathers for Orthodox*. Menlo Park, CA: Monastery Books, 1990.

Maloney, Francis J. *Belief in the Word: Reading John 1–4*. Minneapolis, MN: Fortress Press, 1993.

_____. *The Gospel of John*. Vol. 4 of Sacra Pagina, edited by Daniel J. Harrington. Collegeville, MN: Liturgical Press, 1998.

Marsh, John. *Saint John*. The Pelican New Testament Commentaries. London: Penguin Books, 1971.

Mary, Mother and Archmandrite Kallistos Ware. *The Festal Menaion*. London: Faber, 1969.

Matthew the Poor. *The Communion of Love*. Crestwood, NY: St Vladimir's Seminary Press, 1984.

Meyendorff, John. *Marriage: An Orthodox Perspective*. Crestwood, NY: St Vladimir's Seminary Press, 1993.

Miegge, Giovanni, translated by Waldo Smith. *The Virgin Mary: The Roman Catholic Marian Doctrine*. Philadelphia, PA: The Westminster Press, 1955.

Morris, Leon. Reflections on the Gospel of John, vol. 1, *The Word Was Made Flesh, John 1–5*. Grand Rapids, MI: Baker Book House, 1986.

_____ *The Gospel According to John: The New International Commentary of the New Testament*. Grand Rapids, MI: Zondervan, 1979.

McHugh, John. *The Mother of Jesus in the New Testament*. Garden City, NY: Double Day & Company, 1975.

Nalbandian, Zenob. *The Sacrament of Marriage in the Armenian Apostolic Church*. New York, NY: St Vartans Press, 1987.

Ng, Wai-Yee. *Water Symbolism in John: An Eschatological Interpretation*, Studies in Biblical Literature 15. New York, NY: Peter Lang, 2001.

O'Carroll, Michael. *Theotokos: A Theological Encyclopedia of the Blessed Virgin Mary*. Wilmington, DE: Michael Glazier, 1988.

The Orthodox Syrian Church of the East: The Service Book of the Holy Qurbana (Qurbanakramam). Mathews I, Baselius Marthoma. Kottayam, India: MOC Publications, 2009.

Papanikolaou, Aristotle and Elizabeth H. Prodromou, eds. *Thinking Through Faith*. Crestwood, NY: St Vladimir's Seminary Press, 2008.

Paulos Mar Gregorios. *Glory and Burden: Ministry and Sacraments of the Church*. Noida, India: ISPCK & MGF, 2006.

Pelikan, Jaroslav. *The Emergence of the Catholic Tradition (100–600): The Christian Tradition.* Chicago, IL: University of Chicago Press, 1971.

Perry, John Michael. *Exploring the Evolution of the Lord's Supper in the New Testament.* Kansas City, MO: Sheed & Ward, 1994.

Phillips, John. *Exploring the Gospels: John.* Neptune, NJ: Loizzeaux Brothers, 1989.

Puthuparampil, Joseph. *Mariological Thought of Mar Jacob of Serugh (451–521).* Baker Hill, Kottayam, Kerala, India: St Ephraim Ecumenical Research Institute, 2005.

Quasten, Johannes. Patrology, vol. 3, *The Golden Age of Greek Patristic Literature from the Council of Nicaea to the Council of Chalcedon.* Utrecht, Antwerp: Spectrum Publishers, 1966.

Ratzinger, Joseph (Benedict XVI). *Jesus of Nazareth.* New York, NY: Double Day, 2007.

Richardson, Cyril C. *Early Christian Fathers.* New York, NY: Touchstone, 1996.

Samuel, V. C. *An Orthodox Catechism on the Faith and Life of the Church.* Kottayam, India: MGOCSM, 1983.

Schmemann, Alexander. *For the Life of the World.* Crestwood, NY: St Vladimir's Seminary Press, 2004.

———. *Celebration of Faith*, vol. 3, *The Virgin Mary.* Crestwood, NY: St Vladimir's Seminary Press, 1995.

Schaff, Philip, editor. Nicene and Post-Nicene Fathers of the Christian Church: First Series, vol. 14, *Saint Chrysostom: Homilies on the Gospel of John and the Epistle to the Hebrews.* Reprinted by Peabody, MA: Hendrickson Publishers, 1994. Originally printed, 1886.

Sheen J. Fulton. *Life of Christ.* New York, NY: Image Books, 1977.

Stern, David H., trans. *Jewish New Testament.* Jerusalem, Israel: Jewish New Testament Publications, 1989.

Stevenson, Kenneth W. *To Join Together: The Rite of Marriage.* New York, NY: Pueblo Publishing Company, 1987.

Tarazi, Paul Nadim. *The New Testament Introduction: Johannine Writings,* vol. 3. Crestwood, NY: St Vladimir's Seminary Press, 2004.

Tavard, George H. *The Thousand Faces of the Virgin Mary.* Collegeville, MN: Liturgical Press, 1992.

Theophylact of Ohrid. *The Explanation of Holy Gospel According to John.* House Springs, MO: Chrysostom Press, 2007.

Thurian, Max, translated by Neville B. Cryer. *Mary, Mother of the Lord, Figure of the Church.* London: The Faith Press, 1963.

Thurston, Bonnie. *Women in the New Testament: Questions & Commentary.* New York, NY: Crossroad Publishing, 1998.

Towns, Elmer. *The Gospel of John: Believe and Live.* Philadelphia, PA: Fortress Press, 1978.

Vanier, Jean. *Drawn into the Mystery of Jesus through the Gospel of John.* Mahwah, NJ: Paulist Press, 2004.

Vincent, Marvin R. Word Studies in the New Testament, vol. 2, *The Writings of John.* Grand Rapids, MI: Eerdmans Publishing, 1973.

Waetjen, Herman C. *The Gospel of the Beloved Disciple.* NY: T & T Clark International, 2005.

Yannaras, Christos, translated by Elizabeth Briere. *The Freedom of Morality.* Crestwood, NY: St Vladimir's Seminary Press, 1984.

Periodicals

Aikya Samiksha, 7.1 (May 2010, Trivandrum, Kerala, India: M.S. Publications).

Coptic Church Review, Special Issue, 32 (2011, East Rutherford, NJ).

Sourozh: A Journal of Orthodox Life and Thought 37 (August 1989, Cowley, Oxford, England: Russian Patriarchal Diocese of Sourozh).